Immigration and Discrimination

Immigration and Discrimination

(Un)Welcoming Others

SAHAR AKHTAR

OXFORD
UNIVERSITY PRESS

Great Clarendon Street, Oxford, OX2 6DP,
United Kingdom

Oxford University Press is a department of the University of Oxford.
It furthers the University's objective of excellence in research, scholarship,
and education by publishing worldwide. Oxford is a registered trade mark of
Oxford University Press in the UK and in certain other countries

Published in the United States of America by Oxford University Press
198 Madison Avenue, New York, NY 10016, United States of America

British Library Cataloguing in Publication Data
Data available

Library of Congress Control Number: 2023948254

ISBN 978–0–19–889869–6

DOI: 10.1093/oso/9780198898696.001.0001

Printed and bound in the UK by
Clays Ltd, Elcograf S.p.A.

Contents

Preface and Acknowledgments

In 1947, a 9-year-old boy and his Muslim family were among the numerous people attacked by a group of mainly Sikh men. The boy and his family were living in what would become the Indian side of the newly created Indian-Pakistani border, in a village called Panjawa where the boy's stepfather was a teacher of Islam. During the attack, the boy's infant brother was fatally impaled on a sword, and his mother's neck was deeply gashed. She somehow survived, as did the 9-year-old boy, though he sustained extensive sword wounds in four different parts of his body, including his forehead, back, stomach, and hand, leaving him permanently disabled. To escape, he and the surviving members of his family, along with a few women from the village who also survived the attack, began the long trek from Panjawa to another village called Guria in the former Indian state of Bikaner, and from there ultimately to an area on the Pakistani side in southeast Punjab, where there was a refugee camp. The travel from Panjawa to Guria was the most challenging, but they had help. A young man, who was a stranger to the group, hid them during the day, guided them at night in their walk to their destination, and brought them whatever food he could manage along the way. He told the little boy that he had a sister on the Pakistani side, and that he hoped someone was guiding her to safety in the way he was trying to help the boy and his family. The young man was a Sikh, and the little boy would eventually become my father.

Stories like this one are not uncommon. During the partition of India, countless atrocities were committed by Muslims, Hindus, and Sikhs alike, as people on both sides of the newly created border scrambled to flee a place where they were unwelcomed to a place where they hoped to be welcomed. The reason they were unwelcomed was their different identity—as a Muslim, as a Hindu, as a Sikh; the reason they were welcomed someplace else was that same identity. Similar identity-based atrocities have occurred, and continue to occur, too often in other parts of the world; but, more common perhaps, the messages of unwelcomeness or welcomeness are conveyed through the everyday policies and actions of immigration bureaucracies.

My interest in writing this book is, like many academics writing on migration, ultimately inspired by my own experiences and background—not only by the devastating events my father lived through, but by my mother's circumstances and the experiences of my entire family moving across borders multiple times. Though never consequential in the way of my father's experience, we all encountered varying forms of both welcomeness and unwelcomeness, including the (horribly termed) "paki-bashing" my brother experienced, based in our religion, ethnicity, or nationality. It's with this background that I sought to write this book, attempting to understand when and why it is morally wrong for a state to exclude people because of their identity. I don't conclude that identity-based exclusion is always wrong; rather I argue it is often permissible, especially when it is done by disadvantaged groups. But, of course, even when it is permissible, that far from justifies any method in its service or any attitude motivating it. For inspiring my understanding of this point early in my life, I owe deep thanks to what I hope is a very old Sikh man, one who was safely reunited with his sister.

I owe thanks to many others for their direct help and support. For fueling my efforts in the initial phases of writing this book, I'm grateful to: Deborah Hellman for being the first to encourage me on the book's ideas and provide feedback on a paper that forms part of the book's argument; audiences at the Legal Studies and Business Ethics Workshop at the University of Pennsylvania, the Georgetown Institute for the Study of Markets and Ethics at Georgetown University, the Political Theory Workshop at Stanford University, and the Economics and Ethics of Immigration Conference at New York University for their helpful questions and comments, especially my fellow panelists at the NYU conference, Joseph Carens, Sarah Song, and Kit Wellman, for inspiring me to pursue my ideas in book form. I also owe thanks to several people for their assistance in completing the book: Harry David, for his careful and effective copyediting; Sulabh Newatia, for his always-timely research; two blind reviewers for Oxford University Press for their probing questions and valuable insight; and the editorial team at Oxford, especially Peter Momtchiloff, for seeing this book through to publication.

Parts of Chapter 7 were either adapted or copied from Sahar Akhtar, "The Claim-Right to Exclude and the Right to Do Wrong," *Critical Review of International Social and Political Philosophy* (2023).

Since acknowledgments for a book are typically never just about the book, on a personal note, I am grateful for many people: Lisa, for our lasting friendship and many (mis)adventures crossing borders; my friends at M&A—Hicham, Drew, Kat, Greg, and Rebecca—for providing distractions when I needed it most (and Greg and Rebecca, for our deep friendships too); Jonny, for being a dear friend and reminding me that smart people can be really dumb sometimes; Anna and Bruce, for their limitless support and affection; numerous faculty at Georgetown University, for making me feel welcomed; my mother-in-law, for always being proud of me; my brother-in-law Isaac, for his constancy; and my entire family—especially my parents, for their resilience and compassion, and Bill, for making life amazing.

Introduction: Immigration and Identity

1. Race, Ethnicity, and Religion Take Center Stage

Anti-immigration attitudes appear to be on the rise in many parts of the globe.[1] From South Africa[2] to India,[3] Hungary to Israel,[4] and Colombia to Thailand,[5] receptiveness toward immigrants has recently declined and hostility has increased. In Europe and the United States, while the numbers of those opposed to immigration have been relatively stable in the last decade or so, the perceived salience or importance of immigration as a political issue has sharply increased among its opponents.[6] Though there are many possible explanations for these attitudes, including economic explanations, there also seem to be growing concerns in many places about a diminishing shared identity or, more specifically, about the different race, ethnicity, or religion of potential or new immigrants.[7]

The history of attitudes and policies on immigration has been inextricably linked to race, ethnicity, and religion.[8] Notoriously offensive immigration and citizenship policies are in the somewhat-distant past. These include: the United States' 1882 Chinese Exclusion Act,[9] which barred the admission of Chinese workers; Australia's Immigration Restriction Act of 1901, called the White Australia Policy and designed to exclude nonwhites from Australia;[10] and, Uganda's sudden expulsion of South Asians, primarily Indians, in 1972 under President Idi Amin.[11] More recent policies may be less objectionable and might not reflect hostility toward any groups, but many still raise moral concerns, and

[1] Polling data are certainly not always reliable. For concerns about immigration polls specifically, see Blinder and Allen, *UK Public Opinion*. But in the discussion that follows, I try to rely on data for which there is broad consistency both across time and across different polls.
[2] Crush and Pendleton, "Regionalizing Xenophobia?"
[3] Singh and Mitra, "Millions of Indians"; Gaikwad and Nellis, "Majority-Minority Divide."
[4] Gonzalez-Barrera and Connor, "Around the World."
[5] Esipova, Ray, and Pugliese, "World Grows Less Accepting."
[6] Dempster, Leach, and Hargrave, "Public Attitudes towards Immigration," 11.
[7] Gaikwad and Nellis, "Majority-Minority Divide"; Alesina and Tabellini, "Political Effects of Immigration"; Hainmueller and Hopkins, "Public Attitudes toward Immigration."
[8] For some of this work, see: Lake and Reynolds, *Global Colour Line*; Givens, Terri E. 2007. "Immigration and Immigrant Integration"; d'Appollonia and Reich, "Immigration, Integration and Security"; Fine, "Immigration and Discrimination"; Song, *Immigration and Democracy*, 34.
[9] "Chinese Exclusion Act: Primary Documents in American History," Library of Congress, https://guides.loc.gov/chinese-exclusion-act.
[10] "The Immigration Restriction Act 1901," National Archives of Australia, Australian Government, https://www.naa.gov.au/explore-collection/immigration-and-citizenship/immigration-restriction-act-1901.
[11] Segawa, "Tension between Indians."

Immigration and Discrimination: (Un)Welcoming Others. Sahar Akhtar, Oxford University Press. © Sahar Akhtar 2024.
DOI: 10.1093/oso/9780198898696.003.0001

some are still in effect today. Japan reversed its 1990 policy favoring the admission of Japanese descendants (from such places as Brazil and Peru).[12] But Israel's Law of Return, implemented in 1950, still grants automatic admission and citizenship to all and only Jewish people. Kiribati, a nation made up of three small Pacific Island groups and expected to be the first state to lose its territory because of changing climate patterns, has, since gaining independence in 1979, automatically conferred citizenship on anyone whose ancestry is linked to the I-Kiribati people.[13] And from 1986 to today, Liberia has granted citizenship exclusively to people who are Black African.[14]

But in very recent years, we have again seen a surge of anti-immigration sentiments tied to race, ethnicity, religion, and identity more generally. Indeed, aside from concerns about potential job displacement, race, nationality, ethnicity, and religion seem to be at the *heart* of recent immigration anxieties. Survey data from some areas of the world, including Europe, demonstrate that a majority prefer immigrants who share a similar identity.[15] In the UK, for instance, researchers note that "at the preferred end of the scale are those who are white, English-speaking, Europeans and Christian countries while at the least preferred are nonwhites, non-Europeans and Muslim countries."[16] And all around the world, we have seen upswings in discrimination and antagonism toward particular racial, ethnic, or religious immigrant groups: Asian and African migrant workers in Saudi Arabia and the United Arab Emirates,[17] African and Muslim refugees in South Korea,[18] indigenous Bolivian and Peruvian immigrants in Chile and Argentina,[19] and African migrants in Mexico.[20] Moreover, we have seen a fairly recent ascendancy of populist movements, political parties, and political figures that more or less explicitly focus their rhetoric on issues related to race, ethnicity, and religion while campaigning to restrict immigration. Such figures have included Donald Trump in the United States,[21] Narendra Modi (and the

---

[12] Chung, *Immigration and Citizenship*.

[13] See the Constitution of Kiribati, Articles 19 and 23.

[14] See Tannenbaum, et al., "Aliens and Nationality Law." The authors note that Article 27(b) of the constitution limits citizenship to "a person who is a Negro, or of Negro descent, born in Liberia and subject to the jurisdiction thereof" or "a person born outside Liberia whose father (i) was born a citizen of Liberia; (ii) was a citizen of Liberia at the time of the birth of such child, and (iii) had resided in Liberia prior to the birth of such child." p. 13.

[15] Dempster, Leach, and Hargrave, "Public Attitudes towards Immigration," 14. The data may in fact be worse than what the surveys suggests because of social desirability bias. See Janus, "Social Desirability Pressures."

[16] Blinder and Allen, *UK Public Opinion*, 5.

[17] US Department of State, *Human Rights Report*; Sönmez, et al. "Human Rights."

[18] Rich, Bison, and Kozovic, "Survey."   [19] Valente, "Argentina."

[20] "Concluding Observations on the Combined Eighteenth to Twenty-First Periodic Reports of Mexico," Committee on the Elimination of Racial Discrimination, UN Office of the High Commissioner for Human Rights, https://tbinternet.ohchr.org/_layouts/15/treatybodyexternal/Download.aspx?symbolno=CERD/C/MEX/CO/18–21.

[21] See the discussion in Anderson, *White Rage*, 173. Also see her more general discussion of concerns about who might be "taking over our country" (59–60).

Bharatiya Janata Party) in India,[22] and Sebastián Piñera in Chile,[23] and such parties—not only right-wing but also center-left—thrive throughout Europe, including in Sweden,[24] Poland, Germany,[25] Slovakia,[26] and Austria (in Joerg Haider's Freedom Party, expected to gain even more momentum[27]).[28]

Some of the opposition and rhetoric have had strong undertones of ethnocentrism or even racism. Consider the heated debates in 2005 about women wearing burqas in France's public spaces. While antagonism to burqas was couched in terms of women's rights, at least some of the opposition was against the increasing influx of Muslim immigrants.[29] When he was campaigning for the US presidency in 2015, Trump made atrocious remarks about immigrants from south of the border, saying that "when Mexico sends its people, they're not sending their best. They're bringing drugs. They're bringing crime. They're rapists. And some, I assume, are good people."[30] Though far less explicit, Republican presidential hopeful Vivek Ramaswamy's 2023 comments have echoed such sentiments.[31] There was also, of course, then president Trump's 2017 policy all but banning admission from seven Muslim-majority states and explicitly preferring that any admitted refugees be Christian rather than Muslim.[32] And on the heels of that policy, the majority of surveyed Europeans agreed that "all further migration from Muslim countries [to Europe] should be stopped."[33]

Other contentious immigration issues at the forefront of national debates have been only slightly more subtle in racial or religious subtext, such as Indian prime minister Modi's 2019 Citizenship Amendment Act, which makes religion a basis for granting Indian citizenship for the first time and fast-tracks asylum claims to undocumented minorities but excludes any Muslims from consideration.[34] Still-other developments, such as Britain's 2016 Brexit vote, have not been racially, ethnically, or religiously focused on their face but nonetheless seem at least partly explainable by such factors.[35] What's more, an emerging political science literature suggests race, ethnicity, and religion played an implicit role

---

[22] Kim, "New Nationalism."   [23] Doña-Reveco, "Chile Turns Rightward."
[24] Becker, "Global Machine."   [25] Economist, "Right-Wing Anti-immigrant Parties."
[26] See Kaufmann, Whiteshift, 247.
[27] https://www.worldpoliticsreview.com/austria-politics-fpo-freedom-party-haider-europe-far-right/
[28] For more on this specific example and on trends in Europe overall, see Givens, "Immigration and Immigrant Integration"; Givens and Case, Legislating Equality. Also see BBC News, "Europe and Right-Wing Nationalism."
[29] See Kaufmann, Whiteshift, 255–56.   [30] Korte and Gomez, "Trump Ramps Up Rhetoric."
[31] See, for instance: https://www.nbcnews.com/news/asian-america/vivek-ramaswamy-celebrates-immigrant-family-pushing-far-right-border-p-rcna101592; https://thehill.com/homenews/campaign/4195861-ramaswamy-says-hed-deport-children-of-undocumented-immigrants-born-in-the-us-calling-14th-amendment-contested/
[32] Kaufmann, Whiteshift, 129.   [33] Goodwin and Raines, "What Do Europeans Think?"
[34] Human Rights Watch, "'Shoot the Traitors.'"
[35] See Kaufmann, Whiteshift, 194–95, 200–2.

in recent immigration restrictions based, purportedly, on security reasons and welfare concerns.[36]

In thinking about the ethics of immigration, what are we to make of these sorts of attitudes, debates, and policies? Must any relationship between race, ethnicity, or religion and immigration always be ruled out as morally unjustified? Unlike the popular discourse in many places, scholarly discussions, with very few exceptions, condemn virtually any connection immigration restrictions bear to race, ethnicity, or religion. But does this stance take into account the many nuances present in these issues? Are there some cases, whether imagined or actual (perhaps Kiribati's, Japan's, and Israel's), in which characteristics like race, ethnicity, and religion may rightfully factor into decisions about whom to admit and how? If so, are there moral limits to the role they may play in immigration decisions? And what is the best explanation for any limits to using race, ethnicity, or religion as grounds for restricting immigration?

Employing recent economic literature and empirical research where available, this book seeks to answer such questions. More generally, it is motivated by both the distant and more recent developments and sentiments about immigration around the world that center on race, ethnicity, and religion—and other identities—to try to understand what states may or may not base their admission decisions and policies on, and why.

2. The Argument of This Book

As noted, commentators in scholarly discussions of immigration nearly always denounce the use of any criteria related to race, ethnicity, and religion, whether explicit or implicit. Just as often, they appeal to the terminology and ideas of wrongful discrimination by expressing the view that racial, ethnic, or religious criteria, even when implicitly used, violate fundamental nondiscrimination principles.[37] But there has been little to no effort to examine whether the idea of wrongful discrimination—traditionally applied to interactions among people *within* the same state—is applicable at the global level or to interactions among people in different states.

In this book, I will try to fill this gap by exploring whether the idea of wrongful discrimination can be applied to states' admission decisions, and what this means for states' rights concerning immigration. I will argue that one of the central approaches to understanding when and why discrimination is wrong provides an

---

[36] D'Appollonia and Reich, "Immigration, Integration and Security," 4–5; Givens, Freeman, and Leal, *Immigration Policy and Security*, 3; Rudolph, *National Security and Immigration*, 9.

[37] See, for instance: Carens, *Ethics of Immigration*, 174–75; Miller, *Strangers in Our Midst*; Fine, "Immigration and Discrimination"; Lim, "Selecting Immigrants by Skill."

appealing framework for considering the morality of major aspects of states' admission decisions. Under this global "antidiscrimination" approach, and its underlying view of relational equality, what matters is not simply or always that states use or avoid certain criteria, such as race, but that states' decisions factor in what I call the *global social status* of an identity group, or a group's (dis)advantages in material, political, or way of life terms, or with respect to the social bases of their self-respect, compared with cognate groups outside the social context of a particular state. Social status is a scalar concept, with groups being more or less (dis)advantaged than other groups depending on the dimension of (dis)advantage. Moreover, there are certainly within-group differences, determined by issues such as citizenship, global region, and the role of multiple identities. Though all of this complicates the analysis, I will demonstrate how the conceptual resources of the antidiscrimination approach provides tools to effectively navigate it.

My primary argument will be that states' admission decisions are constrained by certain antidiscrimination duties to globally vulnerable groups—those that face significant disadvantages compared with other groups—and that the status differences between groups often figure into understanding whether an immigration policy violates these duties. However, as I will explain (in Chapter 6), I don't believe that *identity* characteristics necessarily occupy a morally distinctive place in the arguments and the book's analysis can be extended to any groups of people facing significant disadvantages, including the poor and those with serious health conditions. Moreover, I will explain (in Chapter 7) why the book's analysis implies that states are *not morally entitled* to make their own immigration decisions. This result is important not only for the use of admissions criteria such as race, ethnicity, and religion but also, more pressingly, for addressing the refugee crisis and helping people with urgent needs for admission.

Importantly, I will not attempt to provide an overall moral theory of migration. The simple reason is that I believe that states, and therefore what they imply for questions about migration, are complicated. In writing on the ethics of migration, one may be tempted to provide a primary defining characteristic of states or life in the state and then proceed to demonstrate its implications for migration. There are many reasons to favor such an approach, and below we'll explore many of the valuable insights gained from views that have taken such an approach. But it seems to me that attempting to put our finger on a single thing that predominantly characterizes states, or life within one, may miss important nuances and complexities in migration issues—issues that are often best addressed by attending to both historical and current social, political, and economic contexts and by reflecting on empirical research and particular normative judgments.

Consider some of the various features of a state—not to mention of *different* states—and what it means to be a member of some state. Through a state's network of laws and institutions, we coerce another, but we also engage in meaningful forms of cooperation toward the production of the state's public goods. States are political projects, but they also are sites for different ways of life, popular cultures, lifestyles, and national traditions. Living in a state means we interact with others in common public spaces and neighborhoods, but also within private commercial institutions and with family and friends. States ideally protect our human rights, but they also engage in illegitimate wars, conquest, and domination of others, and most (all?) are saddled with a long history of injustice. Some states are organized around a particular religious doctrine or view, while others are organized around a set of political beliefs. Finally, many states occupy vast stretches of territory, spanning multiple climate zones, natural environments, and geographic regions, while others are located on small territories with a single climate or terrain.

Because of the numerous things that living in a state signifies, and because of the variation across states, reasons for and patterns of migration also vary considerably. The vast majority of migrants seem to seek temporary admission into a new state—to take a short-term job, seek temporary employment, or attend school for a few years—with far fewer people seeking to relocate on a permanent basis.[38] A large number of people around the world move for economic reasons,[39] but this isn't necessarily limited to the pursuit of a particular job; it can also include an interest in the broader economic institutions and commercial norms in a place.[40] Some seek to move their families to a stable political and legal environment, but many people appear to be drawn to some state not primarily for either economic or political reasons, but for a particular lifestyle or way of life, perhaps one structured around a distinct geographic feature.[41] Millions of others seek to migrate not because they are especially drawn to anything, but rather to flee oppressive conditions or persecution in their source states.[42]

---

[38] For instance, over three times the number of documented permanent migrants were admitted into OECD states on temporary contracts in 2006. If we consider undocumented migrants, this difference is likely much greater since undocumented migrants tend to be temporary. See Borodak and Piracha, "Who Moves," 4.

[39] Budnik, "Temporary Migration," 21.

[40] Neoclassical economic theory predicts that the movement of labor depends on wage differentials: people will move where wages and employment are higher. This seems right as an explanation for the broad pattern of movement that we observe from poorer states to richer states. But it doesn't explain many of the *particular* patterns we observe, such as people from South Asia moving to the UK and Canada. See Salt, *International Migration*. More generally, see de Haas, "Determinants of International Migration." The various "network" theories do a far better job of explaining the observed patterns of migration. See, for instance, de Haas, "Internal Dynamics"; and Massey et al., *Worlds in Motion*.

[41] Khoo, Hugo, and McDonald, "Which Skilled Temporary Migrants?" I have discussed these reasons and their normative implications in Akhtar, "Being at Home."

[42] Currently, the number of refugees and asylum seekers is estimated to be anywhere between about thirty-five and one hundred million worldwide. "Refugee Data Finder," UNHCR, last modified October 27, 2022, https://www.unhcr.org/refugee-statistics/; "World's Refugees," Amnesty International, https://www.amnesty.org/en/what-we-do/refugees-asylum-seekers-and-migrants/global-refugee-crisis-statistics-and-facts/. The variance is due mainly to morally irrelevant definitional issues. The traditional conception of a refugee refers to someone who has departed their original state and includes about 26 million people, with another 12 million added because of the recent crisis in Ukraine. But, additionally, about 53 million forcibly displaced people remain in their original states, and their

Finally, a large number pursue life in a new state to join family or other loved one(s).[43]

The variety of reasons people have for migrating suggests that a range of different normative considerations come into play depending on the reason for migration and duration of stay in the new state. Those seeking to escape oppression and persecution, or dire economic or natural circumstances, have the strongest and most urgent moral claims to be admitted into a different state—though, as I will discuss in Chapter 6, not necessarily into any state of their choosing or on a permanent basis. There we'll also discuss why migration for family-reunification purposes is likely best justified by a state's duties to its existing members and not by any outsider's moral claims to, say, be free to move (where their loved ones reside). Moreover, the different moral demands rightfully placed on those who migrate to a new state likely also vary depending on the duration and reason for moving: for instance, permanent relocators might have obligations to become familiar with the language and customs of a place (whereas those moving on a temporary basis might not) and possibly have residual obligations to (a subset of members in) their former states. Finally, concerns about people's ability to exit a state might not be best explained by the same moral rationale(s) as people's interest in entering a particular state.

I only mean to suggest, and not defend, the above stances. My point is to illustrate the complexity of states and therefore of migration and the moral demands it may place both on a state and an immigrant. And, in general, this complex picture is why I won't try to offer a single moral theory of migration. Instead, I will focus on just one piece of migration, but I do believe it is a central piece: what states may or may not base their admission and exclusion decisions on, and why. Additionally, because of the complex picture of migration, I also believe we should not hope for a single way to precisely diagnose *the* wrong of any type of admission criteria, though I will argue that a family of wrongs best characterizes the relevant concerns. Relatedly, I do not believe that we can hope to uncover a one-size-fits-all answer for all states concerning whether some basis for admission or exclusion, whether explicit or implicit, is right or wrong.

On this last point, when reading work on the ethics of migration, I have often had the impression that the analysis starts by taking the standpoint of what life is like in some wealthy state—a state that also happens to be majority-white—such as the USA, considers individuals' reasons for wanting to move to such a state, and then proceeds to delineate a general moral theory of migration. While there are

conditions and circumstances typically mirror those of traditional refugees. For more, see "About Internally Displaced Persons," UN Office of the High Commissioner for Human Rights, https://www.ohchr.org/en/issues/idpersons/pages/issues.aspx.

[43] "Migration Trends and Families," UN Department of Economic and Social Affairs, October 14, 2022, https://www.un.org/development/desa/dspd/2022/10/migration-families/; OECD, *International Migration Outlook 2018*, chap. 1; https://www.migrationdataportal.org/themes/family-migration.

excellent reasons for having such states in mind when thinking about the ethics of migration—in particular, such states, especially the United States, are often the primary destinations for migrants,[44] and wealthy states arguably have significantly greater obligations to accept people with urgent admission needs—this book will try to explore the ethics of admission criteria and policies with a wide variety of states in view, both majority-white and non-majority-white states. One reason for this broader perspective is that many non-majority-white states contain vast migrant communities; for example, the United Arab Emirates has the highest proportion of immigrants in the world, as migrants constitute about 88% of its total population.[45] And other states that are not majority white, such as Equatorial Guinea, have recently experienced a surge in migrant populations—from less than 1% of its total population in 2005 to about 16% today.[46] Additionally, many states that are neither majority white nor wealthy host large groups of refugees—such as Bangladesh, which by most accounts contains the largest refugee camp in the world, accommodating the Rohingyas who fled Myanmar's genocide against them.[47] And these sorts of issues seem to matter for thinking about the ethics of immigration. But another significant, perhaps related, reason for exploring the ethics of admissions criteria with a wide variety of states in view is that, as explained in the beginning of this introduction, antimigrant attitudes seem to be on the rise *throughout* the world, not only in wealthy, majority-white states.

As a result of exploring the ethics of admissions criteria from a more global perspective, however, my book will not address many important questions, at least not directly. For instance, it will not discuss whether states must confer citizenship on their residents or what states owe them more generally.[48] Moreover, it will not directly explore how we determine *which* states must help any particular refugees or, more generally, any person experiencing significant and urgent basic human rights deprivations (though as I will discuss shortly, it indirectly does so).[49] Likewise, there are many emerging pressing issues concerning the rights of undocumented immigrants and the treatment of those attempting to gain admission that I will also be unable to directly examine, many of which depend on prior questions about the ethics of immigration selection. For instance, some of the important debates taking place on these issues involve the ethics of human smuggling,[50] interactions with border authorities,[51] and, relatedly, whether the

---

[44] Edmond, "Global Migration."

[45] McAuliffe and Triandafyllidou, *World Migration Report 2022*, 75.

[46] McAuliffe and Triandafyllidou, 62.   [47] McAuliffe and Triandafyllidou, 86.

[48] I have written on this issue elsewhere. See "Stripping Citizenship."

[49] For seminal work on this topic, see Shacknove, "Who Is a Refugee?"; Cherem, "Refugee Rights"; Matthew Lister, "Who Are Refugees?"; Gibney, *Ethics and Politics*; Gibney, "Refugees and Justice." Also see the proposals outlined by Kaufmann, *Whiteshift*, 236–39.

[50] Hidalgo, "Ethics of People Smuggling"; Müller, "Commercial Human Smuggling."

[51] For different issues related to this subject, see Hidalgo, "Unjust Immigration Restrictions"; Laine, "Ambiguous Bordering Practices"; Dickerson, "Secret History."

border (plausibly) does not merely consist of a state's territorial division from other territories but also includes the means of immigration enforcement within the state's territory[52] and even immigration application agencies and detention centers outside the state.[53]

At the same time, there is a significant practical outcome of the arguments in this book—one that has direct implications not only for the use of admissions criteria such as race, ethnicity, and religion but also, more importantly and relatedly,[54] for addressing the crisis facing the millions of people around the world living in conditions in which their basic human rights are significantly and urgently threatened. Specifically, in the final chapter, I will demonstrate that the arguments in this book imply that states are *not* morally entitled to unilaterally make their own immigration decisions. Put differently, states do not have a right against interference to make membership decisions however they choose.

Even beyond this direct implication, however, the analysis I propose will provide conceptual resources for understanding how some state's interaction with a particular group of, say, residents, refugees, or either undocumented or prospective immigrants, often through border enforcement, morally matters for its use of certain admission criteria. In this way, what I explore in this book will have some indirect implications for many important questions about immigration beyond those that I directly consider.

3. Chapter Outlines

This book begins, in **Chapter 1**, by critically examining the conventional position that states have extensive moral rights to make admission decisions as they choose or even to close their borders altogether ("states' choice"). The central justifications for states' choice are generally based in the value of preserving either a state's culture or its members' collective freedom to decide the terms of their political association. I will demonstrate that neither type of general rationale, nor the

---

[52] See the valuable work by Mendoza, "Presumptive Rights of Immigrants"; Mendoza, *Moral and Political Philosophy*. Also see Hing, "Institutional Racism"; and Bier, "US Citizens Targeted."

[53] For instance, see Albahari, *Crimes of Peace*; Sager, "Private Contractors." Also see Shachar, "Shifting Borders."

[54] See the valuable discussion in Song, *Immigration and Democracy*, chap. 7. See also: https://www.npr.org/2022/03/03/1084201542/ukraine-refugees-racism; "UNHCR Guidance on Racism and Xenophobia," UN Office of the High Commissioner for Human Rights, https://www.unhcr.org/en-us/protection/operations/5f7c860f4/unhcr-guidance-on-racism-and-xenophobia.html; International Labour Office, International Organization for Migration, and Office of the United Nations High Commissioner for Human Rights. *International Migration*; Esipova, Ray, and Pugliese, "Syrian Refugees Not Welcome"; "Are Some EU Countries Wrong to Only Want Christian Refugees?", Debating Europe, September 8, 2015, https://www.debatingeurope.eu/2015/09/08/are-some-eu-countries-wrong-to-only-want-christian-refugees/#.Y-v4tXbMLEY; Alexander et al., "How Race and Religion"; Watson, "United States' Hollow Commitment"; Lipka, "Most Americans Express Support."

particular views under each type, can adequately explain why central kinds of cases involving racial and ethnic criteria are wrong while others may be permissible. Moreover, though the particular states'-choice views I will explore have much in their favor, their shortcomings—some of which are revealed by recent economic analysis—will help us appreciate the need for something like the global antidiscrimination approach. This chapter will also discuss why and how I will use this approach rather than closely related ideas, including views that broadly stress concerns about subordination or domination and views that directly appeal to relational equality without necessarily invoking antidiscrimination principles.

Chapter 2 turns to the fundamental ideas and principles of normative discrimination theory. My goal in this chapter is not to specify a particular reason why discrimination might be wrong (whether in the context of states' admission decisions or domestic associations' decisions) nor to say specifically *when* it is wrong. Instead, my goal is to develop and motivate a primary approach to understanding when and why discrimination is wrong—namely, the antidiscrimination approach—and begin to argue why we should comprehend central features of immigration in these terms. I will provide several reasons in favor of the antidiscrimination approach while highlighting some of the shortcomings of the major alternative approach—anticlassification—in order to establish groundwork for applying antidiscrimination principles to states' admission decisions.

These principles stress that the social status of a group, or its comparative (dis)advantages in material, political, and way-of-life terms and in terms of the social bases of self-respect, matters for determining when and why discrimination is wrong. Broadly speaking, antidiscrimination is concerned with not contributing to a vulnerable group's disadvantages in order to avoid creating, sustaining, or perpetuating subordination. On the whole, there are two primary respects in which discrimination, and selective exclusion more specifically, might contribute to a group's vulnerability. One is by comparatively reducing the group's opportunities, and the other is by "degrading" it. As I use the term here, degradation can take multiple, related forms, including acts which express a demeaning message, acts that undermine the self-respect of others, and acts that perpetuate stigmas against others—each of which will be discussed in this chapter. While both reduced opportunities and degradation can be important reasons to object to selective exclusion in many cases, in this chapter I will explain why concerns about degradation are more critical for understanding whether an act contributes to a group's vulnerability in ways related to the moral concerns about subordination— that is, treating or regarding someone as morally inferior or expressing that they are. Additionally, both in my description of Chapter 4 below and in Chapter 5, I will discuss further reasons for this book's relative emphasis on degradation as opposed to reduced opportunities.

A second aim of this chapter is to demonstrate that the antidiscrimination approach is rooted in broad concerns associated with relational equality—the idea that we should relate to and interact with one another as equals in social, political, and economic life. Theories of relational equality direct us to the moral basis of antidiscrimination duties, which will enable us to understand why (some of) these duties apply to states' admission decisions while at the same time understanding the limits of these duties.

The aim of **Chapter 3** is to show that there is a meaningful sense of social status that extends beyond the boundaries of a particular state. I call it "global status," but we will see that sometimes it is more accurate to refer to regional status. The central point is that there is a kind of social status that is not equivalent to—and may substantially differ from—a group's domestic status. Global status refers to a group's (dis)advantages in material, political, or way-of-life terms or in terms of self-respect, under a broad range of international relations and institutions, compared with those of other groups outside the social context of a particular state. Like domestic status, global status is a continuum notion, as there is no hard line between a globally secure and a globally vulnerable group (though we can often identify clear cases of each). Moreover, a group's global status may vary not only in terms of dimension of (dis)advantage but also according to specific international contexts, comparison groups, and regions of the world. In Chapter 5, I will explore the implications of all of this for determining when a state's antidiscrimination duties are violated.

Chapter 3 advances two further goals. First, through exploring the significance of global status, we will see that there are important social, political, and economic relations at the global level and that all of this seems to matter to the moral assessment of a variety of immigration cases. Indeed, such relations, and the notion of global status, are already implicitly invoked in some important discussions of actual cases of selective immigration, including Israel's Law of Return. Second, by illustrating global status's role in explaining the moral evaluation of a variety of immigration cases, this chapter begins to demonstrate that the antidiscrimination approach provides a more compelling way to think about states' admission decisions than the anticlassification approach. The focus of this chapter is on exploring how global status matters for determining when immigration criteria wrong a state's *members*. But with this general explanation in view, we will be able to examine when such criteria wrong excluded nonmembers.

I will then proceed, in **Chapter 4**, to explain how, in general, states are relevantly like the domestic associations, organizations, and communities to which antidiscrimination duties apply, such as many businesses and large clubs. The main consideration in determining whether an association has these duties is whether it occupies a position of power over access to important opportunities; and states, especially wealthy states, control access to a significant range of life options.

In combination with the findings of Chapter 3, the analysis based in the normative similarity to the relevant domestic associations suggests that states are subject to at least global antidiscrimination's *primary duties*—duties owed to any person, member or nonmember, not to exclude on the basis of identity when it contributes to a group's global vulnerability in ways that treat the group's members as morally inferior—or, more simply, when it degrades them. Such duties are arguably antidiscrimination's most central duties since they concern exclusion on the basis of identity and so concern direct forms of discrimination; but they also seem to be fairly minimal compared with other duties states might have, some of which will be discussed in Chapter 6. I will then respond to the major ways of pushing back at the analogy between domestic associations and states, including different challenges suggested in recent books by Ryan Pevnick and Michael Blake, and explain how each of these challenges can easily be dealt with. Finally, this chapter will show why the implicit acceptance of the moral importance of global status in prominent immigration discussions already suggests that states are morally bound by something like antidiscrimination's primary duties.

As I mentioned, for most of the book—indeed up until Chapter 6—I will be concerned with establishing that states have these primary duties—not to exclude on the basis of identity when doing so degrades the excluded group(s)—and not with duties not to exclude simply when it contributes to a group's global disadvantages, including economic or material disadvantages. It might seem odd to give more attention to concerns about what I am calling degradation than to comparatively reduced opportunities for excluded migrants or, more broadly, to their material interests, given that the latter sorts of issues might be far more significant to the excluded migrants themselves. One reason for this book's emphasis is that, as will be discussed in Chapter 2, subordination bears a conceptual connection to degradation, whereas there is no such connection to comparatively reduced opportunities. But there are also additional reasons, three of which I will mention here.

First is a point about the economic and philosophical literature on migration: a primary emphasis of much of this work is the material interests and concerns of potential migrants and of nonmembers more generally.[55] In contrast, relatively little sustained attention has been given to the idea that a state's immigration policies can express a demeaning message about, undermine the self-respect of, and perpetuate stigmas against excluded migrants.[56] Thus, even though, as I observed before, scholars and media commentators seem to frequently appeal

---

[55] For some of these see Caplan and Weinersmith, *Open Borders*; Carens, *Ethics of Immigration*; Brennan and van der Vossen, *In Defense of Openness*; Clemens and Bazzi, "Golden Door"; Clemens, "Economics and Emigration"; Huemer, "Right to Immigrate?"; Kukathas, "Case for Open Immigration"; Miller, *National Responsibility*; Oberman, "Immigration as Human Right"; Wellman, "Freedom of Association."

[56] There are relatively few such treatments. For examples, see Fine, "Immigration and Discrimination"; Lim, "Selecting Immigrants by Skill." Also see Hosein, *Ethics of Migration*, chap. 4, esp. 91–92.

to such concerns, they remain significantly undertheorized. Second, aside from certain cases of nonmembers, such as refugees, we will see that a variety of theorists reject the idea that a state's immigration criteria and policies can wrong (groups of) nonmembers, which, if correct, would imply that states are not bound even by the comparatively undemanding duties associated with degradation concerns. Alternatively, several prominent commentators think that even if nonmembers can be wronged by a state's criteria and policies, a state nonetheless has the right to wrong nonmembers in those ways. We will see in Chapter 7 that if either of these positions is correct, states have a moral right against any external interference, including even diplomatic or economic pressures, to determine their immigration policies in any way they choose. And this important issue has also been relatively unexplored and unchallenged. Finally, in a variety of cases, selectively excluding people in a vulnerable group might not meaningfully alter the landscape of available opportunities for them but remains morally troubling nonetheless, and concerns about degradation will help us to see why.

Starting with a focus on race, ethnicity, and related categories including nationality, religion, and ethno-religion, **Chapter 5** will explore the implications of saying that states have the primary duties; it will examine when criteria generally violate those duties and when they generally do not. As discussed in Chapter 3, a group's status can vary in multiple respects, including in terms of global region and dimension of (dis)advantage. So, determining whether the primary duties are violated in any specific case will depend on a variety of both empirical issues and normative judgments concerning historical relations, present social contexts, and immigration rates to the relevant state. More than providing definitive answers, what I hope to do in this chapter is demonstrate how the conceptual resources provided by the global antidiscrimination approach can effectively assist in thinking through complex immigration cases. Though the inability to conclusively evaluate cases might be seen as a flaw of the antidiscrimination approach, I believe it is a virtue. It would be far less messy to say that racial, ethnic, and related criteria are either always wrong or never wrong, but those stances seem unappealing when we consider the full range of potential cases.

That said, there are some important findings to state up front. One is that not all racial and ethnic criteria violate the primary duties. Moreover, even if a state's identity criteria selectively exclude globally *vulnerable* racial or ethnic groups, this does not mean that the state violates its primary duties. Finally, even if such an exclusion violates the state's primary duties, this does not imply that it degrades, and therefore wrongs, all the vulnerable groups that are excluded.

This chapter also expands the discussion to other central categories of identity—in particular, gender, sex, sexual orientation, and disability—and demonstrates both how these categories of groups clearly have a global social status and why, under the antidiscrimination approach, states' admission decisions are morally constrained by them. Finally, Chapter 5 will discuss how the primary duties are not corrective duties based in past injustices. More generally, the antidiscrimination approach I argue for is not a backward-looking framework that aims to repair past wrongs, but one concerned with current (and future) social status.

Chapter 6 turns to whether *non*-identity criteria, such as health mandates, professional qualifications, or language requirements, can violate the primary duties. I argue that at times such criteria constitute the use of proxies designed to select against particular groups. When they do so, their use may violate the primary duties, and they are subject to the same sort of normative analysis for determining when identity criteria violate the primary duties; but when they do not amount to proxies, non-identity criteria are generally permissible from the standpoint of the primary duties. This discussion has implications for actions related to broad immigration proposals and policies beyond the use of criteria, such as the proposal to build a wall along the United States' southern border.

Chapter 6 then explores what further analysis is required for maintaining that states have antidiscrimination duties beyond the primary duties and when such duties might be violated, in the process outlining some important differences between the kinds of social relations inside a state and those among members of different states. I will focus on two possible types of duties: to not selectively exclude when it contributes to a group's global disadvantages (and not only when it degrades), with implications for both identity and non-identity criteria; and to not exclude anyone who faces significant disadvantage (material, political, or otherwise), with implications for non-identity groups such as the global poor and people with significant health conditions. As a general matter I do not believe that there is anything especially morally significant about identity characteristics when it comes to immigration. The book focuses on these characteristics because, as discussed in section 1 of this chapter, they have often taken center stage in debates about immigration. But any group that is subordinated or at risk of becoming subordinated is of concern from the standpoint of global antidiscrimination duties. It may be that subordination more closely tracks identity than it tracks other characteristics, such as poverty and health, but I do not believe there is otherwise any reason to concentrate the analysis on groups formed around identity. More broadly, I will discuss how there does not seem to be any reason to limit our concern only to identity criteria that degrade or to identity criteria at all if other sorts of criteria or admission policies more generally prompt the same underlying anxieties. However, even if more demanding sorts of antidiscrimination duties could be established, a variety of immigration policies would remain morally unobjectionable.

Related to this last point, a final goal of Chapter 6 is to highlight the distinctions between the antidiscrimination approach and the open-borders view, while critically evaluating the main deontological arguments for the latter, which attempt to establish something like a moral right to international freedom of movement (a right to migrate). Though the case for such a right is powerful, I will argue that the central question for establishing such a right, especially from a liberty standpoint, must still be addressed for these arguments to be successful. This question is whether states, or their members, collectively own the relevant territories or the goods and institutions within the territories.

Finally, **Chapter 7** examines the implications of both my book's analysis and the dominant open-borders view for the idea that states have a right to exclude. We will see that this right is distinct from the idea of states' choice examined in Chapter 1 and amounts to the claim that states have a right against interference to make even wrongful admission decisions. Focusing on criteria such as race, ethnicity, and religion, as well as, relatedly,[57] the exclusion of people with urgent admission needs, including refugees and asylum seekers, I will offer a reductio of this position. A major implication of this last chapter is that states are *not* unilaterally entitled to make membership decisions. This result is significant not only for the use of identity criteria in admissions decisions but also, more importantly, for addressing the admission needs of people around the world experiencing significant and urgent threats to their basic human rights. As an alternative to unilateral control by each individual state, I suggest that the morally appropriate way for states' membership decisions to be made is similar to the way in which membership decisions are made for a variety of domestic associations, including businesses and large social clubs—namely, through the collective establishment of rules governing admission, with violations subject to economic or political penalties and sanctions.

---

[57] See again the valuable discussion in Song, *Immigration and Democracy*, chap. 7. See also "UNHCR Guidance on Racism and Xenophobia," UN Office of the High Commissioner for Human Rights, https://www.unhcr.org/en-us/protection/operations/5f7c860f4/unhcr-guidance-on-racism-and-xenophobia.html; International Labour Office, International Organization for Migration, and Office of the United Nations High Commissioner for Human Rights. *International Migration*; Esipova, Ray, and Pugliese, "Syrian Refugees Not Welcome"; "Are Some EU Countries Wrong to Only Want Christian Refugees?," Debating Europe, September 8, 2015, https://www.debatingeurope.eu/2015/09/08/are-some-eu-countries-wrong-to-only-want-christian-refugees/#.Y-v4tXbMLEY; Alexander et al., "How Race and Religion"; Watson, "United States' Hollow Commitment"; Lipka, "Most Americans Express Support."

1

Race, Ethnicity, and Religion under States' Choice

1. Introduction

With a preliminary description of the book and its motivation in mind, I want to begin this first chapter by considering dominant ethical positions on immigration restrictions. Critically examining these views and what they imply for various kinds of restrictions will set the stage for pursuing what I will call the "global antidiscrimination approach," which I will go on to explain and argue for in the rest of the book.

The main subject of this chapter is the conventional position that states have extensive moral rights to make admission decisions as they choose or even to close their borders altogether ("states' choice"). In a later chapter, I will explore in greater detail the opposing position that maintains states' borders must be open ("open borders").

2. Some Cases and Terminology

I wish to start with a focus on points of agreement across the range of immigration views. In particular, there are two key intuitions that virtually all normative immigration theorists share. First, as mentioned in the introductory chapter, there is near-universal agreement that racial and ethnic immigration criteria are generally morally wrong.[1] Second, almost everyone appears to regard restricting immigration for security- and safety-based reasons as *not* generally morally wrong—at least, that is, when such concerns are empirically plausible and not simply motivated by animus or bias against certain groups of people.[2]

---

[1] See (for example) Carens, *Ethics of Immigration*, 174, 179, 182; Miller, *Strangers in Our Midst*, 102, 103. David Miller, "Immigrants, Nations, and Citizenship," 389; Fine, "Immigration and Discrimination," 146; Blake, *Justice, Migration, and Mercy*; Wellman, "Freedom of Association,"; Lim, "Selecting Immigrants by Skill"; Mendoza, "Presumptive Rights of Immigrants"; Blake, "Immigration, Association, and Antidiscrimination"; Song, *Immigration and Democracy*, 34–35.

[2] This is clearly the position among those who advocate for broad state rights over immigration ("states' choice" views), but it is also the position of most open-border theorists. For instance, Carens writes that "a principled use of national security as a criterion of exclusion is morally permissible."

Immigration and Discrimination: (Un)Welcoming Others. Sahar Akhtar, Oxford University Press. © Sahar Akhtar 2024.
DOI: 10.1093/oso/9780198898696.003.0002

Let me clarify that, despite widespread agreement, these two stances might simply be mistaken. Perhaps racial and ethnic restrictions are *not* generally wrong, contrary to what most seem to think, and perhaps empirically grounded security reasons for limiting immigration are in fact wrong.[3] While I do not think the above positions are mistaken, neither do I wish to simply take for granted that they are correct. Rather, I will attempt to eventually vindicate them—though not necessarily as applied in any particular instance. But points of agreement may be a good place to start our examination, and we can at least tentatively treat such points as normative "data" in need of explanation—an explanation for why certain restrictions almost always raise moral flags while others characteristically do not. In certain ways, the approach that I will adopt in this book is similar to Joseph Carens's "contextualist" approach to assessing the ethics of political questions. In particular, I will consider not only points of agreement among a variety of theorists, but, like under Carens's approach, also a wide range of cases, including certain actual cases, to examine the implications of theoretical positions and to prompt reflection on whether one's ethical position on a particular case is compatible with one's theoretical view.[4]

Returning to the two key intuitions from above, we should of course not be surprised that while security bases for restrictions are generally not regarded as impermissible, racial and ethnic restrictions generally are. The latter sorts of criteria used in any context or for any purpose in any society typically raise numerous concerns, especially considering the history of injustices against certain groups in a given society. Accordingly, it's likely that there are a number of potential views available for explaining the differences between using, say, racial criteria and using almost any other sort of criteria. So, to narrow the range of suitable explanations, we can add more "data," so to speak—that is, more fine-tuned positions on different types of immigration restrictions.

One important nuance we can mine is that while racial and ethnic criteria are generally considered wrong, a range of prominent authors writing on the ethics of immigration, including Joseph Carens, David Miller, Michael Blake, and Christopher Wellman, suggest that there are *certain* cases in which such criteria

---

Carens, *Ethics of Immigration*, 176. Also see Kukathas, "Case for Open Immigration." Kukathas argues that a security rationale does not justify a stance against open borders as such, but he does suggest that security grounds are permissible for restricting *particular* persons' movement (see esp. 217–18). For a final example, see Huemer, "Right to Immigrate?" Huemer suggests that if a sudden and large influx of immigrants were to lead to "serious harmful consequences" (29), which would seemingly include safety and security problems, then (at least temporary) limits on immigration could be justified.

[3] Walzer, whose position I discuss in section 3.1, suggests that racial and ethnic criteria may be used in connection to protecting the state's dominant culture, potentially justifying the White Australia policy discussed in the introductory chapter and below. While I will argue that racial and ethnic criteria do not always seem wrong, I disagree with his diagnosis of the White Australia case and his more general claim that such criteria may be permissible whenever they protect the state's dominant culture.

[4] See Carens, "Contextual Approach."

are potentially morally permissible. For instance, despite arguably being the leading proponent of the view that states' borders should be open, and despite regarding racial and ethnic criteria as distinctively wrong, Carens has proposed that Japan's past policy excluding people who do not share the dominant ethnicity is permissible; he suggests that any wrong(s) involved with such exclusions may have been outweighed by the moral value served by the Japanese people's protection of their distinct culture.[5] David Miller, Michael Blake, and Christopher Wellman all consider the use of racial and ethnic immigration preferences morally wrong (though for different reasons), but they, along with several others,[6] express support for Israel's Law of Return, which, similarly, grants automatic admission to all and only Jewish people; they suggest that any wrong done by the policy is potentially outweighed by the Jewish experience of the Holocaust.[7] One question we can ask then is: what, if anything, accounts for why *these* examples of racial and ethnic immigration restrictions might be morally acceptable, or, at least, why do they appear to look different to supporters?

But before beginning to consider explanations, I think it will be helpful to have a greater variety of types of immigration restrictions in mind. Consider the following cases.

Security Control:

A state excludes any person who poses a national-security threat, as determined by a rigorous multi-institutional screening process.

Population Limits:

A state accepts everyone on a first-come-first-serve basis, but with numerical caps.

Occupational Preference:

A state's immigration policy prioritizes workers in one industry, disfavoring other occupations.

Linguistic Criteria:

A state excludes people who fail its language criteria.

Racial Ban:

A wealthy state composed only of European-descendant white members decides to admit people of all races but explicitly disfavors the admission of Black people.

---

[5] Carens, "Migration and Morality," 37–39. He does not claim to have *established* the case's permissibility, but instead suggests it is potentially permissible.

[6] See (for example) Coleman and Harding, "Citizenship." Likewise, Carens suggests Israel is a "special case," though I'm not entirely clear he thinks it potentially permissible. Carens, "Who Should Get In?," 109, note 19. Also see Carens, "Migration and Morality," 45.

[7] Miller, "Immigration," 204. Miller associates Israel's policy with religion not ethnicity, but that distinction is far from clear. See Fine, "Immigration and Discrimination," 147; Blake, "Discretionary Immigration," 286; Wellman, "Freedom of Association," 140–41.

The above cases seem to range not only in content but also in objectionableness. While Security Control looks clearly permissible and Racial Ban seems clearly wrong, the other types of immigration cases intuitively seem to fall somewhere in between those. For instance, of all the other examples, Population Limits seems the least objectionable; indeed, there may be nothing wrong with the case whatsoever. In contrast, how we think about the other cases may very much depend on which particular details are filled in. If we imagine that under Occupational Preference, the state prioritizes the high-tech or IT industry and disfavors, for example, the nursing, home-cleaning-services, and child-care industries, it may raise some potential concerns or at least some issues that require further analysis; on the other hand, if the state prioritizes the admission of low-skilled farmers over scientists and accountants, the policy may be commendable in some respects. Similarly, Linguistic Criteria may stir unease if the state's policy is that immigrants must be fluent in, say, German, but far less so, perhaps not at all, if it requires fluency in either Samoan, Cambodian, or Lao. More clearly, though less realistically, if the state's criteria (whether expressed or not) specifically exclude speakers of a particular language, such as Arabic, it would seem very troubling.

While considerably more analysis is warranted to determine whether any of the above cases *are* either wrong or not wrong, for now it's worth seeing whether we can identify broad normative considerations to account for why these types of immigration restrictions might at least *look* very different. And the first thing we can note is that the existing dominant philosophical views do not seem to offer satisfactory explanations. For instance, the open-borders position, which will be discussed in detail in Chapter 6, suggests that, just as people are free to move to different domestic sub-units within legitimate states (for example, someone is free to move from Virginia to California), people should be free to move across states, aside mainly for security and safety concerns.[8] Among other things, this suggests that not only was Japan's past policy wrong (contrary to Carens's position on the policy), but, more importantly I believe, that Population Limits, Occupational Preference, and Linguistic Criteria are all wrong regardless of any details that are filled in.

Since we'll explore the open-borders position in Chapter 6, I want to shift to the conventional position of states' choice. This position claims that states (or their current members) have extensive moral rights to determine their admission as they choose. More specifically, states' choice refers to states having liberty-rights

---

[8] As we will see, proponents maintain that just as within a state, movement can be legitimately constrained for certain important reasons (such as protecting property rights and public safety), so too can international movement. See Carens, "Migration and Morality," 36–37. Importantly, however, as we will explore in Chapter 6, at least for the most prominent proponent—Joseph Carens—it is far from clear whether any of these reasons amount to grounds for *excluding* people. Rather, drawing from the example of similar domestic restrictions, they seem to constitute grounds for constraining the speed and ease of people's ability to move. See *Ethics of Immigration*, 246–48; for analog domestic scenarios, see 251.

(or permission-rights) to choose criteria or not admit anyone altogether. If there is a liberty-right to do X, there is no duty not to do X and, thus, doing X is not wrong. Typically, people use the term "right to exclude," rather than "states' choice," to describe this idea, but, as we will see in Chapter 7, in many discussions the right to exclude means something far stronger than a liberty-right to choose criteria or not admit anyone.[9] While the open-borders position seems to automatically condemn policies that may, in the end, prove acceptable—or at least deserve further exploration—accounts of states' choice, as we'll see, face a great deal of difficulty explaining what, if anything, is wrong with certain policies that appear *straight-forwardly* wrong, such as Racial Ban. Before going further to show the specific difficulties that the major states'-choice variants face, let me briefly clarify further terminology and discuss important ideas that all such views, and this book, share.

First, both under states'-choice accounts and in this book, the term "member" is used broadly to include both a state's citizens and any residents in the state, and "nonmember" refers to someone who neither is a citizen nor resides within the state's territory. Second, proponents of states' choice maintain that extensive immigration rights are something that only "legitimate" states rightfully enjoy. Though some authors define a legitimate state in very broad terms,[10] states'-choice theorists use the notion to refer to a state that protects the basic human rights of all its members and also does not violate the basic human rights of nonmembers.[11] There's been significant discussion concerning exactly what constitutes our basic human rights, but they are largely taken to refer to those conditions that are necessary to have a minimally decent life. Examples typically include physical security, subsistence, free expression, and free association.[12]

Third, though it is separate from the requirements for a legitimate state, proponents of states' choice maintain that states have some moral obligation to provide help to nonmembers whose basic human rights are in jeopardy. Since it may be impractical or ineffective to help these nonmembers in their home states, this will often mean that states have some obligation to admit certain

---

[9] It seems to also refer to a claim-right against others not to interfere with the state's criteria, or not to admit anyone, even if the criteria or closure is wrong. So, to keep the two types of rights distinct, I will use "states' choice" to refer to liberty-rights and "right to exclude" to refer to the claim-right against interference even when a state's policy is wrong.

[10] For a prominent description along these lines, see the work of Allen Buchanan, who defines "recognitional," or international, legitimacy as requiring that a state satisfy both internal and external conditions of minimal justice and also that it not displace or destroy another legitimate state by coming into existence. See *Justice*, 266, chap. 6. He moreover argues that the external conditions of justice that would apply in ideal circumstances require not only satisfaction of human rights but also distributive justice. See Buchanan, 193, chap. 4.

[11] See (for example) Miller, *Strangers in Our Midst*, 59–62; Wellman, "Freedom of Association," 127–29; and Altman and Wellman, *Liberal Theory*, 4.

[12] This list of basic human rights is inspired by Rawls's list. See *Law of Peoples*. For a more comprehensive list, see Buchanan, *Justice*, 129.

nonmembers, especially victims of oppression and persecution,[13] such as refugees
and asylum seekers, but also, more broadly, anyone whose basic human rights are
significantly and urgently threatened.[14] Importantly, however, Chapter 7 will
demonstrate that at least many states'-choice theorists, among others, also maintain that states have the moral right to violate their moral obligation to admit these
nonmembers.[15] Finally, another idea shared by proponents of states' choice is that
states have fairly robust obligations to admit family members of the state's current
members.[16]

As I will discuss in Chapter 6, I entirely agree that states have extensive moral
obligations regarding both categories of nonmembers—both people whose basic
human rights are significantly and urgently threatened and family of existing
members (and under my view, family is construed broadly, including, for instance,
unmarried long-term partners). I label such categories of nonmembers "nondiscretionary" since both proponents and opponents of the conventional position
maintain that states are often not at their moral discretion to choose whether to
admit them. But my agreement with the conventional position does not go much
further than this. For outside of these categories—that is, when it comes to
"discretionary" nonmembers—the conventional position is that a state's admission decisions are not morally constrained by any duties to nonmembers.[17]
Focusing on two prominent types of states'-choice accounts, in the next section
I'll demonstrate that they do not provide satisfactory explanations for potential
moral differences in the range of immigration-restriction cases I described above.
I'll also discuss more general problems with each approach.

3. States' Choice

Variants of the states'-choice position commonly appeal to the foundational idea
that, just like most other communities and associations, states have the moral
right to self-determination—that is, the collective moral right to define for

---

[13] See Walzer, *Spheres of Justice*, 31–34, 44–48; Blake, "Discretionary Immigration," 281–82; Miller,
"Immigration"; and Wellman, "Freedom of Association," 127–29.
[14] Pevnick extends the idea of refugee to people who are unable to meet their basic subsistence
needs. See Pevnick, *Constraints of Justice*, esp. 139–58. Wellman also suggests that the traditional
understanding of refugee, as someone fleeing persecution, may be too narrow. See Wellman, "Right to
Exclude," 119.
[15] The distinction between liberty-rights and claim-rights will be important for that discussion.
[16] Moreover, I think we may presume that for most proponents of states' choice, a state's rights over
immigration are also limited in cases of explicit agreements between states (for example, as in the case
of EU states) or agreements between states and external nonstate actors or international organizations.
Michael Blake, for instance, explicitly recognizes such limits. See Blake, "Immigration, Jurisdiction, and
Exclusion," 122–25.
[17] Though Miller's view, discussed in section 3.1, might seem an exception to what I have just said,
this is far from clear.

themselves the terms of their community or association and to control access to its set of goods and resources. And control over the state's membership is regarded as a central component of what it means to be self-determining. Appeals to self-determination are made on different grounds, but I will discuss two dominant types of accounts in the literature: cultural and associational.

3.1 Culture

This first account maintains that states have broad moral rights to decide their admission in order to retain control over the dominant character or distinctive culture of their members,[18] especially perhaps when the dominant culture has historical ties to the territory.[19] Generally speaking, the cultural account emphasizes the value of a common way of life or cultural identity to individual agency or flourishing, and it claims that having control over admission enables the state to protect or promote this common identity.[20]

This account may best capture popular opinions about immigration and any beliefs about why states should be at liberty to choose whatever criteria for admission they want. And there is certainly much to be said for the account, especially if we focus not on temporary migrants but people seeking to move to a new state on a permanent basis or those seeking membership. For starters, authors in both the nationalist and liberal traditions have for some time believed that living in a *particular* culture—as opposed to any culture that meets one's basic needs or provides adequate options—is important because of the central relationship between culture and autonomy (or agency).[21] One's culture is thought to provide the background context that gives meaning to our values, goals, and plans. Based on this understanding of culture's relevance, it seems a certain kind of cultural continuity is important for individual flourishing. And it's possible that new members who fail to share at least central values and beliefs of the existing culture could pose threats to its integrity if they arrive in high numbers.[22] Perhaps more importantly, if the social scientific research is correct, then a common culture and the mutual identification that comes along with it may be important for fostering trust and hence for facilitating the conditions of social and economic

---

[18] Walzer, *Spheres of Justice*, 62; Miller, "Immigration."

[19] Miller, *National Responsibility*, 216–18.

[20] Miller, 213–22. Miller even ties state legitimacy to the state's protection or promotion of its distinct culture.

[21] For important discussions of these ideas, see Kymlicka, *Liberalism, Community, and Culture*; Kymlicka, *Multicultural Citizenship*; Parekh, *Rethinking Multiculturalism*; Sandel, *Liberalism*; Taylor, *Sources of Self*; and Young, *Politics of Difference*.

[22] A very recent, important book argues along these lines, especially that immigrants' attitudes on, for instance, trust, frugality, and the importance of living near family bear fairly strong correlations with origin-state members' attitudes on these things. See Jones, *Culture Transplant*.

justice.[23] The idea is that solidarity and social cohesion are important for people's willingness to support various redistributive goals and the state's political institutions, and if citizens adopt an us-versus-them attitude toward other members, this undermines their support for state programs and services they consider to primarily benefit the "other side."

The cultural account, however, also confronts challenges and faces some important limitations that will matter for this book's purposes. First, some researchers have pushed back on the idea that a common culture is critical for a durable welfare system, arguing that, ultimately, it is stable institutions, and not common identity, that determine the kind of cooperation needed to sustain a robust welfare system, including the provision of public goods.[24] At most, they argue, any correlation between mutual identification and a stable welfare system suggests that states should do more to help integrate immigrants and foster solidarity between existing members and newcomers, not that states may choose the characteristics of new members in any way they choose.[25] A related issue is that, in most cases, what seems to matter for individual well-being is that one's culture not change *abruptly*; and it can easily be argued that as long as there are numerical limits on who is admitted, new members who might not possess the "right" cultural characteristics (more on this soon) do not pose threats to cultural integrity in ways that matter.[26] So it seems we may need more theoretical material to determine when criteria protecting a culture are justified. Additionally, the account's reach may be very limited. Most modern states do not contain a single national or linguistic culture (consider the United States, Brazil, and India, for instance). So, for this account to have the greatest application, we would have to allow common state culture to be interpreted very broadly to include public or popular cultures.[27]

---

[23] See Bowles and Gintis, "Reciprocity"; Lindbeck, Nyberg, and Weibull, "Social Norms"; Fehr, Fischbacher, and Gächter, "Strong Reciprocity." For a very recent discussion, see Jones, *Culture Transplant*.

[24] In their new book, Alex Nowrasteh and Benjamin Powell carefully examine three within-state case studies (pre-First World War USA, Israel, and Jordan) to argue that neither high-skilled nor low-skilled labor migration significantly impacts either formal or informal institutions. See Nowrasteh and Powell, *Wretched Refuse*.

[25] See the valuable discussions in Pevnick, *Constraints of Justice*, 148–50; Brennan and van der Vossen, *In Defense of Openness*, esp. 38–41. A second, related challenge observes that divergences from a common national identity can often come from within, such as through younger generations.

[26] See Scheffler, "Significance of Culture"; and Pevnick, *Constraints of Justice*, 233–35. Also see the discussion in Kymlicka, *Liberalism, Community, and Culture*.

[27] But then it may be difficult to understand the very rationale behind the view. The more we think of culture in very thin or watered-down terms, the more likely it seems that outsiders will be able to identify with and share in the state "culture," at least its central aspects. In fact, there is emerging evidence that when people move to a new state on a permanent basis, they prefer to relocate to a place with a culture they are already comfortable with, not least because moving to a new state can be emotionally and psychologically costly. Under a regime of open borders, then, in which people can move wherever they choose subject to only minimal constraints, it seems we should expect that states would often attract people who share a great affinity for the state's central culture—again, defined in very thin terms. If this is right, though, it may significantly weaken the original justification for states'

For this book's purposes, perhaps the most central worry about the cultural justification for states' choice concerns whether, and if so how, any moral constraints on a state's admission decisions can be defended as long as some criteria can, even vaguely or remotely, protect the dominant culture. This worry arises for a few reasons. First, aside from language qualifications and testing for knowledge of the state's history, its contemporary events, and the like (which might not demonstrate cultural *affinity* so much as cultural knowledge), determining whether nonmembers share in the state's dominant culture would often seem very difficult—how might we meaningfully measure "culture" without reducing it to one or two variables such as trust attitudes?[28]—so much so that states would likely simply employ rough-and-ready demographic data such as applicants' race, ethnicity, or religion. A more general observation along these lines has been helpfully highlighted by Sarah Song in her insightful new book on immigration. She asks simply, "What if particular racial and ethnic identities are considered significant to dominant narratives of national identity?" As she notes, "Visions of national identity have always been contested, and race and ethnicity have historically played a central role in shaping what it means to be American, British, French, Australian, and so on."[29] Moreover, she notes, and as we saw in the introductory chapter, "racial and xenophobic sentiments are not relics of the past."[30]

Michael Walzer, a primary proponent of the cultural account, also recognizes the historical and contemporary links between characteristics such as race and efforts to protect a culture.[31] But unlike Song, Walzer doesn't altogether condemn even some notoriously objectionable policies, including the White Australia Policy, which was rooted in the belief that whites are superior to other races. While Walzer suggests that the use of race is unfortunate, he also implies that policies such as White Australia may be employed to preserve a state's dominant culture. It seems that for him, the moral limits on any such policy come only from considerations related to people with urgent admission needs, as he claims that such policies are morally permissible if the state in question cedes some territory to provide refuge to people fleeing oppression and the like.[32] Outside of non-discretionary cases, Walzer suggests that using racial criteria is not wrong.[33]

Now, in contrast to what seems to be Song's view on the issue,[34] I will argue that employing racial or ethnic criteria is not *always* morally wrong. But the point is that even in instances in which using those sorts of criteria seems clearly morally wrong, as with the Chinese Exclusion Act and White Australia Policy and the

control over admission criteria. At the very least, it suggests that the cultural justification for states' choice is strongest in cases in which a state is characterized largely by a single comprehensive linguistic culture.

[28] Nowrasteh and Forrester, "Trust," especially the introduction.
[29] Song, *Immigration and Democracy*, 34.   [30] Song, 35.   [31] Walzer, *Spheres of Justice*.
[32] Walzer, 46–48.   [33] Walzer, 46–48.   [34] Song, *Immigration and Democracy*, 34–35.

hypothetical case of Racial Ban, states may resort to using racial or ethnic criteria by appealing to the rationale of protecting and preserving the common identity. Moreover, imagine again that under Language Criteria, the state's criteria specifically exclude people who speak, say, Arabic. As the cultural account currently stands, it isn't clear on what grounds such policies can be condemned.

Let me be clear that the main current philosophical position under the cultural account explicitly condemns using racial or ethnic characteristics in admission decisions (though it does not seem to set any constraints on language standards used in immigration policy). Specifically, David Miller, who has provided the most compelling defense of the cultural account, maintains that race and ethnicity cannot be used as criteria for exclusion by democratic states.[35] Miller claims that since people have strong interests at stake when it comes to immigration, states must show people equal consideration absent any relevant differences between them, which implies that a state must give someone relevant reasons if they are excluded while others are admitted.[36] But, he claims, racial or ethnic preferences are not relevant reasons.[37]

As with the cultural account more generally, there is much to say in favor of Miller's specific view. Of particular note here, Miller maintains that while choosing immigrants on the basis of race, ethnicity, or national origin conveys a wrongful message to existing members who share the disfavored characteristics, such as the message that they are second-class citizens, the primary injustice is the one done to the nonmembers who are excluded by the criteria.[38] This would seem to allow him—but as we will see shortly, not some other states'-choice proponents—to say that, along with the Chinese Exclusion Act and White Australia, the policy in Racial Ban is wrong. A more general way to describe the point is that, unlike other states'-choice proponents, Miller seems to suggest that the interests of even discretionary nonmembers place some constraints on states' immigration preferences. At the same time, however, it's unclear what exactly such constraints amount to because it is unclear what it means, under his view, to show equal consideration to nonmembers seeking admission.

These points can be appreciated by examining central examples Miller provides to motivate the idea.[39] He imagines a case in which two people are stranded in a remote place and suffering from dehydration, and he stresses that we must show them equal consideration, which implies helping them both regardless of their racial identities.[40] Miller's conclusion here is certainly correct, as it is unthinkable to deny either person help for almost any reason at all (let alone because of their

[35] Miller, *Strangers in Our Midst*, 104–6.   [36] Miller, 105.

[37] Miller, 105–6. More specifically, he claims that race and ethnicity cannot be tied to legitimate goals for democratic states, and he says he is relying on an "intuitive" understanding of which goals are legitimate. See Miller, 197n35.

[38] Miller, 104, 106.   [39] He calls this idea "weak cosmopolitanism."

[40] Miller, *Strangers in Our Midst*, 30–33.

race). But this case involves urgent claims, much more akin to the claims of certain *nondiscretionary* nonmembers, such as those seeking refuge from persecution or facing other significant and urgent basic human rights deprivations. The application to discretionary nonmembers is much less obvious. In the example he provides that comes closest to the non-urgent interests of discretionary nonmembers, Miller considers a hiker who requests to have one of Miller's books because she has run out of reading material. He thinks he must consider her request and, if he refuses her, provide her some reason; failing to do so would disrespect her. However, he does not believe he owes it to her to *justify* himself.[41] Accordingly, it's unclear what sort of moral *obligation*, if any, is at play. Now, as we will discuss further in Chapters 3 and 4, states control access to a wide range of important life opportunities, so the interests at stake for prospective immigrants are appreciably more significant than the interests of a hiker requesting a book out of boredom. But, as the view stands, it does not seem these differences should matter. As long as a state is not turning away people whose basic human rights are significantly and urgently threatened (or perhaps, more generally, any nondiscretionary nonmembers[42]), it would seem that what extending equal consideration to nonmembers means is, at most, that states must simply provide *some* reason for refusing them admission. Put differently, if the demand to offer reasons to those denied admission doesn't amount to a demand to provide justification, why must the state's reasons rule out racial preferences?[43] We will examine Miller's view further in Chapter 7, but it seems we need additional conceptual resources to answer such a question. Without them, it's difficult to assess whether Miller's view, the most sophisticated of the cultural accounts, can in fact condemn Racial Ban and similar policies.

3.2 Association

The second type of account that appeals to self-determination to ground states' choice has far broader application to contemporary states since it is not limited to those with a dominant culture or character. This *associational* account maintains that states have a right to choose their associates, and they vary depending on the

---

[41] Miller, 37. Rather than illustrating moral obligations, this example seems to suggest that outside of urgent need, we should follow norms of etiquette and the like.

[42] Miller would also presumably reject the idea that a state may use racial criteria in family-reunification cases, the other category of nondiscretionary cases.

[43] Relatedly, it's also not obvious how the fact that a state is a democracy is supposed to bar it from implementing criteria that are thought to wrong *nonmembers*. If the concern were about how certain members are wronged, it might be easy to see how the state's democratic character is supposed to rule out racial criteria as illegitimate (for instance, racial immigration screens might perpetuate the minority status of a group of members). But wrong done to members is not the primary reason Miller thinks a state may not use racial preferences.

underlying moral basis for why states are considered to have this right. But in this chapter, I'll focus on the view cogently defended by Christopher Heath Wellman. In an influential article, Wellman argues that all legitimate states, or their members, simply have the collective *freedom* to associate with whomever they choose or refuse association altogether. This freedom to associate, he argues, implies the moral right to choose immigration criteria in any way a state chooses, as long as the state does not wrong its current members, and (regarding discretionary nonmembers) it implies states may simply exclude all nonmembers.[44] I'll call Wellman's particular position the "associational freedom" view.

To make his case, Wellman first points out that in the context of marriage, people clearly have the freedom to reject a potential associate on whatever basis they choose: since one has the moral right to get married to a willing partner of one's choice, one also has the freedom to reject marrying whomever one chooses. Similarly, Wellman argues, states have the freedom to associate with whatever willing party they choose, and this freedom implies their right to reject potential associates on whatever grounds they choose. Although Wellman recognizes that "freedom of association is much more important for individuals in the marital context," he argues that the freedom to reject potential associates is important and compelling for collective associations as well.[45] He cites religious, sports, and identity associations such as the Boy Scouts as examples of groups that enjoy freedom of association and thus the right to reject potential associates.

This is an attractive position. In general, there is something intuitively compelling about the idea that, as members of a common state, we have the collective freedom to associate with others or not. For instance, as Wellman argues, it seems it should be up to a state's members to decide whether to join regional associations with other states and especially whether to merge with another state to become a single state. Some critics, however, respond that this account is not persuasive in the context of accepting *new members*. For instance, they note that it is difficult to understand how members' freedom of association is damaged by the "mere presence" of immigrants in the society.[46] This concern, however, is largely dependent on interpreting the relevant interests as *associational interests* and, perhaps more narrowly, the interests in consorting or socializing. But even when considering private associations, such as clubs, we needn't think of the interests at

---

[44] Wellman, "Freedom of Association," 127–29.

[45] Like other defenders of states' choice, Wellman maintains that all states have an obligation to help secure the basic human rights of every person regardless of their residence or membership, and he recognizes that to do this, states may sometimes have to admit nonmembers onto their territories. But this is only a contingent or conditional obligation; if a state is able to help protect a nonmember's basic human rights in other ways—such as by helping to secure stable political and economic conditions where they currently live or by granting them temporary refuge—the state need not admit them on anything more than a short-term basis. See Wellman, 113.

[46] Miller, *National Responsibility*, 210–11. Also see Fine, "Freedom of Association," 343; Song, *Immigration and Democracy*, 44–45.

stake in terms of club members' preferences for engaging in or avoiding direct interaction or socialization. Instead, members' freedom of association can simply be interpreted as their collective freedom to structure the shape and nature of their association, or more specifically, their freedom to decide its membership, relationships, affiliations, partnerships, and the like.

There remain, however, some central concerns about this view, all of which suggest that states' freedom of association should not be considered in the broad terms proposed by Wellman. For instance, one question we can ask is why, if states may deny association to whomever they choose, this does not also imply they are free to *disassociate* from whomever they choose.[47] More specifically, if the justification for the moral right to reject potential associates is that states ought to have control over their shape and character as part of their freedom of association, then this freedom would also seem to support a state's moral right to disassociate from people with whom it no longer wishes to associate. This is undoubtedly a component of collective freedom of association for many clubs and private associations; it is permissible for a club to expel certain members if, for instance, they are not abiding by the bylaws or general culture of the club. And we think the freedom to disassociate is especially important in the context of marriage. One partner should have the freedom to divorce the other partner when he or she chooses. Now there is certainly a difference between evicting club members or divorcing a marriage partner, on the one hand, and disassociating from fellow members, on the other hand, insofar as the latter forces people to move from their homes, communities, and families.[48] One might say, as Walzer does, that current residents have something like a locational right against being evicted from their homes and from the territory where they reside.[49] Moreover, forcing someone off the territory could cause (other) violations in their basic human rights, such as violations in their property rights, and this is something that is ruled out for legitimate states. However, to reinforce the analogy, a state could reject someone from the *political* community by, for instance, revoking their citizenship and providing them with a weaker bundle of welfare and political rights (residence rights) or, less drastically, taking away some of their voting rights, without requiring them to move. And this could be done simply because the majority of

---

[47] Although Wellman initially suggests the possibility of this right to disassociate, later in the paper he simply denies that *states* have this right. See Wellman, "Freedom of Association," 109, 139.

[48] In general, there will plausibly be constraints on states' ability to disassociate that do not apply in the case of private associations. This is because of the function that legitimate states perform: providing the basic goods needed for developing a plan of life. But while legitimacy conditions establish *constraints* on disassociation, it's not obvious that they automatically prohibit it. In particular, revoking people's citizenship without deporting them remains a possibility as long as people's basic human rights are secured, especially if the state ceases to exercise most, if not all, of its power over those it strips of citizenship. See Akhtar, "Stripping Citizenship."

[49] Walzer, *Spheres of Justice*, 43. Stilz also defends occupancy rights. See Stilz, "Occupancy Rights."

members prefer to limit their political affiliation with certain other members.[50] All of this suggests that states' freedom of association faces certain moral limits beyond those facing other sorts of associations. At the very least, it certainly faces greater limits than Wellman recognizes.

In her persuasive response to Wellman's article, Sarah Fine focuses on additional reasons for thinking that states' freedom of association is morally constrained.[51] Though she discusses a range of objections in this vein, let me focus on that which is most directly connected to this book's purpose. Fine has argued that states are not like most other sorts of associations, intimate or collective, because of the valuable opportunities and resources present in any state. Rejection from a state has a very significant impact on the life plans of a potential immigrant (again, even limiting our focus to discretionary nonmembers).[52] And she writes that "when particular clubs or associations start to look a bit more like states in the sense that outsiders have significant interests in becoming members and exclusion brings with it high costs to the nonmembers without serving clear expressive or intimate purposes, the argument in favor of exclusion seems weaker."[53] For support, she considers the exclusion of women from the Jaycees, a large social club with career-advancing networks. I think her point is exactly right and that such organizations' freedom of association is morally constrained in certain ways, at least when it comes to excluding people on the basis of their identity characteristics such as gender or race. Thus, there is *some* reason to think that states are also so constrained. Importantly, if they are, it hardly robs them of their right to deny joining regional associations or their right not to be annexed.[54]

It's important to clarify that like most other states'-choice proponents, Wellman explicitly states that using racial and ethnic immigration criteria is wrong. But his reason for this position is different both from Miller's reason

---

[50] Elsewhere, Wellman, along with his coauthor Andrew Altman, considers this kind of challenge to the view and suggests that it betrays a misunderstanding of the obligations of legitimate states. See Altman and Wellman, *Liberal Theory*. They claim that the main consideration that limits a state's ability to evict current citizens is that states exercise nonconsensual coercive power over their citizens. Because it is nonconsensual, the justification for state coercion is, first, that states secure citizens' basic human rights (namely, they perform the necessary legitimating functions) and, second, that in doing so they do not require unreasonable sacrifices from their constituents (183–84). The second idea—which is only briefly mentioned—seems to be that since coercion already imposes burdens on members, the state must avoid placing additional burdens on them. They write that legitimacy requires a state to "treat everyone within its territorial confines as equal citizens who, among other things, are equally entitled to remain citizens of the territory in which they have resided." This second condition is violated, the authors believe, if a state expels members (184). However, as we've just seen, there is a difference between expelling people from the territory (deportation) and expelling them from the political community (which would involve removing, or downgrading, their membership). Their focus seems to be specifically on the permissibility of deportation.

[51] Fine, "Freedom of Association."   [52] Fine, 350–51.   [53] Fine, 351.

[54] In general, these sorts of rights look quite different from rights over immigration, if for no other reason than that states retain far greater control over the shape of their association when accepting new immigrants than when being forced to join outside associations or states. I will discuss this point further in Chapter 6. See Fine's point about how states can establish "membership" policies in numerous ways outside of their decisions about *whom* to admit. See Fine, 353.

and from what I will propose in this book. Following Michael Blake,[55] Wellman locates the wrong of racial and ethnic criteria not in how they wrong the excluded nonmembers, but rather in how they wrong the state's current members who share the disfavored criteria. He writes that such criteria "would wrongly disrespect those citizens in the dispreferred category" and thus violate our "special duty to respect our fellow citizens as equal partners in the political cooperative."[56] Since, Wellman argues, we lack a similar duty to nonmembers, if the state has no disfavored members, racial or ethnic criteria are not wrong.[57] While Wellman is most drawn to Blake's particular explanation for the wrongness of immigration policies employing criteria such as race and ethnicity, at the same time he has doubts about the explanation. One doubt he raises is whether immigration policies would in fact always be wrong if the state had current members sharing disfavored criteria. For instance, he contemplates a hypothetical Norwegian policy that welcomes 100,000 additional Pakistani immigrants to bolster the existing Pakistani community in Norway but, because of social and political concerns about integration and the like, closes Norway's doors to all further Pakistanis. Wellman suggests that he is not sure whether this policy would be wrong even though many existing Pakistani residents in Norway "might understandably be insulted by the policy" (p. 150).

In later chapters, I will explain why I agree with Wellman that such a policy might not be wrong, and I will discuss his and Blake's views in much greater detail in Chapters 3 and 4. But here I want to simply observe what the position that racial and ethnic criteria do not wrong excluded nonmembers, and more generally, this sort of rationale for why certain types of criteria are morally wrong, implies for the hypothetical policy with perhaps the clearest moral status. Here I'm referring again to Racial Ban, which seems patently wrong. But under this position for why racial and ethnic criteria are wrong, Racial Ban would not be wrong since there are no members in the state sharing the disfavored race—an implication that Wellman himself raises significant concerns about, as I will discuss shortly.[58] Likewise, if under Linguistic Criteria, the state excludes either, say, Arabic or Spanish speakers, it would presumably not be wrong if there are no current members who are or who speak, respectively, Arabic or Spanish. Finally, under both Wellman's particular view and the associational account more generally, it is not clear whether there are any grounds to be concerned, or even raise questions, about Occupational Preference if the state prioritizes the high-tech and IT industries while disfavoring the nursing, home-cleaning-services, and child-care industries.

[55] Wellman, "Right to Exclude," 145–48.
[56] Wellman, "Freedom of Association," 139.   [57] Wellman, 139, 140.
[58] Wellman (140) writes, concerning Australia's former White Australia policy, "unless Australia were already composed exclusively of white constituents (and no state is completely homogenous), it would be impermissible to institute immigration policies designed to [exclude non-whites]," clearly suggesting that, if a state did lack members in the excluded categories, racial policies would not be wrong.

Focusing again on race and ethnicity, Wellman, along with Blake, may well respond with a similar outlook to that of Walzer in response to White Australia. That is, they may think that while policies like Racial Ban are *regrettable*, they are not wrong. I won't be able to defend the contrasting position (that such policies are wrong and, moreover, because of how they wrong the excluded *nonmembers*) in this chapter—though I'll attempt to do so throughout most of the rest of the book. But here it's simply worth noting the implication of their position: Racial Ban is not wrong. Moreover, it's also worth noting that, in later work, neither Wellman nor Blake seems altogether satisfied with the idea that racial and ethnic criteria never wrong the excluded nonmembers. Blake's doubt about this position comes across in his engaging work on immigration in a very recent book.[59] In it, he writes that "the use of racial animus in migration policy is morally impermissible," seemingly independently of whether any members are wronged.[60] Blake stops short of claiming that such a policy would *wrong* the excluded nonmembers, but he does suggest that the reason the policy would be morally wrong has to do with how nonmembers would experience the policy as a statement of their "moral infirmity."[61]

Wellman does not go so far as to say that racial and ethnic immigration policies can be wrong independently of how they wrong the state's current members. However, he does state that he "continue[s] to worry" that the position that such policies are never wrong unless they wrong current members "supplies no ground on which to criticize racist selection criteria of an entirely homogenous country."[62] Contemplating a hypothetical similar to Racial Ban, he writes, "most of us would be horrified even if a homogenously white state explicitly excluded all prospective black immigrants."[63]

Wellman is undoubtedly right, and, moreover, there are many reasons to be horrified about such a case. In this book, I'll focus on arguing for a central underlying reason, which is that whites, as a group, have a very secure global social status, while Blacks around the world are substantially disadvantaged compared to many racial and ethnic groups in a wide range of global interactions. Unlike Blake's suggestion, however, my argument that racial and ethnic policies can be wrong independently of any effects on, or implications for, a state's

---

[59] I've included Blake in this brief section on association for two reasons. First, he shares in common with Wellman the position that racial and ethnic criteria do not wrong the excluded nonmembers. Second, Blake notes the connection between the associational account and what he takes to be the basis of states' choice, which he describes not in terms of members' right to refuse unwanted associations but in terms of members' right to refuse unwanted obligations toward others (to protect and fulfill their human rights). See Blake, *Justice, Migration, and Mercy*, 68–78. As with both Wellman and Blake, this book could be seen as adopting some version of an association account, but on my view the relationship between fellow state members is not limited to either the social (as some interpret Wellman's view) or the political (per Blake's view). Rather, it includes the full range of social, economic, political, and cultural relations. For, as discussed in the introductory chapter, life inside any particular state is characterized by multiple, overlapping relations.

[60] Blake, 129.   [61] Blake, 128–30.   [62] Wellman, "Right to Exclude," 149.
[63] Wellman, 149.

members is not limited to cases in which we can infer a kind of animus in the background nor to cases in which the excluded nonmembers experience the policy as derogatory. Indeed, in later chapters, I'll describe several cases in which neither of these conditions seem to be met and yet the cases appear clearly wrong. Maybe more importantly, however, as briefly alluded to, Blake's suggestion for *why* such cases may be wrong, or at least criticizable, does not seem to be based in how they wrong the excluded nonmembers, but seemingly on how they impugn the character of the state in question.[64] I believe both reasons are important for why certain policies may be wrong, but highlighting how and why they can wrong the excluded nonmembers opens space for broader theorizing about a state's obligations to vulnerable groups around the world.

Though I have mainly focused my discussion of the associational account on Wellman's associational-freedom view, in a later chapter I will explore in greater detail the variant recently defended by Blake and the view articulated by Ryan Pevnick. Both authors argue that if states have the right to choose their associates, we need to say far more about the basis of this right than the associational-freedom view offers. For Blake, the right is best conceived of not as the right to be free from unwanted associations, but (more specifically) as the right to be free from unwanted *obligations*.[65] For Pevnick, an association's right to choose its associates is based in members' mutual contributions to the association's collective goods.[66] On either way of conceiving the basis of the right to choose associates, however, I will argue that states, just like other associations, may not use any criteria they choose free from the moral claims of nonmembers.

4. Why Discrimination, and Why Antidiscrimination?

The rest of the book is devoted to arguing that we can understand central aspects of states' admissions and border policies with the antidiscrimination interpretation of when and why discrimination is wrong and its underlying view of

---

[64] Blake discusses the use of race in immigration selection and claims that "a full theory of morality in migration" might allow us to condemn its use in certain contexts. Since he distinguishes concerns about justice from concerns about caring for others, or showing them "mercy," as two separate elements of moral theorizing about migration, it seems reasonable to assume that he is referring to the element of mercy rather than justice when he refers to a "full theory." See Blake, *Justice, Migration, and Mercy*, 3–4. Additionally, he writes that he understands mercy "to be the virtue of not giving someone the harsh treatment we are permitted in justice to provide them, out of a moral concern for the effects of that treatment upon the recipient of the harsh treatment" (189). Since he's concerned about how animus-motivated racial policies might be experienced by nonmembers as statements of their "moral infirmity" (128–30), this provides more evidence for thinking that he condemns such policies for reasons having to do with the state's character. I should add that I am very drawn to the idea that concerns about justice and about a state's character are distinct aspects of migration theorizing. However, I do not believe that the wrong associated with certain identity criteria is always best explained by state-character concerns.

[65] Blake, 68–78.   [66] Pevnick, *Constraints of Justice*, chap. 2.

relational equality. According to what I will call the "global antidiscrimination approach," the global social, political, and economic status of groups—that is, their global social status—matters for determining what sorts of state immigration decisions are permissible and what sorts are wrong. Broadly speaking, global social status refers to a group's relative (dis)advantages, in material, political, or way-of-life terms or in terms of the social bases of self-respect, in comparison with other groups outside the social context of a particular state. I will demonstrate that the global status of both the admitting group and the excluded group matter for whether an immigration policy or restriction is morally wrong, including in the sorts of cases we considered at the start of this chapter.

I will devote much of the book to arguing that states have duties not to exclude people on the basis of identity criteria when doing so contributes to a group's vulnerability in particular sorts of ways. A variety of implications will follow from my analysis: what sorts of identity criteria are permissible and when—not only concerning race, ethnicity, and religion, but also concerning gender, sex, sexual orientation, and disability; when it is morally permissible for states to employ *non-identity* criteria such as professional, educational, language, or health criteria; whether it is wrong to use criteria that selectively exclude any significantly vulnerable group, including the poor and those with serious health conditions, not only groups sharing an identity; and whether states have the moral right against interference to exclude. In some cases, the analysis can be incorporated into existing theories of migration. For instance, as alluded to earlier, I will argue that states face much more significant moral limits than those accepted by states'-choice adherents; but these views can be supplemented with the global antidiscrimination approach and retain some of their basic shape. In other cases, however, if my arguments are correct, they prompt the need for a fundamental rethinking of existing views on migration. In particular, I will demonstrate that the approach argued for in this book challenges both the ideas that states have the moral right to exclude and that borders should be open. Concerning the last view, though I am drawn to the open-borders position for many reasons, I will offer independent reasons to doubt whether it is correct.

Before I turn, in the next chapter, to describing the antidiscrimination approach in the discrimination literature, and its underlying view of relational equality, I want to say a few words about why and how I will use this framework rather than others. For there are connected ideas that could potentially be substituted for the book's approach,[67] including those that more broadly stress concerns about

---

[67] The closest alternative is outlined in a book by Peter W. Higgins. See Higgins, *Immigration Justice*. This is a rich book for many reasons, including its effective use of empirical evidence and the feminist literature to convincingly show how current patterns of immigration seem to entrench women's disadvantages. Like my book, Higgins's gives a central place to social identity in the discussion of immigration. Specifically, he argues that states may not implement immigration policies that avoidably

subordination or domination[68] and views that directly appeal to relational equality without necessarily invoking antidiscrimination principles.[69] There are a few reasons this book centers on the antidiscrimination approach. The first is simply discursive: as indicated in the introductory chapter, discussions of the ethics of immigration frequently refer to core ideas found in the discrimination literature, though not necessarily the antidiscrimination approach (more on this shortly). Indeed, since immigration centers on *admission* and *exclusion*—often a primary subject of discrimination theories—ideas concerning when and why discrimination is wrong seem a natural place to position the analysis.

The second reason is that norms against wrongful discrimination are generally designed to protect persons defined by certain social categories—that is, identity groups.[70] In contrast, concerns about, say, domination or arguments that appeal directly to relational equality often focus on the interactions among individuals as such. While the focus on individual interactions is warranted in most contexts, I will explain in various places throughout the book, especially Chapters 3, 4, and 6, that it may be less apt in the global context, in which interactions are often mediated by group membership.

Third, especially as compared with the relational-equality literature, which is in relative infancy, the topic of discrimination has garnered far more attention from legal, moral, and political theorists and consequently has many worked-out concepts and principles, as we will see in the next chapter.

harm already unjustly disadvantaged groups (see Chapter 4 especially). However, there are several major differences between Higgins's analysis and my approach. A central difference is that he seems to define disadvantaged groups primarily in domestic terms and suggests that most social groups (perhaps aside from women) are disadvantaged relative to a particular domestic context (esp. 113–14). Thus, he does not argue for something akin to the concept of global social status and so does not examine its implications for immigration decisions. Less significant, but still important, he also includes citizenship itself as a social group (111) and defines disadvantage in capability terms, seemingly excluding self-respect disadvantages (122–25), which play an important role in my analysis. Finally, his view that immigration policies are wrong if they avoidably harm already-disadvantaged groups does not distinguish between different categories of policies, such as direct, proxy, and indirect, something I spend some time on, especially in Chapters 5 and 6. There is certainly other work on the intersection of immigration and identity, but it is quite distinct from the central analysis in this book. See Amy Reed-Sandoval's chapter, which discusses how some of the recent analyses of immigration ethics focus on race and ethnicity. Reed-Sandoval, "Open Borders Debate." However, for an earlier expression of this book's central view, see an article written by Adam Hosein in the *Boston Review*. Hosein, "Do Outsiders." Discussing the United States' 2017 executive order temporarily banning nonrefugee immigration from seven predominantly Muslim states, Hosein directly connects concerns about discrimination, immigration, and relational equality when he writes, "It is as morally repugnant to create a *global* political order of superiors and inferiors, of lords and vassals, as it is create a *domestic* political order of racial castes" (original emphasis). He elaborates on this point in his clear and comprehensive examination of a wide range of issues concerning the ethics of migration. See Hosein, *Ethics of Migration*, chap. 4, esp. 91–92.

[68] For relatively recent work, see Buckinx, Trejo-Mathys, and Waligore, *Domination*.

[69] For an analysis of how the notion of relational equality could be applied globally, see Nath, "Social Equality"; Ip, *Egalitarianism and Global Justice*.

[70] See Kasper Lippert-Rasmussen's related discussion on how discrimination theories may be more helpful than views on, say, domination or oppression in explaining many of the relevant issues. Lippert-Rasmussen, *Born Free and Equal*, 49–53.

A related issue is worth emphasizing. I will be attempting to demonstrate that a particular approach to understanding when and why discrimination is wrong—antidiscrimination—provides an attractive framework for thinking about the ethics of immigration criteria. In order for the book to focus mainly on immigration and not discrimination theory, I am unable to devote much more than sections of a chapter to trying to show the relative merits of this interpretation over its main competitor—anticlassification. I will try to do this by directly discussing the antidiscrimination approach's relative merits, but also by arguing that even if the anticlassification approach (or, more likely, some mix of the two interpretations) presents the correct picture of our duties not to engage in wrongful discrimination within the domestic context of a particular state, the antidiscrimination approach seems normatively appropriate for the global context. This is so mainly for two reasons, discussed in the next chapter and in Chapters 3 and 4. First, anticlassification seems best suited to contexts in which individuals directly and regularly interact; and global social relations are not as dense and regular as relations within a state, nor are they best characterized by individual interaction. Second, while the (dis)advantage differences between groups domestically speaking can sometimes be fairly substantial, there are often vast differences between groups globally speaking, making the antidiscrimination approach more obviously relevant to the global case. I will now turn to exploring the different interpretations of when and why discrimination is wrong and begin my arguments for the antidiscrimination approach.

2

Core Elements of Antidiscrimination

1. Introduction

In order to demonstrate why we should understand central aspects of states' borders and admission decisions in terms of the ethics of discrimination—or, more specifically, antidiscrimination grounded in the idea of relational equality—we need to first understand the fundamentals of normative discrimination theory. Since this book's aim is not to invent a novel theory of wrongful discrimination, and since a rich literature already exists, we can begin by looking to this literature. As we will see, the specific reasons discrimination is considered wrong, when it is wrong, are contested matters even when it comes to the domestic context—that is, within the confines of some particular state. But my goal is not to specify a particular reason why discrimination (in any context) might be wrong, nor to say specifically when it is wrong. Instead, my goal in this chapter (and the next) is to develop and motivate the antidiscrimination understanding for when and why discrimination is wrong and begin to argue for it in the context of immigration. This approach, whose underlying concern is to avoid treating, regarding, or relating to others as moral inferiors, stresses that the social status of a group matters for when and why discrimination is wrong.

Importantly, I will not try to establish that this approach is the best way to think about the ethics of discrimination *inside* states, or in the domestic context, but rather that it is useful for thinking about states' admission decisions. In this chapter, I will provide several reasons in favor of the antidiscrimination approach, while highlighting some shortcomings of the major alternative approach (anticlassification) in order to establish the groundwork for applying antidiscrimination principles to states' admission decisions. This approach will be described in broad outline in this chapter and its aptness for immigration selection will gain support in successive chapters. Among other things, we will see in the following chapters that the antidiscrimination understanding provides an appealing explanation for the normative differences among the various cases of immigration criteria discussed in Chapter 1 as well as other cases, both hypothetical and real.

A second aim of this chapter is to demonstrate that the antidiscrimination approach is rooted in broad concerns associated with relational equality (also called "social equality"). In general terms, relational equality refers to the idea that

Immigration and Discrimination: (Un)Welcoming Others. Sahar Akhtar, Oxford University Press. © Sahar Akhtar 2024.
DOI: 10.1093/oso/9780198898696.003.0003

we should relate to and interact with one another as equals in social, political, and economic life. Because of the considerable overlap between antidiscrimination principles and the idea of relational equality, the powerful moral intuitions behind relational equality strengthen the reasons for endorsing the antidiscrimination interpretation. Perhaps more importantly, theories of relational equality direct us to the moral basis of antidiscrimination duties, which will enable us to understand why (some of) these duties apply to states' admission decisions while at the same time understanding the limits of these duties.

2. Wrongful Discrimination

The first thing I must do is briefly discuss the general idea of wrongful discrimination as pertaining to the domestic context. The exact definition of wrongful discrimination is a contested one, and I will survey particular views later in the chapter. But broadly speaking, wrongful discrimination is differential treatment that disadvantages people with certain characteristics or treats them in an inferior manner.[1] Such characteristics—called prohibited grounds—include race, ethnicity, religion, gender, sexual orientation, and disability.[2] What these characteristics have in common is that they are considered *socially salient* and *identity-constitutive*.

Socially salient characteristics are traits that shape interaction across a wide range of social contexts.[3] These traits influence how one is perceived by others (often in stable, predictable ways) and, in turn, how one is regarded and treated. Often, these characteristics are easily visible, such as skin color or physical disability, but sometimes even nonvisible traits, such as religion, can take on social salience if a group sharing the characteristic is associated—rightly or wrongly—with certain modes of acting or stable patterns of belief or if the group has been subject to discrimination. As Lippert-Rasmussen notes, "Some of the most infamous forms of discrimination consist in rendering membership of a certain group easily perceived . . . e.g., the way people classified as Jewish people were forced by the Nazis to wear the Star of David."[4] Saying that a trait is identity-constitutive means that it is important to the way one forges values and, typically, to one's sense of self.

---

[1] "Disadvantage" (for example) might be construed very broadly to include disadvantages in respect (for example, Hellman's *When Is Discrimination Wrong?*). However, below we will both discuss different forms of discrimination and examine different reasons why discrimination is thought wrong, when it is wrong.

[2] For other potential grounds, see Khaitan, *Theory of Discrimination Law*, 49–56.

[3] This aspect of nondiscrimination is, it seems, critical. See the valuable work by Lippert-Rasmussen, "Badness of Discrimination," 169; Lippert-Rasmussen, *Born Free and Equal*.

[4] Lippert-Rasmussen, *Born Free and Equal*, 31.

A trait's being socially salient and being identity-constitutive are, in principle, separable. For instance, consider blue hair, which because of its high visibility might structure numerous social interactions even while it might not be identity-constitutive. Typically, however, these aspects go hand in hand since what contributes to a characteristic's status as identity-constitutive is often its social salience. This is in large part what distinguishes having an identity trait from having certain other attributes, such as a particular eye color. An identity trait is partly constituted by group members' self-understandings of a given identity, which are in turn a response to how others have perceived, interacted with, and treated the group members.[5]

For the sake of brevity, I will simply refer to identity and, frequently, identity groups. To speak of identity groups does not necessarily mean to say that the wrong of discrimination is a group wrong. As I will discuss shortly, under some views, discrimination, when it is wrong, is a wrong committed against individuals. Moreover, to speak of identity is not to suggest that the individuals falling into a group *identify with* one another, certainly not in every way, or that they share common interests, desires, and plans. They may, of course, but any member of a particular identity group typically has multiple identities (or, put differently, membership in multiple groups), and these other identities often influence how someone conceives of any one of their identities.[6]

Several types of duties might be born from concerns about discrimination, including positive duties to provide assistance to those who experienced past discrimination and duties to avoid policies, practices, and institutions that have a disproportionate disadvantageous impact on people with certain identities—often called "indirect discrimination."[7] A canonical example of the latter is in the US case of *Briggs v. Duke Power Company*, where the use of a written test disproportionately disqualified Black people from promotions.[8] I will begin, however, by focusing on what is often considered the paradigm case of discrimination—namely, "direct discrimination."

There are different ways to define direct discrimination, some of which seem to render all cases of it wrong.[9] But I will define it broadly and in the non-moralized sense—capturing what seems to be the central elements of the idea in recent prominent literature—so that it can be applied to a wide range of immigration

---

[5] Young, *Politics of Difference*, esp. 43–48; Fiss, "Equal Protection Clause," 148–49.

[6] Appiah, *Ethics of Identity*.

[7] More precisely, this is thought to involve the imposition of "a disproportionate burden on a group of people, where this does not involve any bias or discriminatory intention on the part of the agent." See Lippert-Rasmussen, *Born Free and Equal*, 55. He calls this a "rough description" and offers a more precise understanding on p. 72. The rough version is sufficient for my purposes here.

[8] Khaitan, *Theory of Discrimination Law*, 73–74.

[9] Under one influential account, it is defined as *aiming* to impose a disadvantage on someone because of their identity. See Altman, "Discrimination."

cases and yet leave open the question whether it is wrong in any given case. So, direct discrimination is defined here as differential treatment on the *basis of* or *in virtue of* identity, where this roughly means that someone's (perceived[10]) identity figures in the discriminating agent's reason for the treatment.[11] But this does not necessarily mean that the discriminating agent has an objectionable reason, or objectionable mental state more generally, such as contempt or prejudice. For instance, a company that either explicitly does not hire men or that explicitly favors hiring women for a particular position are both examples of direct discrimination since the fact that one is (perceived to be) a man (or not a woman) figures in the company's reason for the differential treatment.[12] But if the position is, say, a fitting-room assistant, this may not necessarily reflect any prejudice against, or contempt for, men.[13] More generally, as defined here, direct discrimination need not always be wrong.

Before exploring when it is wrong, however, it's important to narrow the scope of the discussion further since a variety of duties might be generated from concerns about direct discrimination that are not typically related to immigration decisions, such as duties not to engage in certain speech acts.[14] Of primary importance to this book is differential or selective admission or membership, or, conversely put, "selective exclusion," on the basis of people's identities. Both criteria disfavoring some identity group(s) for admission and criteria favoring some identity group(s) for admission involve selecting against or selectively excluding a certain group (or groups). As might be expected, criteria disfavoring a group, especially when done in an explicit manner, typically raise greater moral concerns—something I will discuss in Chapter 5—but for now nothing hinges on the distinction between favoring and disfavoring.

In the domestic context, moral concerns about selective exclusion on the basis of identity are normally thought to constrain the admission or membership decisions of a wide variety of associations, communities, and organizations, such as most businesses and large clubs. I will explore what makes such associations

---

[10] What matters is not that one has (or does not have) the relevant trait, but rather that the actor believes this to be the case. See the discussion in Lippert-Rasmussen, *Born Free and Equal*, 15, 20.

[11] Eidelson, *Discrimination and Disrespect*, 17–24. See related definitions in Lippert-Rasmussen, *Born Free and Equal*; Khaitan, *Theory of Discrimination Law*, 69. This definition is broad enough to treat cases in which an identity is explicitly marked out for differential disadvantageous treatment (for example, a company that explicitly refuses to hire Asians) and cases in which an identity is not marked out for such treatment but is nonetheless differentially treated disadvantageously (at least partly) on the basis of the identity (for example, Asians in the case of a company that mainly favors Blacks), both as instances whereby people are directly discriminated against. At the same time, the definition is not so broad that it does not permit a distinction between direct discrimination and indirect discrimination, in which an identity group experiences a disproportionate impact. I discuss indirect discrimination in Chapter 6.

[12] On how instances of both disfavoring and favoring can count as direct discrimination, see Eidelson, *Discrimination and Disrespect*, 17, 229.

[13] I leave it open whether the differential treatment is wrong in this case.

[14] Such duties could be related to immigration decisions, of course, but are not the primary focus.

and communities, and not others, morally bound by these constraints in Chapter 4. But here it is sufficient to note that many are so constrained.

Turning to the different understandings of nondiscrimination, there are two broad interpretations: anticlassification and antidiscrimination (the latter often called antisubordination[15]).[16] Much of the discussion of these different understandings has focused on determining which is the more accurate interpretation of the Fourteenth Amendment of the US Constitution (more specifically, the Equal Protection Clause).[17] For a variety of reasons (not least that I will not focus exclusively on migration to the United States), this book has little connection to that debate. Rather, this book is concerned with which interpretation better *morally* captures the broad reasons for why and when selective exclusion looks wrong, with a special focus on the *global* context.

The anticlassification interpretation stresses that the selective exclusion of people on the basis of their membership in identity groups (especially race and sex) is wrong, regardless of the particular group in a prohibited-ground category.[18] So, for instance, it maintains that selecting against whites and men can be just as wrong as selecting against their cognate or corresponding groups, Blacks and women. Its primary concern is that the treatment of individuals be "facially neutral" or, pertaining to race and ethnicity, "color blind."[19]

Several accounts seem to qualify as anticlassification or at least support the anticlassification interpretation. One common type of rationale that I think we can easily dispense with claims that selective exclusion is wrong because it distinguishes between people on the basis of either immutable characteristics or traits beyond their control.[20] However, religion is a commonly invoked counterexample to the idea that differentiating on the basis of immutable traits is wrong. This is because although one's religion can be changed, in many contexts it nonetheless seems morally wrong to select against someone because of their religion.[21] Conversely, in plenty of instances it seems perfectly justified to select against someone for either having or lacking a trait that is beyond their control, such as

---

[15] I avoid this term here since it has strong associations with a particular view (Owen Fiss's) of when discrimination is wrong (namely, when it contributes to a group's subordination) that stresses that discrimination is a *group* rather than individual wrong, which I take no stand on here. Fiss, "Equal Protection Clause." We will see that the concern to avoid subordinating groups centrally animates a variety of views.

[16] For instance, see Siegel, "Equality Talk"; Colker, "Anti-subordination above All."

[17] Epstein, "Black and White and Gray."   [18] Colker, "Anti-subordination above All."

[19] Colker, "Anti-subordination above All."

[20] For instance, see Richard Kahlenberg's discussion suggesting that this is why racial discrimination is wrong. Kahlenberg, *Remedy*, 54–55.

[21] This does not imply that it is never permissible to select against someone based on their religion. But if it is permissible, it is not because one can *alter* their religion. Rather, it is because the selecting association is of a particular type or has morally important interests at stake in making religion-based decisions. For fruitful discussion, see Tebbe, *Religious Freedom*.

not hiring a person who is blind for a position as a bus driver.[22] In short, the immutability concern, by not extending to traits such as religion, includes too little; the involuntariness concern, by rendering wrong many seemingly justified cases, includes too much.

Another traditional type of anticlassification account stresses that positions and offices should be open to those who *merit* them, where merit is defined as having the best qualities and traits for the role.[23] One problem with this account is that although it may be appropriate for job selection, school admissions, and the like, it is not relevant for the topic of this book since we are not discussing positions and offices. As with, say, selecting residents for apartment rentals or other housing, state-admission decisions do not seem to fall into the range of applicable decisions.[24] But could we take a very broad view of what counts as a "position" and argue that membership in a state is a kind of position for which people with certain traits may be more or less fitted or suitable? Even if this were a promising way to think about state-admission decisions (and I don't believe it is), we have several independent reasons to reject merit accounts along with the related idea that selective exclusion on the basis of identity is wrong because it selects against someone on the basis of irrelevant characteristics.

One concern about all such accounts is that what counts as most qualified, fit, or relevant for any given position or role is typically vague since it depends on how exactly we ought to construe the position or role (its function, needs, or purpose), which will usually require competing considerations that need to be assigned weights.[25] More importantly, even if that issue can be resolved, many have argued that while, for instance, hiring someone who is less qualified or choosing an applicant who is less suited for a position may be less efficient, productive, or rational, that does not mean it is morally wrong.[26] For associations and organizations, including businesses, are certainly morally permitted to pursue goals other than those we typically associate them with, such as profit maximization in the

---

[22] See Bernard Boxill for these sorts of examples and for related discussion. Boxill, *Blacks and Social Justice*, 12–17.

[23] Prominent proponents include Goldman, *Justice and Reverse Discrimination*; Miller, *Principles of Social Justice*.

[24] The discussion in Lippert-Rasmussen's *Born Free and Equal* (108–9) is helpful.

[25] Wasserman, "Discrimination, Concept of," 807; Hellman, *When Is Discrimination Wrong?*, chap. 4, esp. 97–101. Also see Shin, "Substantive Principle." It can also license the permissibility of reaction qualifications, many of which may be wrong.

[26] Cavanagh, *Against Equality of Opportunity*, 20, 99–101, 156–57. Also see *When Is Discrimination Wrong?*, chap. 5, where Hellman extends this and other criticisms to the related idea that selective exclusion is wrong when and because it is irrational, arbitrary, or based on inaccurate views. Also see Shin's critique of the role of "relevance." Shin, "Substantive Principle," 153. Additionally, saying that those who are most qualified for a role are *entitled* to or *deserve* it encounters further concerns, including how these notions are themselves defined and on what bases people are entitled to or deserving of some position. Hellman, 105–12. Additionally, as John Gardner argues, hiring on the basis of reaction qualifications—the qualifications a candidate is thought to have in light of how others, including customers, will react to them—is often rational but may nonetheless be morally wrong. Gardner, "On the Ground."

case of businesses, and it is often even morally praiseworthy or obligatory for them to pursue other goals.[27]

A third type of anticlassification account stresses that selective exclusion is wrong when and because it reflects the discriminator's morally objectionable mental states, such as disrespect, prejudice, or animus.[28] Many have argued that while paradigm cases of discrimination often involve attitudes such as prejudice, such attitudes do not seem *necessary* for an act to count as wrongful discrimination.[29] Moreover, as we will see in Chapter 4, while objectionable mental states are often central for evaluating decisions made in personal contexts, they do not seem necessary for assessing the moral status of differential-selection decisions made in large and impersonal associations, which are certainly characteristics of states.

Despite flaws in these anticlassification rationales, some broad considerations count in the interpretation's favor—especially in cases where someone is explicitly disfavored or rejected from an opportunity on the basis of their identity since it seems there is typically[30] some sort of morally objectionable hostility or animus behind such decisions. And hearing of any individual being denied an opportunity in virtue of, for instance, their race or sex prompts general concerns about fairness. At the same time, however, I share the widely accepted view that evaluating fairness includes not just attending to the details of a particular denied opportunity but assessing the broader political, economic, and social context, both current and historical, and the fundamental background institutions that shape opportunities.[31]

More importantly, I think, while some rationales in favor of (or at least supportive of)[32] anticlassification seem quite appealing, reflecting on the reasons why steers me in the direction of the antidiscrimination approach, which I will describe in the next section. In particular, a set of related rationales that seem especially attractive claim (1) that we should be free to deliberate about important life options without having to consider our (for example) race or gender a

---

[27] For instance, even if there is a presumption in favor of businesses' pursuit of economic productivity, this does not mean they may do so at the expense of committing moral wrongs such as exploiting people or polluting the environment.

[28] Alexander, "What Makes Wrongful Discrimination Wrong?"; Cavanagh, *Against Equality of Opportunity*; Arneson, "What Is Wrongful Discrimination?"

[29] In particular, see Lippert-Rasmussen's discussion (2014, pp.), in which he raises such an objection against the particular mental-state account (based on disrespect) offered by Larry Alexander. Lippert-Rasmussen, *Born Free and Equal*; Alexander, "What Makes Wrongful Discrimination Wrong?" However, see Eidelson's account of disrespect, which he describes as an "absence of appropriate recognition of someone's personhood, whether that absence comes about willfully or by neglect." Eidelson, *Discrimination and Disrespect*, 75. For Eidelson, disrespect need not be an occurrent mental state and does not entail animus or prejudice in the way these are commonly conceptualized.

[30] There may be some exceptions, such as a women's locker room with a sign that states "No men allowed."

[31] The canonical expression of this view is made in Rawls, *Theory of Justice*.

[32] It's unclear whether Moreau's view, discussed shortly, is intended to support anticlassification, but insofar as the anticlassification interpretation is attractive, I think it is because some such related view lends support for it.

barrier to pursuing those options, since these characteristics are "normatively extraneous,"[33] (2) that any race- or gender-based selective exclusion undermines our individual freedom to define our race or gender for ourselves or simply reject such characteristics' central place in our lives and in our conceptions of ourselves,[34] or (3) that being classified on such bases violates our individual dignity.[35] However, the primary reason these sorts of ideas are attractive concerns how tightly scripted the identities of *certain* groups, such as (to use the United States as an example) Blacks and women, have been, to the particular detriment of individuals in those groups. A similar point can be made about merit and mental-state accounts. I believe that much of the appeal of these accounts is that, historically, certain groups, such as (again in the United States) Blacks and women, have had fewer opportunities or have been denied positions on the basis of their identity despite seemingly having the relevant qualifications and, additionally, have all too often been the object of mental states like prejudice and contempt. Relatedly, in order to appreciate why *indirect* forms of discrimination may be morally concerning (at least in the domestic context), we need to attend to the historical injustices that certain identity groups have characteristically faced.

Finally, and very importantly, recall the sorts of characteristics that are commonly given the status of prohibited grounds, including race, ethnicity, religion, disability, sexual orientation, and gender. More specifically, consider why these sorts of traits, and not (typically[36]) such traits as eye color, are thought to be socially salient and identity-constitutive in the first place. It seems it largely has to do with a historical and current context of inferior treatment and regard toward *particular* groups in any one of these categories. For instance, as a result of the historical and often-ongoing mistreatment of Black people (among others) in the United States, race has become relevant to the structure of social interactions there, often serving as the basis for attributing certain qualities to people and responding to them in particular ways. Thus, the reason that race typically shapes interaction across a range of social contexts and (thereby) becomes identity-constitutive seems to turn on how *certain* racial groups have been the objects of prejudice, harmful stereotyping, and scorn, have had their basic rights and liberties violated, or have been marginalized or alienated.[37] All of this leads me

---

[33] Moreau, "What Is Discrimination?," 147.   [34] See Suk, "Quotas and Consequences."
[35] Bickel, *Morality of Consent.*
[36] Since a certain eye color, or any other ascriptive trait, could come to be associated with, for instance, a particular race or ethnicity and be used as a proxy to selectively disadvantage people of that race or ethnicity, I don't wish to completely rule out the significance of ascriptive traits.
[37] Put differently, it seems there must typically be a significant advantage differential between some group (for example, Blacks) and a cognate group (whites) before the characteristic counts as a prohibited ground. Khaitan, *Theory of Discrimination Law,* 49–56.

to conclude that anticlassification does not put the normative emphasis in quite the right place—something I believe the antidiscrimination understanding does.[38]

3. Antidiscrimination

Reflecting on the above sorts of considerations and the cogency of recently developing theories of relational equality (discussed in the next section), I am led in the direction of the antidiscrimination approach—if only in the context of *states'* admission decisions, for reasons that will begin to emerge in the next chapter. This approach to understanding when and why discrimination is wrong is animated by the central concern that certain groups have been, or are at risk of becoming, subordinated. As I will elaborate shortly, subordinated groups are those that have been systematically and persistently treated in inferior ways— such as through the imposition of obstacles in multiple, significant spheres of life, the maintenance of institutions that express that the group is morally inferior, or, most obviously, the denial of equal rights and privileges to the group.

Although there are several antidiscrimination views with their own understanding of the wrong of selective exclusion (when it is wrong), some important considerations are common to all of them. Chief among these considerations are (1) the social, political, and economic status ("social status") of an identity group matters, and (2) a central aim to avoid treating others as moral inferiors, or expressing that they are inferior. Putting these together, whether a group has a *vulnerable* or *disadvantaged* social status is important for determining whether it is wrong to select against people in that group on the basis of their identity.[39]

Vulnerable groups are defined as those that face substantial disadvantages in material, political, or self-respect terms, or even in terms of culture, in comparison with their cognate group(s)—which, because of the relative power they command over such goods and resources, can be described as comparably advantaged or secure.[40] Material disadvantages most obviously refer to reduced access to income and wealth, but also to reduced education, employment, longevity, and health.[41] Political disadvantages refer to lower quality and strength of representation and

---

[38] For how the anticlassification interpretation, and some of its prominent defenders in the United States, can sometimes be seen as steering in the direction of antisubordination, see Dorf, "Equal Protection Incorporation"; Dorf, "Partial Defense," 116. Also see Epstein, "Black and White and Gray."

[39] The relevant vulnerability would attach to groups but might not be *caused* by group membership.

[40] See the seminal discussion in Fiss, "Equal Protection Clause," 151–52. While Fiss seems to mainly explicitly refer to groups whose vulnerability is due to a history of oppression (that is, historically disadvantaged groups), he also discusses groups whose disadvantages are relatively recent or are not due to others' mistreatment of them (see 151n67). Also see Sunstein's discussion of these categories of disadvantage. Sunstein, "Anticaste Principle," 2429–30. For a relatively recent overview, and a discussion of the broader notion of vulnerability, see Khaitan, *Theory of Discrimination Law*, 49–56.

[41] See Khaitan, *Theory of Discrimination Law*, 54–56; Sen, *Inequality Reexamined*, 28–30.

political standing and comparatively weak consideration given to the group's interests by political and legal institutions. Furthermore, groups might face substantial disadvantages with respect to their self-respect, whether because of disadvantages in one of the other senses or because of the lingering effects of past disadvantages. A clear example of a group that is vulnerable along several of these dimensions of (dis)advantage is Black people in the United States, especially in comparison with whites.

Finally, I include cultural disadvantages, which largely refer to a compromised or threatened capacity to pursue the group's distinct way of life, including central aspects such as its language.[42] With this inclusion of cultural disadvantage, my understanding of vulnerability might be broader than typically intended by antidiscrimination theorists. But I believe that, in general, cultural disadvantage has been insufficiently attended to in the antidiscrimination literature.[43] This might be because the other forms of disadvantage are thought to overlap significantly with cultural disadvantage, but as we will see in the global context, this is not always the case. Thus, it will be important for purposes of discussing discrimination in the global context that we include cultural disadvantage. For instance, we will see that a group might have a vulnerable global status in light of its substantial population decline and consequent damage to its way of life but not suffer any major material or political disadvantages in comparison with other groups.

The relative disadvantages that vulnerable groups face might not be due to any wrongdoing on the part of others, but simply to, for instance, the group's numerical, political, or economic minority status. However, a group's relative disadvantages often (also) arise because, like Black people in the United States, they have experienced abiding and pervasive injustices or continue to experience the lingering social, political, and economic effects of past injustices.[44] If so, then the group counts not just as vulnerable but also as subordinated.[45] Subordinated groups experience relative disadvantages in a persistent and systematic manner (that is, across multiple dimensions of [dis]advantage) as a result of unjust moral relations. What such moral relations have in common is that the relevant groups are treated as *moral inferiors*. More specifically, these relations treat someone as

[42] This emphasis on culture is partly inspired by Iris Marion Young's discussion of cultural imperialism and Will Kymlicka's argument that certain cultures should have special group-differentiated rights. See Young, *Politics of Difference*, 59–61; Kymlicka, *Multicultural Citizenship*, 108–13.

[43] My understanding of cultural disadvantage combined with disadvantages in self-respect seems related to what Khaitan combines under the heading of "socio-cultural disadvantage." Khaitan, *Theory of Discrimination Law*, 53–54. Also see his discussion of self-respect (126–28).

[44] Fiss, "Equal Protection Clause," 151–52.

[45] While some antidiscrimination theorists might not make a distinction between vulnerable and subordinate groups, doing so allows for the possibility that some groups (those that are also subordinate) may deserve greater or more urgent moral attention in our deliberations and actions than other groups.

lacking the capacity to develop and exercise moral responsibility, cooperate with others, or form and pursue a conception of the good.[46] Examples of such relations include, but are certainly not limited to, oppression (inflicting violence on others or denying them equal rights and benefits), domination (arbitrarily wielding power over others), marginalization (excluding or segregating others from social life or regarding them as outcasts), and exploitation (the nonreciprocal procurement of others' goods or labor).[47]

The specific reasons that vulnerability matters for differential treatment vary across particular antidiscrimination views, but broadly speaking, such views are concerned with not contributing to a group's vulnerability in order to avoid creating, sustaining, or perpetuating a group's subordinate status.[48] For although a group's vulnerability does not mean its members are necessarily subordinated, it may make it far more likely that they will become so.[49]

On the whole, there are two primary respects in which selective exclusion is thought to contribute to the vulnerability of a group. One is in terms of comparatively reduced *opportunities*, and the other is in terms of what I will describe as *degradation*. Most straightforwardly, selective exclusion can comparatively reduce material, political, or cultural opportunities and, especially if the opportunities are significant, compound the disadvantages faced by a vulnerable group relative to secure groups.[50]

More importantly, a variety of views are concerned with the social structure and expression of what I will call "degradation." Under one major type of view, for instance, discrimination wrongs someone when and because it expresses a demeaning or denigrating message about them or sends the message that they are morally inferior.[51] And selecting against people on the basis of their identity is more likely to demean them if their group is vulnerable (especially if it has or had a

---

[46] See Elizabeth Anderson's discussion. Anderson, "What Is the Point?," 312.

[47] My description of these ideas largely follows the description by Young, *Politics of Difference*, chap. 2; Young, *Imperative of Integration*, chap. 1.

[48] Fiss, 1976; Ely, John Hart. 1980. *Democracy and Distrust*, Cambridge, MA: Harvard University Press; Sunstein, Cass. "The Anticaste Principle," *Michigan Law Review*, 92 (1994): 2410–55; More recently, Sophia Moreau has argued for a related account, providing more content to the notion of subordination (2019. "Discrimination and Subordination," in *Oxford Studies in Political Philosophy*, Vol. 5, ed. David Sobel, Peter Vallentyne, and Steven Wall. New York: Oxford University Press, 117–46).

[49] As I understand antidiscrimination views, because of this concern vulnerable groups should garner greater protection than nonvulnerable groups; that is, we should not only attend to groups that already are, or have been, subordinated. See, for instance, Fiss' discussion, 1976: 151–3 (and note 67); 155–7.

[50] Fiss, "Equal Protection Clause," 139, 148–54; Ely, *Democracy and Distrust*; Sunstein, "Anticaste Principle," 2419, 2430–31.

[51] Anderson and Pildes, "Expressive Theories of Law"; Hellman, *When Is Discrimination Wrong?* (Under Hellman's view, the message must also have the effect of lowering the social status of the object.) See also Shin, "Substantive Principle." Stuart White can be partly interpreted along these lines as well; see White, "Freedom of Association," esp. 384–85.

subordinate status) and if, by comparison, the selecting group enjoys a secure or powerful status.[52] The sense of demeaning here is an objective one.[53] We must ask whether it is plausible to interpret the action as *expressing* a demeaning or degrading message, and not whether it is either intended or subjectively experienced as demeaning. And to answer this, we would primarily look at the differences in social power between the relevant groups and at past and current social practices to see whether, for instance, the relevant classification has been used to marginalize or exploit people or whether their identity has been the object of prejudice or scorn.

A connected view under the degradation category is concerned with how differential treatment can (further) undermine the social bases of self-respect of certain groups or, relatedly, (further) *reasonably* make their group members feel socially inferior.[54] And a common understanding of the social resources required for one's self-respect is others' recognition of one's moral personhood and the value of one's chosen ends.[55] A final account connected to degradation highlights concerns about stigma, or how certain social meanings associated with a particular group (stereotypes) undermine our ability to see the identity group as our moral equals.[56] Moreover, this sort of view worries that if social institutions are arranged in a way that reflect such stereotypes, the group may behave in a manner consistent with them, thus reinforcing those very stereotypes.[57]

While the three forms of degradation just described are closely related, whether, and to what extent, any one of them occurs often depends on the particular kind of action. For instance, if the owner of a small business tells one of their employees who has some disability that the latter is a burden, that single act would seem to

---

[52] Anderson and Pildes, "Expressive Theories of Law"; Hellman, *When Is Discrimination Wrong?* Hellman suggests that the relevant power difference occurs between individuals, but, as Moreau has argued, it seems more accurate to consider the disparity between the groups to which individuals belong. Moreau, "Discrimination and Subordination," 124.

[53] Hellman, *When Is Discrimination Wrong?* This also seems related to Glenn Loury's view on stigma and race. Loury, *Anatomy of Racial Inequality.*

[54] Sunstein stresses such concerns in "Anticaste Principle." Also see White's concerns about dignity interests. White, "Freedom of Association," 384–85. Moreau highlights how certain "structures" (institutions, policies, and physical structures) can tacitly accommodate the interests and concerns of the powerful group(s) and, in this way, can sometimes condition self-respect (or its relative absence) for more vulnerable groups. An example concerns how buildings with wheelchair ramps in the back might make the person using a wheelchair feel that they are regarded as "not to be seen" or that they should be "out of sight." See Moreau, "Equality and Discrimination." The feeling that one's group is treated or regarded as socially inferior must be *reasonable.* Speaking in a somewhat different context, Thomas Waligore argues that "what matters is not subjective fear but reasonable distrust" based in the group's experiences of injustice. See Waligore, "Rawls, Self-Respect and Assurance," 46. For the idea of reasonableness as it directly relates to a sense of social or political inferiority, see Hosein, "Racial Profiling." Hosein likewise suggests that whether one's sense of political inferiority is reasonable depends on background conditions, including being the subject of prejudice.

[55] This is a major understanding of Rawls's view. See (for example) Eyal, "'Most Important Primary Good.'"

[56] See Loury, *Anatomy of Racial Inequality,* 60–67.   [57] Loury, esp. 73–91.

express a demeaning message about people who have the disability.[58] But it seems it would take a higher level of act-visibility or more significant consequences for a single act to either undermine the basis of the group's self-respect or perpetuate stigmas against them. So, for instance, if it is the President of the United States who makes such a comment about someone with that disability, then it would certainly not only express a demeaning message about them but also weaken the bases of their self-respect and perpetuate stigmas against them. We will see in Chapter 5 how different immigration-selection cases can give rise to some but not all these different degradation forms.

The emphases on reduced opportunities and degradation both have value, as each of them captures something important about when and why selective exclusion is wrong. Indeed, several prominent authors writing on discrimination either have observed that it may be mistaken to try to identify the single wrong of discrimination or have endorsed a pluralist account.[59] To take a notable example, and one that bears strong resemblance to the focus here on opportunities and degradation, T.M. Scanlon maintains that discriminatory acts are "wrong because of their consequences—the exclusion of some people from important opportunities—and because of their meaning—the judgement of inferiority that they express and thereby help to maintain."[60]

But while I believe that both comparatively diminished opportunities and degradation are important reasons to object to discrimination in many cases, on the whole it seems that concerns about degradation are more critical for understanding whether an act contributes to the vulnerability of a group directly in a way that relates to moral anxieties about subordination—that is, as involving the moral relations associated with treating someone as morally inferior. In considering differential admission or membership into associations and communities, it is often because of comparatively reduced opportunities that concerns about degradation arise. However, a vulnerable group's having comparatively reduced opportunities might not on its own prompt such worries. To clarify, if the group is not only vulnerable but also subordinate, then merely because it is selectively

---

[58] This seems so even if others with the disability are unaware of the comment since whether an expression demeans does not depend on how people subjectively experience the expression.

[59] See comments by, for instance, Eidelson, *Discrimination and Disrespect*, 73. For pluralist accounts, see Alexander, "What Makes Wrongful Discrimination Wrong?"; Khaitan's view of the value and purpose of antidiscrimination laws, especially as outlined in *Theory of Discrimination Law*, chap. 5; and Scanlon, *Moral Dimensions*. While Lippert-Rasmussen believes that discrimination is wrong "first and foremost because of its harmful effects," this suggests that he thinks there may be different reasons why discrimination is wrong. Lippert-Rasmussen, *Born Free and Equal*, 3.

[60] Scanlon, *Moral Dimensions*, 73. Under his view, the meaning of an act depends on the agent's reason for it. I don't share this interpretation, since I have been convinced by the analysis provided by disability-rights theorists, and discrimination theorists such as Hellman, that acts can be "conventionally understood" (to use Eidelson's terms) to have certain meanings. Eidelson, *Discrimination and Disrespect*, 84.

denied important opportunities, selective exclusion can perpetuate the group's inferior treatment. But if a group is not already subordinate, this need not always be the case. Much depends on the details—and in Chapter 5 we will explore a range of considerations that may make a difference for immigration cases. But here consider a large business in the United States that favors the selection of Black employees. Though this might mean that South Asians now have fewer employment opportunities, that might not on its own mean that South Asians are treated as morally inferior. In contrast, if they are also demeaned, if the social bases of their self-respect are compromised, or if any stigmas against them are perpetuated, their differential treatment directly implicates such moral relations. Though the importance of degradation relative to comparatively reduced opportunities will not be especially relevant for much of the discussion here, beginning in Chapter 4 we will see how it can matter for whether a particular case involving immigration criteria is wrong (more specifically, whether it violates what I will call the "primary duties"), especially when considering *non*-identity groups and indirect discrimination. But, for now, we can leave this complication aside.

That a group's vulnerability matters does not mean it is never wrong to select against members of relatively secure groups. As I briefly discussed above, there are several reasons why selecting against anyone on the basis of their identity may be wrong, especially when their identity is *explicitly* disfavored. And it may be that in the *domestic* context, because of the density and nature of social relations (which I will discuss in section 4), in addition to antidiscrimination duties there are also some important *anticlassification* duties, especially to not explicitly disfavor any group, vulnerable or otherwise.[61] Moreover, selection against even members of secure groups can exacerbate the disadvantages experienced by vulnerable groups by causing, for instance, retaliation against them or further damage to their self-respect. To the extent that it does, such selection may be ruled out even under antidiscrimination duties.[62]

But, under the antidiscrimination interpretation, there is an important *asymmetry* built into the understanding of when and why selective exclusion is wrong,

---

[61] However, it may be inaccurate to describe this in terms of *anticlassification*, rather than a particular kind of duty under the antidiscrimination approach. For it seems there must be a significant advantage differential between some group (for example, women) and a cognate group (men) before a given way of classifying people counts as a prohibited ground that confers *both* groups certain rights (making it wrong, in some cases, to discriminate against, say, men as well as women). Khaitan suggests that this is because a category gains expressive salience when there are substantial and abiding advantage differences between the groups under the category. But this plausible suggestion seems to again move us in the direction of antidiscrimination. Khaitan, *Theory of Discrimination Law*, 49–56.

[62] See Khaitan, 171–80. Many of these concerns may apply specifically to affirmative action, but it's unclear whether selecting in favor of one's *own* vulnerable group counts as a kind of affirmative action. For a discussion of some concerns about affirmative action, see Larry Alexander, "What Makes Wrongful Discrimination Wrong?," 217–18.

with the emphasis placed on protecting vulnerable groups.[63] Related to this asymmetry, discrimination's wrong (when it is wrong) is considered comparative in nature: someone is treated wrongly in comparison with others (or in comparison with how others would be treated in similar circumstances), not merely denied something to which they are independently entitled.[64] More substantively, the wrong involves a failure to treat people as moral equals.[65] Of particular importance in later chapters, this can mean it is permissible for vulnerable groups, in contrast to their cognate groups, to favor the admission of their own group members since such favoring may not amount to treating selectively excluded cognate groups as inferior but rather as helping to secure the conditions of their own equality. For instance, it might be thought that in the United States, women and Black people are, or were in the past, morally permitted to favor their own group members for admission decisions in certain social and educational organizations to help address their disadvantages.[66]

All of this will prove important when I analyze antidiscrimination duties in the context of immigration: in particular, given the (as we will see) often-considerable differences in the social status of different groups globally speaking, antidiscrimination's built-in evaluative asymmetry seems especially compelling.

Though I will use particular examples of vulnerable groups in certain domestic contexts to highlight some of the important steps in this book's arguments, my concern will not be to determine which groups with respect to the social contexts of particular states count as either vulnerable or subordinate. That would require, among other things, attending to the advantage differences between groups and to the historical and current social, political, and economic circumstances in that state—something that I will not always be able to do in this book. The major exception to what I have just said, however, is where there is

---

[63] If nothing else, in the domestic context at least, this asymmetry can be interpreted as suggesting that while selecting against any group may be wrong, all else equal it may be morally worse when the group in question is vulnerable. Though I'm unsure whether to characterize harm-based theories as antidiscrimination views (as I use the term here), this version of asymmetry is suggested by some prominent harm theorists. See, for example, Lippert-Rasmussen, *Born Free and Equal*, 148, 170n38, 174–76.

[64] Although Khaitan's account might seem to be an exception here, on closer reflection it appears not to be. According to Khaitan, discrimination is wrong when it compromises a bundle of basic goods to which everyone is entitled, including sufficient self-respect and secure access to an adequate range of valuable opportunities. Khaitan maintains that the underlying rationale for these goods is that their possession makes one free and enables one to pursue their conception of the good life. Importantly, however, he also argues that what counts as, say, "sufficient" or an "adequate range" depends in part on what others have, and he discusses how a similar point is true of other freedom-based accounts of antidiscrimination. So, while freedom-based accounts are not egalitarian, they are nonetheless *comparative*, preserving a central feature of the notion of antidiscrimination. Khaitan, *Theory of Discrimination Law*, esp. chap. 4.

[65] See Fiss, "Equal Protection Clause," 157; Hellman, Deborah. "Two Concepts of Discrimination."

[66] For some discussion, see Sellers-Diamond, "Serving the Educational Interests," 1877; Weeden, "Historically Black Colleges," 1.

overlap between domestically vulnerable groups and what I will describe as globally vulnerable groups—the subject of the next chapter.

4. Antidiscrimination and Relational Equality

Having described the antidiscrimination interpretation and provided initial support for it, I will now show that its central concern seems to be rooted in the broader idea of relational equality. Theories of relational equality stand mainly against theories of distributive equality, which emphasize the equal distribution of a set of (basic) goods, liberties, or resources. Relational-equality theories, in contrast, stress that the fundamental moral concern is how we interact with and regard each other in social, economic, and political relations.[67]

In broad terms, the idea of relational equality refers to the notion that we must relate to each other as equals or stand in equal relations. Most often, it is expressed negatively as refraining from or avoiding the creation of unequal relations. And it is expressed in terms that deeply resonate with antidiscrimination accounts. In particular, concerns about relational equality are thought to generate not just obligations to avoid the most egregious injustices, such as inflicting violence on others, but also, more generally, obligations to avoid establishing or sustaining certain kinds of hierarchical relations or stratification between people (unequal status).[68] The literature on the antidiscrimination approach helps to bring into focus which kinds of hierarchy may be especially concerning—namely, those that attach to identity groups. But additionally, relational-equality theories also seem to at least implicitly underscore the importance of identity groups to understanding objectionable hierarchical moral relations. For instance, Viehoff stresses that for differences in status to violate conditions of relational equality, they must pervade society as a whole, which is perhaps most likely when differences occur between different identity groups rather than between individuals as such.[69] More broadly, when relational-equality theorists seek to illustrate their concerns about

[67] Anderson, "What Is the Point?," 314. Though they are seen as distinct conceptions of equality, relational equality certainly has implications for distributive equality, and some argue that to secure the ideal of relational equality, distributive equality (for example, equal voting and welfare rights) is needed. For instance, see Miller, "Equality and Justice," 234–35. Miller may be correct, but as my primary attention will not be on what is needed for the ideal of relational equality (especially within a state), I believe we can leave this issue aside.

[68] I discuss the qualification "certain kinds" below. For descriptions to this effect, see Miller, "Equality and Justice," 224; Fourie, "What Is Social Equality?," 110; Scheffler, Equality and Tradition, 225; Schemmel, "Distributive and Relational Equality"; for a relatively recent discussion of how this description seems to be common to all relational-equality views, see Fourie, Schuppert, and Wallimann-Helmer, "Nature and Distinctiveness," 4.

[69] Viehoff, "Power and Equality." This might not always be true. Consider, for instance, the roles of lord and servant. It does not seem that these roles constitute different identity groups (though they may strongly correspond to different identity groups). Still, it does seem that any status differences between them could pervade all of society, or at least those societies in which the roles are salient.

hierarchy or caste, they often refer to the different statuses of identity groups as paradigmatic examples.[70]

Relations characterized by unequal social status are thought to be troubling for a variety of reasons. Important instrumental concerns largely refer to the connection between relational inequality and distributive justice[71] and, relatedly, to the effects of relational inequality on civic relationships, self-respect, mental health, and crime.[72] But many relational-equality theorists observe that unequal social status is also inherently objectionable. As Kolodny writes, they "propose for consideration, since it is not the sort of claim that admits of much articulate argument—that we have reason to avoid relations of social superiority and inferiority for their own sake, not simply as a symbol of, or means to, something else." Kolodny elaborates that "we begin with an intuitively felt concern about certain paradigms—such as the kindly master—and then argue that it is best interpreted as a concern about relations of social superiority and inferiority."[73] Similarly, Anderson notes that the idea that we have obligations not to create or worsen status inequalities between people, and may have obligations to address and rectify them, should already have a grip on us.[74]

At bottom, antidiscrimination accounts seem grounded in concerns about unequal social status.[75] Sunstein, for instance, refers to antidiscrimination law's implicit "equality principle," which, he writes, "should be understood as an effort to eliminate, in places large and small, the caste system rooted in race and gender."[76] He adds that "a law is therefore objectionable on grounds of equality if it contributes to such a caste system. The controlling principle is that no group may be made into second-class citizens."[77] Similarly, Hellman connects the idea of relational equality with her expressivist account of discrimination's wrong, writing that "the point of equality is to treat one another as equals, and thus the wrong of

---

[70] To be sure, they often define the relevant groups more broadly to include not just groups characterized by identities, including race, ethnicity, religion, gender, and so forth, but also groups based on family membership (or inherited statuses) and socioeconomic class. See Anderson, "What Is the Point?," 312. But as will be explained in Chapter 6, groups based on *identity* are far more salient in the context of international interactions and relations.

[71] John Rawls, *Justice as Fairness*, esp. 440–44; O'Neill, "What Should Egalitarians Believe?," esp. 126.

[72] Scanlon, "Diversity of Objections"; Wilkinson and Pickett, *Spirit Level*.

[73] Kolodny, "Rule over None II," 299–300.

[74] Anderson, "What Is the Point?" Also see O'Neill, "What Should Egalitarians Believe?," esp. 121–22.

[75] For early statements to that effect, see Colker, who writes, "This approach seeks to eliminate the power disparities between men and women, and between whites and non-whites...From an anti-subordination perspective, both facially differentiating and facially neutral policies are invidious only if they perpetuate racial or sexual hierarchy." Colker, "Anti-subordination above All," 1007–8. Siegel writes, "The antisubordination principle is concerned with protecting members of historically disadvantaged groups from the harms of unjust social stratification...Because the antisubordination principle focuses on practices that disproportionally harm members of marginalized groups, it can tell the difference between benign and invidious discrimination." Siegel, "From Colorblindness to Antibalkanization."

[76] Sunstein, "Anticaste Principle," 2428.   [77] Sunstein, 2429.

discrimination is to fail to treat people as equals. We do that when we differentiate among people in a manner that ranks some as less morally worthy than others."[78] And in a very recent paper, Sophie Moreau relates nondiscrimination more generally to the idea of relational equality. She observes that "the kinds of discrimination that usually give rise to the greatest moral indignation involve the creation or perpetuation of different classes of people, with some having a superior status and others an inferior one, in circumstances where we think that everyone ought to have an equal status."[79]

To clarify, there are certainly variations among the views that can be described as relational-equality theories[80] and between such theories and antidiscrimination accounts.[81] Attending to all such distinctions will not be important for my purposes; however, I want to address one potentially important source of divergence. This concerns the issue of whether, under relational-equality theories, mere differences in advantage or power—material, political, or cultural—among people constitute unequal statuses.[82] Insofar as they do, relational equality's central concern diverges from the concern of antidiscrimination views to avoid subordination. Having a subordinate status, recall, entails that the comparative disadvantages experienced by a group are due to relations that have treated its members as morally inferior.

It is very unclear, however, whether the mere-difference interpretation of unequal status captures what most theorists of relational equality maintain, especially in more recent works.[83] For instance, Viehoff writes that as long as there is a justification for advantage or power differences that "does not treat one person (or her fundamental interests and claims) as more important than another, the [differences] are compatible with our status as social equals."[84] For another prominent example, Kolodny suggests that unequal social status is not to be defined merely in terms of material differences.[85] Moreover, though Kolodny is

---

[78] Hellman, *When Is Discrimination Wrong?*, 47–48, 172. As described in a relatively recent volume on relational equality, there is a decidedly expressive or attitudinal dimension to status inequalities, conveyed through both behavior and institutions—something that is also at the heart of many antidiscrimination views, including Hellman's. See Fourie, Schuppert, and Wallimann-Helmer, *Social Equality*, 7.

[79] Moreau, "Discrimination and Subordination," 117.

[80] For instance, many theorists are concerned with status hierarchies between individuals, which do not necessarily attach to groups. See Kolodny, "Rule over None II," 292.

[81] While antidiscrimination is principally concerned with identity groups, this is not always true of relational-equality views. See notes 69–70 in this chapter.

[82] It is unclear whether this is even the correct way to read the very early theorists of relational equality, such as Miller and Norman. See Miller, "Equality and Justice"; Norman, "Social Basis of Equality"; Fourie, Schuppert, and Wallimann-Helmer, *Social Equality*, 5.

[83] Early statements of relational equality by authors such as Anderson and Scheffler were very vague on this issue. (See Anderson, "What Is the Point?"; Scheffler, "What Is Egalitarianism?") They can largely be read as sufficitarian with respect to differences in material and resource conditions and differences in power.

[84] Viehoff, "Democratic Equality and Political Authority," 30.

[85] Kolodny, "Rule over None II," 292–93.

known for advancing the connection between equal political power and relational equality, he does not maintain that even political-power differences necessarily violate conditions of relational equality. On the contrary, he stresses that if those with greater power also possess the determined disposition to refrain from exercising their greater power over others—not out of some sort of magnanimity to bestow gifts on them, but as something to which others are fundamentally entitled—then relational equality is preserved.[86]

In general, it seems that violations of relational equality are typically described not merely in terms of differences in advantage or power, but as differences in advantage or power as a result of some experiencing inferior regard, consideration, or treatment by others, who in turn experience superior regard, consideration, or treatment. Putting the emphasis on institutions, unequal social relations occur when social norms, structures, and arrangements across a range of social contexts treat some as morally inferior or express that they are inferior. In other words, it seems that antidiscrimination views and theories of relational equality are, on the whole, concerned with the same central idea: that some are relegated to an inferior class or are liable to become so relegated.

Having said this, however, there may still be other differences between the central demand of the antidiscrimination approach—avoiding subordination—and the demands of relational-equality theories.[87] In particular, the latter demands may be much broader, especially when considering what the *ideal* of relational equality requires.[88] If so, antidiscrimination duties do not exhaust the full scope of duties that are generated under theories of relational equality, but instead concern what we might describe as relational equality's most egregious violation.[89]

The point of the foregoing discussion was only to illustrate how antidiscrimination accounts share affinity with, and seem to ultimately be grounded in,

---

[86] Kolodny, 295, 298. For another example, although Moreau writes that "in most situations of social subordination, members of the subordinated social group have less power than members of other groups," she does not seem to be maintaining that mere power differences constitute subordination, but rather that power differences often cause, and accompany, a subordinate status. Moreau, "Discrimination and Subordination," 23. Assuming it is the latter claim, this is entirely compatible with the positions of prominent antidiscrimination theorists. See, for instance, Fiss, "Equal Protection Clause," 151–53 (including his note 67), 155–57.

[87] For instance, it might be thought that two groups can be characterized as having unequal social statuses without the (dis)advantage differences between them (that result from objectionable moral relations) being either *systematic* or *persistent*, which are important notions for describing subordinated groups.

[88] As we've seen, relational-equality theorists describe their view primarily in negative terms—as the absence of unequal social status—but they have been less clear on what the *ideal* of relational equality looks like, and there may in the end prove to be important differences between what relational equality as an *ideal* requires and what the antidiscrimination approach requires. (My own view, following Jonathan Wolff's analysis, is that the ideal of relational equality just is the absence of unequal social status. See "Social Equality.")

[89] See Wolff's discussion (in "Social Equality"), following Amartya Sen's, on how even though we do not have a theory of relational equality fully worked out, we can nonetheless identify *manifest* status inequalities. Sen, *Idea of Justice*.

concerns about relational equality, not to suggest that the two types of views are one and the same.[90] And because of the deep connection between them, theories of relational equality can be used to further our understanding of when and why selecting against some people, but not others, is wrong. As we will see next, they do this by directing us to the *basis* of obligations (namely, social, economic, and political interactions and institutions) and by shedding light on the *scope* for different sorts of obligations by suggesting that what treating people as social equals requires depends on the density and type of relations and interactions. These issues will be important for appreciating how antidiscrimination concerns at the global level demand our attention and thus why we should maintain that states are subject to (at least certain) antidiscrimination duties when making admission decisions. But they will also be important for understanding the limits of such duties—in particular, why such duties do not seem to imply open borders.

5. Are Such Concerns Restricted to the Domestic Context?

I have suggested that, on the whole, the antidiscrimination approach is grounded in broader concerns about unequal social relations and hierarchy. But, from the outset, one might worry that antidiscrimination based in the notion of relational equality cannot be extended to evaluate states' admission decisions. For, one might think, concerns about status differences, caste, hierarchies, and the like are inappropriate for understanding the global moral landscape since such concerns depend on the shared relations among members of the same state.[91]

Indeed, the terms "relational equality" and "social equality" are, for some, interchangeable with "democratic equality," which may seem to bolster the previous worry since there is no shared democracy outside of individual states. Elizabeth Anderson in particular has aligned the two notions. In her noteworthy work, she generates support for relational equality by appealing to the claims and demands of egalitarian political movements within societies. Describing these movements, she writes, "They seek to live together in a democratic community,

---

[90] Despite potential differences between the ideas of unequal social status and subordination, for most of the remainder of the book, I will not distinguish these ideas. First, even if the nature and density of social, economic, and political relations in the domestic context support an understanding of relational equality that suggests the existence of duties surpassing those born from concerns about subordination, there may be much less support for such an understanding in the global context given, as we will see, the weaker and less dense relations that obtain in the global context. Second, antidiscrimination duties concern not only groups that are considered subordinate but also, more minimally, those characterized as vulnerable. And recall a vulnerable status need not be due to objectionable moral relations and involves experiencing substantial, though not necessarily persistent, disadvantage. So even if the idea of unequal status includes weaker or less persistent disadvantages than those suggested by subordination, antidiscrimination duties will, by focusing on vulnerable groups, also focus on weaker forms of disadvantage.

[91] See, for instance, Miller, 1997. However, see Hosein, "Do Outsiders."

as opposed to a hierarchical one. Democracy is here understood as collective self-determination by means of open discussion among equals, in accordance with rules acceptable to all. To stand as an equal before others in discussion means that one is entitled to participate, that others recognize an obligation to listen respectfully and respond to one's arguments, that no one need bow and scrape before others or represent themselves as inferiors to others as a condition of having their claim heard."[92]

If relational equality is considered in such terms and is equivalent to Anderson's idea of democratic equality, we may have great difficulty seeing how antidiscrimination principles could be normatively appropriate ideas for the global level.[93] Simply put, not only is there presently no system of global democracy or global democratic community, or any single community at all, but individuals do not interact with each other through transnational or global institutions in anything like the way members of the same state interact. Fellow members are joined together by shared political, civil, and social institutions under which they mutually cooperate.[94] Perhaps most distinctively, fellow members live together under a common network of coercive laws.[95] And there do not seem to be equivalent sorts of interconnections among people in different states.

However, in response to this potential objection, I will briefly demonstrate that a democratic notion of equality is far from the only understanding of relational equality. More specifically, it is entirely compatible to uphold the democratic notion within a state while claiming that different, and very likely weaker, duties apply at the global level.

To start, discussions of relational equality, as with discussions of related concepts such as nondomination, often begin with or gain support from reflecting on the context of personal or intimate relations. These include relationships in the strong sense of face-to-face interactions. For instance, authors appeal to the objectionableness of the hierarchical relations between lord and servant, slave-owner and slave, and, in more traditional societies, husband and wife.[96]

---

[92] Anderson, "What Is the Point?," 313.

[93] Nath has more generally argued that using any kind of formal criteria to ground the significance of relational equality is immensely problematic. She writes, "To illustrate, it would follow from limiting the domain of egalitarian justice [to co-citizens] ... that during the reign of slavery in the United States inegalitarian relations between blacks and whites were not unjust precisely because blacks were not counted as citizens of the political order to which whites belonged ... By the same token, this view also implies that until women gained the right to vote, a distinctly social egalitarian complaint regarding the conditions that undergirded their perceived inferior status was baseless. These examples show that pinning the demands of social egalitarianism to *official* membership is perverse. It renders us unable to criticize some of the gravest distributive inequalities that make social egalitarianism an appealing view in the first place." See "Equal Standing," 607.

[94] Sangiovanni, "Global Justice."

[95] Blake, "Distributive Justice"; Nagel, "Problem of Global Justice."

[96] Kolodny, "Rule over None II," 292; Scheffler, "The Practice of Equality," sect. 1.2; Gosepath, "Principles and Presumption," 173.

Or, authors point to the *equal* character of genuine friendships.[97] Indeed, even those who argue for democracy on grounds of relational equality invoke relationships such as friendships as models of nonhierarchical relations.[98] But although such personal relationships are standardly invoked, proponents recognize that the appropriate conception of relational equality varies across different relations—and even across different personal relationships. For instance, what relational equality requires in friendship and marriage seems quite different from what it requires among neighbors or at the workplace.[99]

Likewise, they recognize that what relational equality requires in personal relationships is certainly distinct from what it requires in anonymous, indirect interactions—namely, those mediated through the state's institutions.[100] In short, the appropriate demands of relational equality depend on the nature and density of the relevant relations. So, while close, dense relations may provide the laboratory, so to speak, for reflecting on and developing our intuitions about hierarchical relations, hierarchical relations are not only a moral concern when they occur in close relationships. (If that were so, relational-equality theorists—and domination theorists—would seem to face significant difficulty explaining why unequal status is a concern at the *statewide* level.)

And a similar point can be made when extending the idea of relational equality past the state level to the global level. For the state can then be used as a laboratory for reflecting on what status inequalities among anonymous interactions look like and why they raise concerns to argue for a conception of relational equality among people engaged in interactions of an even-more-indirect nature. Of course, this book does not seek to determine the full range of relational-equality duties at the global level but is concerned only with what might be characterized as a subset of such duties: antidiscrimination duties pertaining to states' admission decisions. The important point here is that there is nothing with the idea of relational equality that insists that the only relations mattering for equality are those among members of the same state. As Anderson herself comments, this understanding of equality is a concern whenever some are vulnerable to oppressive relationships—those relations "by which some people dominate, exploit, marginalize, demean, and inflict violence upon others."[101] As we will see in the following chapter, many groups are indeed vulnerable to such relationships at the global level, and moreover, such vulnerability is important for explaining why some

---

[97] Viehoff, "Democratic Equality"; Kolodny, "Rule over None II," 304.

[98] Ibid. However, for a plausible discussion of how the social relations of friendship do not apply to whole societies, see Viehoff, "Power and Equality."

[99] Viehoff, "Power and Equality." Also, for discussion, see Baker, "Conceptions and Dimensions."

[100] See especially Viehoff, "Democratic Equality"; Viehoff, "Power and Equality"; Kolodny, "Rule over None II."

[101] Anderson, "What Is the Point?," 313. And Anderson herself claims that relational equality is an ideal not only among state members but among (at least) workers in the world at large (see 321n78).

groups seem morally permitted to make admission decisions on the basis of identity when other groups are not so permitted.

Having articulated the central notions of the antidiscrimination approach based in relational equality, I will now take initial steps toward demonstrating that this approach is applicable at the level of states' admission decisions. The next chapter will address the primary issue: focusing first on racial, ethnic, and related groups, I will show that there is a meaningful sense of social status that extends beyond the boundaries of a particular state. In doing so, we will also see that there are important social, political, and economic relations at the global level and that all of this seems to matter to the moral assessment of a variety of immigration cases. Chapter 4 will then explain how, in general, states are relevantly like the domestic associations and communities to which antidiscrimination duties apply and, building on the work of Chapter 3, demonstrate the plausibility of maintaining that states' admission decisions are constrained by at least some antidiscrimination duties.

3

Race, Ethnicity, and Religion in the Global Context

1. Introduction

The last chapter developed and motivated the central ideas of the antidiscrimination approach. To maintain that this approach should be applied to state-admission decisions, the first thing needed is to demonstrate that identity characteristics are socially salient in the *global* context. Focusing on race and ethnicity (and related categories), I will show that they are globally salient by showing that racial and ethnic groups have a social status that extends beyond the boundaries of a particular state. This idea, which I call "global status," will be initially described in broad terms and become progressively more refined as we proceed to later chapters, especially Chapter 5.

This chapter advances two further goals. First, through exploring the significance of global status, we will begin to see the extent and nature of shared social, political, and economic relations and interactions at the global level. Second, by illustrating global status's role in explaining whether a variety of immigration cases are potentially morally permissible, it demonstrates that the antidiscrimination approach provides a more compelling way to think about state admissions than an anticlassification approach does. The focus of this chapter is on exploring when racial and ethnic criteria wrong a state's current *members*. Once we have this general explanation in view, we can then apply it to examine when racial and ethnic criteria (and other identity and non-identity criteria) wrong excluded nonmembers. This is something I will begin in the next chapter, followed by a more detailed analysis in Chapter 5. Arguing for the idea of global status and demonstrating its importance for morally assessing different types of immigration policies are important steps toward that goal and toward applying the antidiscrimination approach to states' admission decisions more generally.

2. Global Status: An Initial Description

Since we have so far only discussed antidiscrimination in the context of selection decisions inside a state, the emphasis has been on what we might call "domestic

Immigration and Discrimination: (Un)Welcoming Others. Sahar Akhtar, Oxford University Press. © Sahar Akhtar 2024.
DOI: 10.1093/oso/9780198898696.003.0004

status," or an identity group's social status relative to other groups *within* the same state. This section's main claim is that it is coherent to discuss a type of social status outside of a group's status within a state. I call it "global status," but we will see that sometimes it is more accurate to refer to it as regional status. The central point is that there is a kind of social status that is not equivalent to—and may substantially differ from—a group's domestic status.

Let me first briefly explain the importance of demonstrating that groups have a global status, focusing first (for reasons explained shortly) on racial and ethnic groups and related categories such as religion, ethno-religion, and nationality. We can see the significance of global status most clearly if we again consider the domestic context. Recall that a central factor explaining why antidiscrimination principles constrain the admission decisions of domestic associations and communities is that characteristics such as race and ethnicity are socially salient. And, again, socially salient characteristics are characteristics that shape interaction across a wide range of social contexts, often serving as the basis for attributing certain qualities to others and responding to them in particular ways. But in considering the admission decisions of a domestic association, what is needed is not a demonstration that race and ethnicity are socially salient within the context of interactions inside that association. To be sure, they may well be. But even if, for instance, all of some business's current employees are of the same race, that does not bear on whether the business's hiring decisions are subject to antidiscrimination duties. What matters is that race and ethnicity are socially salient more generally—including *outside* the business. In other words, we attend to the broader social, political, and economic facts to understand whether such characteristics are important to the structure of social relations in the society as a whole. And the fact that there are sizable differences in the material, political, and cultural (dis)advantages of different racial and ethnic groups indicates that race and ethnicity are indeed socially salient in the broader society.

To apply antidiscrimination principles to states' admission decisions, then, we must likewise establish not that race and ethnicity are socially salient within any admitting state, but that they are (also) salient outside that state—in the global society as a whole, so to speak, or in the context of global social relations. I will show this by demonstrating, first, that different racial and ethnic groups face substantial differences in (dis)advantages in the broader global context—thereby having different global statuses—and, second, that a group's global status is often important for understanding the normative differences among various immigration cases.

As mentioned, I am beginning with racial and ethnic identities and the related categories of nationality, religion, and ethno-religion. As we will see, these categories might present notable challenges to the idea of global status since it might be thought, for instance, that many racial and ethnic groups do not have a uniform status around the world or in all social, political, and economic

GLOBAL STATUS: AN INITIAL DESCRIPTION 61

contexts. I largely agree with this charge but will argue that it does not undermine the antidiscrimination approach. Moreover, the charge is far less tenable when it comes to identity categories such as gender, sex, sexual orientation, and disability. So, if I can convincingly show that racial and ethnic groups have a global status that helps to normatively explain selective immigration criteria, it should be easy to demonstrate that other types of identities, such as gender or disability, do as well. I return to the latter types in Chapter 5.

Though the concept will gain clarity throughout this chapter (and greater detail in the following chapters), I start by sketching the basic idea. Global status refers to a group's (dis)advantages in material, political, or way-of-life terms or in terms of self-respect, in a range of circumstances, compared with other groups—outside the social context of a particular state. In contrast to groups with a secure global status, those with a vulnerable global status experience any one or a combination of the following: comparatively little power to shape international interactions and relations—including political relationships within international bodies (for example, the United Nations, International Monetary Fund [IMF], and World Bank), treaty negotiations, climate agreements, economic associations, war and armed conflict, trade, and, last but not least, immigration—and to garner international economic, social, and political goods (for example, natural resources, territory, and recognition of sovereignty); a way of life that is substantially compromised or fragile compared with other groups, including central aspects such as its language; or, disadvantages in the social bases of self-respect. (All of this corresponds to the domestic analog.[1]) A group's global vulnerability might be caused by disadvantageous structural and institutional conditions—including common trade practices and monetary policies—and by natural disasters and climate change. Very often though—and perhaps even more than is the case for domestically vulnerable groups—the comparative disadvantages faced by many globally vulnerable groups are due to abiding and significant injustices or the lingering effects of past injustices.

As we'll see in the next section, groups certainly vary in their degree and type of vulnerability or power. To say that a group is vulnerable, for instance, is not meant to imply that it is disadvantaged in comparison with every other group or with respect to every dimension, region of the world, or context more generally. In Chapter 5, we'll see that that variability undoubtedly presents some challenges and makes the analysis of many cases more complex. However, I don't believe it suggests that the analysis is unworkable or impractical. Rather, with the resources provided by the antidiscrimination approach, we will be able to navigate even very complicated cases.

Now certain groups both have a vulnerable global status and are domestically vulnerable in numerous states. To take just one example, the Romanis, an Indo-Aryan

---

[1] See discussion in Chapter 2, section 3.

ethnic group, have experienced oppression and persecution within many European states and parts of Russia and often live in poverty in multiple states. However, and as we will see in more detail shortly, numerous other groups have a secure *domestic* status in many states but nonetheless stand in objectionable moral relations, including oppression, exploitation, or marginalization, with more secure groups across states (or prepolitical territories) and international institutions. A key to distinguishing global from domestic vulnerability is that for the global sense, the relevant disadvantages, including any objectionable moral relations, do not only occur with respect to the social context of a single state.

Though it is not really discussed in the philosophy (or discrimination) literature,[2] primarily for two reasons it should not be especially controversial to claim that groups have a global social status. First, state boundaries have changed significantly over time—with states coming into, and going out of, existence—and virtually every part of the world has experienced mass migration at one time or another. Consequently, we shouldn't expect the contours of objectionable moral relations to neatly map onto the boundaries of present-day states. Second, global history is often marked by the drawing of distinctions among people on the basis of identity traits, especially visible or perceived traits, resulting in major international injustices, including forced relocation, colonialism, genocide, imperialism, and unjust wars.

Race, especially, has been the locus of considerable international social and political differentiation, with members of certain racial groups having experienced significant oppression at the hands of other racial groups, both within numerous states and across state boundaries. Unfortunately, atrocious examples are easy to come by. Consider one of the most devastating: the transatlantic slave trade. During the span of many centuries, over 12 million Black Africans were forcibly and brutally removed from their home territories, *sold* to traders, and transported to North and South America and the Caribbean, where, if they survived the horrific transportation conditions, they endured a lifetime of slave labor. When we add to this picture the oppressive colonial, imperial, and apartheid regimes many Black people were forced to live under in their home territories and the significant discrimination they faced (and often still face) in their new states long after emancipation, and when we consider the lingering effects of each type of wrong,[3] it is not hard to see how Black people constitute a racial group with a

---

[2] Certainly, there are numerous discussions of global injustice, domination, and the like, but these are primarily framed in terms of power differences between wealthy states and poor states (or how global institutions and nonstate actors objectionably relate to people in poor states), not in terms of differences between identity groups as such. A notable exception is Charles Mills's discussion on the global-power differences between whites and people of color. See *Racial Contract*.

[3] For different forms of analysis, see Acemoglu, Johnson, and Robinson, "Colonial Origins"; Meredith, *Fate of Africa*. Also see Wong (Omowale) (esp. *Devastation and Economics*) on the slave trade's and colonialism's relationships to identity.

vulnerable global status,[4] even if they are not *domestically* vulnerable in many states (for example, Kenya, Botswana, and Ghana).

Similar points seem to apply to many religious (or ethno-religious) groups, such as the world's Jewish population, which I will discuss in section 7. Likewise, many Muslims have experienced a (sometimes recent) history of injustice, and multiple conquests and wars, leaving them, on the whole, disadvantaged in many parts of the world, even though they have secure domestic statuses in many states.[5]

3. Global Status: Refining the Idea

Before going further, several points need to be stressed and clarified. First, as with domestic status, global status does not require that members in the same group stand in solidarity or even identify with one another on the basis of sharing the characteristic. To be sure, they frequently do. To offer only one example, the former president of Nigeria stated, "We, as black people, believed and still believe that we would be second-class citizens in the world if we allowed any black people anywhere in the world, not to talk of Africa, to be treated as second-class citizens because of the colour of their skin."[6] As indicated by the recent worldwide Black Lives Matter protests, this may be a sentiment shared among many. More generally, it is not uncommon that when some members of a particular group experience poor treatment on the basis of their identity—or experienced poor treatment in the past—others with the same identity feel disrespected or belittled,

---

[4] A variety of measures demonstrate their global disadvantages, especially in material and political terms. For instance, the bulk of majority-Black states fall near or at (in the case of South Sudan) the bottom of the 167 states in terms of wealth generation, employment, absolute poverty, education and literacy rates, and health care, according to the Legatum Prosperity Index ("Rankings," https://www. prosperity.com/rankings). To take one example—and by no means the lowest-ranked such country— Nigeria, which has the largest Black population in the world, ranks 161st (out of 167 states) for primary education enrollment, 156th for wealth generation, and 163rd for health care (https://docs.prosperity. com/7216/0465/3153/Nigeria_2020_PIcountryprofile.pdf). Moreover, just over 40% of its population lives in conditions of absolute poverty ("Poverty Headcount Rate in Nigeria as of 2019, by Area," Statista, https://www.statista.com/statistics/1121417/poverty-headcount-rate-in-nigeria-by-area/) and at around 54 years, life expectancy is among the lowest in the world. For comparison, the average life expectancy in the top 40 or so countries ranges between 80 and 84 years ("Life Expectancy—Country Rankings," GlobalEconomy.com, https://www.theglobaleconomy.com/rankings/Life_expectancy/). Also see "Health in Nigeria—Statistics and Facts," Statista, https://www.statista.com/topics/6575/health-in-nigeria/.

[5] One measure of the comparative disadvantages that Muslims face concerns the total wealth of Muslim-majority states. For instance, the share of total world GDP generated by the Islamic Cooperation States (OIC), which includes 57 Muslim-majority states, is only 8.2%. Additionally, OIC states are disproportionately affected by protectionist trade policies elsewhere. See Organisation of Islamic Cooperation, *OIC Economic Outlook 2020*. There are also numerous indicators of their relative health disadvantages. During the period 2005–17, only 69% of deliveries were assisted by a doctor, nurse, or midwife (compared to 84% in non-OIC developing states). And between 2000 and 2017, life expectancy increased to 68.1 years, but in the same period it rose to 71.7 in non-OIC developing states and 81.4 years in developed states. See Organisation of Islamic Cooperation, *OIC Health Report 2019*.

[6] Obasanjo, "Xenophobic Attacks."

and this sort of shared experience can cut across state lines. Moreover, transnational solidarity might sometimes serve as evidence that a group is globally vulnerable. It can of course go in the other direction as well, with certain members of secure groups around the world self-identifying with one another. (For an unfortunate and extreme example of this, there has been growing evidence that white supremacists have been uniting in ways that suggest they strongly subjectively identify with one another across societies.[7]) But the idea of global status does not depend on group members' subjectively identifying, or standing in solidarity, with one another.

The second clarificatory point will also prove important to the argument in Chapter 5. To say that a group is globally vulnerable is distinct from saying (all or most of) its members, or the group taken collectively, constitute part of the global poor (that is, people facing absolute deprivation in material terms). Though these issues can certainly overlap, they can also come apart. As we will see in section 7, in virtue of persecution's lingering effects on the social bases of self-respect, the world's Jewish population is arguably globally vulnerable but not part of the global poor.

The third issue is, I believe, most important here. Namely, one might worry that for many groups, there is no one, stable global status, but rather a status that varies according to context and world region, and, moreover, that there often is no single group at issue.

To reply, the idea of global status does not require thinking that a group's social status is uniform throughout the world or across all interactions. Certainly, some groups, including European-descendant whites and Han Chinese, might today count as secure in relation to almost all other groups around the world and in most types of international interactions.[8] And, in contrast, other groups, including Black people (for reasons already expressed) and many indigenous populations (for

---

[7] Soufan Center, *White Supremacy Extremism*.

[8] I will discuss the global advantages of whites and the collective global power they exercise over international interactions in section 4. Here I focus on Han Chinese, who also seem to have a powerful global status, especially in material and political terms. For political terms, in section 4 I discuss how China occupies one of the five permanent seats on the UN Security Council, conferring it substantial influence over international-security issues and military relations, including over the implementation of sanctions. Fasulo, *Insider's Guide*. For material terms, after decades of economic development, there has been a massive increase in incomes in China, with its gross national income per capita having grown more than tenfold since 2000. "How Well-Off Is China's Middle Class?," ChinaPower, https://chinapower.csis.org/china-middle-class/. Also, consider how China is currently ranked second (after the United States) in terms of total household wealth, and Hong Kong, Singapore, and Taiwan are also ranked very highly (Credit Suisse Group, *Global Wealth Report 2020*, 43). All of these states fare very well in terms of educational opportunities ("Best Countries for Education," *US News & World Report*, https://www.usnews.com/news/best-countries/best-education) and health care as well, with Taiwan in particular considered to have one of the best health care systems in the world. According to one study, it has *the* best system in the world ("Health Care Index by Country 2023," Numbeo, https://www.numbeo.com/health-care/rankings_by_country.jsp). There are also several indicators of the success of Chinese members in other states. For instance, in 2016 in the USA, students of Chinese descent had the lowest school dropout rate among all 16- to 24-year-olds (US Department of Education, *Status and*

reasons we'll explore), might today be characterized as disadvantaged in relation to almost all other groups and international interactions. Moreover, what might initially look like differences in the *domestic* statuses of such groups might not, on reflection, always capture the full picture. The Black community in Brazil offers an important case in point. Brazil is often lauded as a mixed-race democracy or "postracial" society in which being Black is not associated with having a vulnerable social status. But in reality, race continues to be strongly correlated with (dis)advantages. For instance, according to a relatively recent census, the wealthiest 1% in the country was over 80% European-descendant white and over 76% of the country's poorest were Black; and racial stigma was still experienced on a wide scale.[9]

For other groups, however, their global statuses might vary considerably along multiple measures. Consider Christians living in the Middle East and North Africa, who seem considerably disadvantaged in relation to groups only in that region of the world (thus, we might refer to their regional status),[10] or Jewish people, who seem disadvantaged in self-respect terms and therefore in certain types of interactions but not in others.[11] Moreover, it may be appropriate to draw distinctions of social status *within* a group, especially when the group is initially described broadly. Take Muslims, whose experiences and (dis)advantages likely vary depending upon region of the world, country of citizenship, and local natural conditions. Arab Muslims, for instance, have far greater power to command international resources than Indonesian or, especially, Chinese Muslims.[12]

Trends, 107). The following data refer to Asians in general (including Hindu Indians), but they are informative nonetheless (and in Chapter 5, we will see that Hindu Indians are similarly globally secure): among US residents with at least a bachelor's degree in 2016, Asians earned more than their white peers ($69,100 compared with $54,700) (US Department of Education, vii). And in 2018, they had the highest SAT scores ("Fast Facts: SAT Scores," National Center for Education Statistics, https://nces.ed.gov/fastfacts/display.asp?id=171).

[9] *Guardian*, "Brazil Census." For a more recent discussion of these issues (with similar statistics), see de Oliveira, "Is Neymar Black?" Also see Telles, "Demography of Race."

[10] Christians experience widespread discrimination, prejudice, and even persecution in the area. According to one report, their treatment in countries such as Algeria, Iran, Iraq, Syria, and Saudi Arabia has recently reached an alarming stage, with numerous reports of attacks on churches, confiscation of property, and arrests. Aid to the Church in Need, *Religious Freedom*. (See the following for more specific instances: Yeginsu, "Turkey's Seizure"; World Watch Monitor, "Turkey Seizes Six Churches"; Gardner, "Iraq's Christians"; Center for Human Rights in Iran, "Christian Property in Iran"; Kuttab, "Israel Urged." In Saudi Arabia, there are strict limitations on all Christian forms of expression, including acts of worship and prayer (and not only in public settings). See also Aid to the Church in Need, *Persecuted and Forgotten? 2017–2019*, http://www.acnuk.org/persecuted; Human Rights Watch, "Saudi Arabia.") For another indicator of Christians' poor treatment and regard in some states, note that since the mid twentieth century, the population of Palestinian Christians in their homeland has declined from 11% to only 2%. (See Institute for Middle East Understanding, "Palestinian Christians"; section "People and Society" at "West Bank," CIA.gov, last updated February 21, 2023, https://www.cia.gov/the-world-factbook/countries/west-bank/#people-and-society.) What this implies for states' antidiscrimination duties will be taken up in Chapter 5.

[11] I discuss this example in detail in Chapter 5.

[12] For instance, according to one global comparison, Qatar is the fourth-richest state in the world, and out of the top 30 richest states, six are Arab-Muslim majority (Ventura, "Richest and Poorest

But one might wonder whether this sort of context dependency and the potential status differences within the (apparently) same group fundamentally pose a problem for the analysis. I don't believe they do. For one thing, all of this is similar to the notion of domestic status, which for many groups can vary according to comparison group, social context, and region within a state. In the United States, Asian Americans might not generally occupy a disadvantaged position compared with, say, Blacks, or in social contexts in the northwestern part of the country, or with respect to higher education opportunities. But they might face disadvantages in relation to whites, in other geographic regions such as the South, and with respect to certain business opportunities such as access to managerial and executive positions. Another example concerns Hispanics, who might not be vulnerable compared with, for instance, native groups, or with respect to employment in the sports and entertainment industries, or in social contexts in Southern California or Florida. But they do face disadvantages compared with Asian Americans and whites, in relation to financial and health opportunities, and in geographic regions such as the Midwest and West.[13]

Moreover, there are often domestic-status distinctions within the same (apparent) group, if for no other reason than the role of multiple identities. Sticking to the United States, if Indonesians are considered as Asians (as they typically are[14]), then since most are also Muslim, in some contexts and regions in the United States they may be differently treated or regarded than, say, Japanese Americans.[15] These points seem amplified for Hispanics within the United States, as it seems their population exhibits significant differences in (dis)advantages, with those originating in South America generally having a far-higher status in the United States than those originating in Central America or the Caribbean.[16] While there are no perfect measures for such status differences, poverty rates, income, and

Countries"). In recent years, Arab states have had some of the world's largest sovereign wealth funds, which consist of state-controlled assets primarily allocated to foreign investments. As a result of such investments, they have significant shares in foreign banking, gas and energy, and technology firms and own considerable amounts of European and US property. (See, for instance, Behrendt, "When Money Talks." Also see Martin and Parasie, "Gulf Sovereign Funds.") Similarly, according to the US Department of Education, Arab donors have contributed almost $7 billion to US colleges and universities since 1981, with Qatar, Saudi Arabia, and the UAE being the largest three foreign donors. See US Department of Education, Foreign Gift; Bard, "Arab Funding." In contrast, Chinese Muslims, in particular Uyghurs, are arguably some of the most vulnerable people in the world. (For recent discussion, see Chan, "I Never Thought China"; Wong and Buckley, "U.S. Says China's Repression"; Economist, "Persecution of Uyghurs"; Serhan, "Saving Uighur Culture.")

[13] Tienda and Mitchell, Hispanics and the Future.

[14] US Census Bureau, Population and Housing Unit Estimates.

[15] Also consider the important role that overlapping identities can play in carving out distinctions of status within a particular group (for example, the way Black women may suffer more disadvantages than either white women or Black men and may experience "double discrimination" or the joint effects of discrimination on the basis of both race and gender). Crenshaw, "Demarginalizing the Intersection."

[16] The point is stronger still for the broader category of Latina/os, which also includes Brazilians. Haslanger makes a related observation concerning the diversity of cultures and histories among certain racial groups, such as Asians and Latina/os. Haslanger, "Future Genders? Future Races?," 17–18. Although her terminology is different from mine and although hierarchical relations are built into

occupations may provide some evidence, and each of these varies considerably with country and region of origin. For example, median incomes of US members originally from Argentina, Chile, and Bolivia are significantly higher than the national US average, in contrast to members who originated from Honduras and Mexico, and the former are far likelier than the latter to hold managerial and other professional jobs.[17]

Finally, there have been (and still are) important internal domestic-status distinctions among whites in the United States, varying according to, for instance, class, place of origin, and current residential region. For instance, both impoverished white workers in the post-Civil War period and Italians (especially Southern Italians) in the early twentieth century were treated and regarded inferiorly to, and by, other whites. More recently, Appalachian whites have had a significantly vulnerable domestic status, not just in terms of considerable economic disadvantage and inadequate access to basic services, but (because of a perceived dialect) being stereotyped as lazy and being regarded with pity and disgust by others, including other whites, in surrounding regions (importantly, Appalachian whites' vulnerability is largely regional, as they unlikely constitute a salient group in, say, the West Coast states[18]).

Given such variation, the question whether we can actually group diverse populations together and assign them a single status arises in the domestic context as well. And I think the answer to that question, for both domestic and global status, must be that it depends. It depends on the purpose of the analysis and on the comparison class. When it comes to the relation between one (loosely bound) group and certain other (loosely bound) groups, we often *can* draw broad distinctions in social status—if only or mainly in certain ways, during particular periods, or in particular social contexts. For instance, white laborers in the post-Civil War United States constituted a vulnerable group compared with wealthy white people, but that doesn't mean they didn't belong to a larger group that, in comparison with Blacks, experienced numerous advantages. Even poor white laborers had access to public spaces and services from which Black people were denied, they experienced deference from Blacks, and major newspapers represented their interests qua whites.[19] And though the white population was hierarchically structured in the early twentieth century and Southern Italians experienced prejudice and marginalization, they were still perceived as, and had

---

her understanding of race, a corollary of her main point in this discussion appears to be that what unifies the members of the group of, say, Latina/os in the United States is that they, on the whole, stand as subordinate to another group, for instance whites.

[17] Among groups categorized as Hispanic, "the poverty rate is highest among Hondurans, Puerto Ricans and Mexicans (27%). They are closely followed by two groups at 26%—Dominicans and Guatemalans." In contrast, "Colombians and Peruvians have poverty rates *below* the total US rate (15%)." Pew Research Center, "Largest Hispanic Origin Groups," sect. V.

[18] See Rhee and Scott, "Geographic Discrimination"; and Pasternak, "Bias Blights Life."

[19] See Dubois, *Black Reconstruction in America*.

the comparative benefits of, being white, relative to other groups.[20] As Charles Mills writes, "'Whiteness' in the period was not a monolith but itself a hierarchically structured category. Nonetheless, even inferior whites were superior to people of color."[21]

Similarly, although there are global-status distinctions among, for instance, Arabs, depending on (for example) country of citizenship and skin color, that does not imply there are no global-status differences between Arabs, on the whole, and members of *other* groups. Arabs, for instance, have far greater advantages than Kurds in international interactions, and might be disadvantaged in comparison to European whites in at least some.[22] I don't mean to suggest that there are not greater complexities at the global level; the size of identity groups, their frequent dispersal around the world, and their differing citizenships certainly compound the problems of identifying coherent groups and determining their social status. But the fact that global social status is contextual and its determination depends on the comparison group and kind of analysis undertaken seems to be not a particular limitation of the view advanced here but an extension of how these complex issues of social identity are best considered in any domestic context.[23]

4. How Does Global Status Matter?

Before considering why global status may matter in specific immigration cases, we should elaborate on why it may be morally significant more generally. In particular, one might think that the idea of social status is only significant insofar as it affects people's lives locally, that is in their states of membership, and think that only domestic status structures people's daily lives. My reply to this concern is that global status can and does affect people's lives in very real ways.

Sometimes a group's global status has that effect because it affects the group's domestic status within particular states. This can in turn affect global status, creating a feedback loop. For instance, the terrorist acts committed in the

---

[20] See Guglielmo, *White on Arrival*.   [21] Mills, "Race and Global Justice," 187n15.

[22] Some ways to measure this include control over international organizations, GDP, and diplomatic influence. See, for example, Novosad and Werker, "Who Runs the International System?"; Bush, "Varieties of International Influence." To understand the relative lack of power that Kurds enjoy in international interactions, one need only note that although they represent the fourth-largest ethnic group in the Middle East, they have yet to secure sovereign territory. For recent discussion, see BBC News, "Who Are the Kurds?"

[23] See Sally Haslanger's prominent view, which seems very relevant here. See especially Haslanger, "Gender and Race." She suggests that what unifies a group is that, along certain dimensions and in particular contexts, individuals in the group are, on the whole, subordinate or powerful compared with those in another group (esp. 44, 47–48). In a related fashion, Khaitan suggests that relative-advantage differences between groups are central to and necessary for norms against discrimination. Khaitan, *Theory of Discrimination Law*, 32–33.

United States on September 11, 2001, contributed to fear and suspicion of Muslims, and violence and attacks against them, within multiple and diverse states, including China, Canada, and many European states.[24] Writing seven years after the attack, the international human rights watchdog Human Rights First stated that "the environment in which Muslims live has deteriorated considerably since September 11, with Muslims and Muslim communities becoming victims of negative stereotyping and manifestations of prejudice."[25] A plausible interpretation is that the events in one state (the United States) affected the ways Muslims were regarded globally, in turn affecting their domestic statuses within many states (their disadvantages compared with other groups in those states). And given how interactions in one part of the globe can affect how people are treated and regarded in other parts, it would not be unreasonable to suppose that if some state had selectively excluded Muslims soon after September 11 (or today[26]), that would have had significant expressive effects and might have further compromised the bases of their self-respect in other states, plausibly further damaging their global status.

Other times, however, a group's global status may directly impact the lives of people in the group without altering, or being mediated by, their domestic status. Numerous authors have observed that global institutions and interactions can deeply and pervasively shape our lives—through economic and trade agreements, conditional aid and loans, diplomatic pressure, security and military operations, and climate change goals and policy—in unmediated and direct ways.[27] Far less attended to, however, is how the global status of differing racial and ethnic groups affects these institutions and interactions. Partly this may be because studies examining and measuring the role of race and ethnicity have been relatively lacking in the field of international relations, and, as a result, definitive evidence is hard to come by (though this has recently begun to change[28]). But there are some differences that seem readily observable, even to the non-political scientist.

The differences in military strength, along with international diplomatic support, among globally secure and globally vulnerable racial or ethnic groups often illustrate the point in dramatic fashion—with serious and tragic effects on

[24] Stahnke et al., *Violence against Muslims*; Carr, *Experiences of Islamophobia*; Ma, "Anti-Islamic Movement."

[25] Stahnke et al., 3.

[26] Consider the United States's 2017 executive order restricting immigration from many Muslim-majority states. I discuss this in Chapter 6.

[27] See (for example) Beitz, *Political Theory*; Cohen and Sabel, "Extram Republicam Nulla Justitia?"; Abizadeh, "Cooperation"; Cavallero, "Coercion."

[28] Early scholars of international relations were very attentive to issues of race and ethnicity. For instance, the idea of the "global colour line" is taken from a 1925 article by W.E.B. Du Bois in which he claimed that questions of racial hierarchy were at the heart of international politics. The article was published in *Foreign Affairs*, which, strikingly, was originally the *Journal of Race Development*. There has recently been an emerging turn toward examining the role of race in global relations.

group members' lives. For instance—though there are certainly counterexamples[29]—those with comparably vulnerable global statuses have been disproportionately killed in numerous wars, especially wars of independence. To take just one example, in three African states' wars of independence from Portugal during the period 1961–74, roughly 122,000 members of the native populations died (in Angola, Mozambique, and Guinea), while only roughly 8,500 Portuguese died.[30]

Beyond specific military and security outcomes, consider how representation is constructed in the United Nations (UN) Security Council—which is, by all accounts, the most powerful body in the UN. The Security Council has five permanent members—China, the United Kingdom, the United States, France, and Russia—any one of whose no vote on a security or military proposal or measure, including sanctions and peacekeeping missions, effectively operates as a veto.[31] That point alone, I believe, demonstrates differing global political and military power among groups.[32]

More generally, globally secure racial or ethnic groups often have significant influence on global institutions, giving them a comparative ability to set agendas, determine policies, gain access to goods, including territory and natural resources, and establish agreements in their favor.[33] And their subsequent advantages are often experienced directly. Some groups, for example, have significant control over natural resources or major multinational companies, which generates enormous economic opportunities and promotes well-being for their members in the states they live in (without altering the groups' domestic statuses).[34] A similar point applies to disparities in power over global economic institutions such as the World Bank and the IMF, in which voting power is proportionate to a state's global economic position, giving wealthy states the ability to forge agreements in their members' favor.[35] Having more votes in the IMF means a state has

---

[29] The Bangladeshi Liberation War of 1971 seems to be an important counterexample (though there are, assuredly, more), as it seems that most of those (brutally) killed were Hindus at the hands of Pakistani Muslims.

[30] Clodfelter, *Warfare and Armed Conflicts*, 599.   [31] Fasulo, *Insider's Guide*.

[32] Another point is also worth attending to: The ten nonpermanent members on the Security Council are elected only for two-year terms and mainly on a regional basis. Representation is distributed according to the following regions: Africa (three seats); Asia-Pacific (two seats); Eastern Europe (one seat); and Latin America and the Caribbean (two seats). However, there is one exception to regional representation, and, at least to some extent, it tracks a common racial identity. Namely, the category of "Western European and Other States" combines states from very different regions of the world, including Australia, New Zealand, Canada, the United States, Turkey, and, since 2004, Israel—aside perhaps from Turkey and Israel, white-majority states. United Nations, "United Nations Regional Groups." While there were some Cold War-related reasons for this alignment, such reasons may have ceased to be important many years ago, and yet the category still exists. Götz, "Western Europeans and Others." (See US Congress, *Expressing the Sense*.)

[33] Bush, "Varieties of International Influence"; Novosad and Werker, "Who Runs the International System?"

[34] For numerous examples illustrating this point, see Kotkin, *Tribes*; Kotkin, "Rise of the Hans"; *Economist*, "From Pearls."

[35] Bretton Woods Project, *IMF and World Bank*.

substantial bargaining power over the lending agreements between states, and having more votes at the World Bank gives a wealthy state sizable power over the rules of global trade, which determine the conditions under which goods and services created in one state can be traded with those from another state.

Based especially on these last points, however, one might worry that this discussion has mainly illuminated how wealthy *states*, not any identity groups, might have relative power over international institutions and access to global resources. However, in most of the world's wealthy and powerful states, globally secure groups constitute the majority. To take one of the clearer examples, the majority of the world's white population lives in states that form roughly half of the top 30 states worldwide by GDP (out of 205 states total).[36] Similarly, the primary states in which the world's white population resides constitute 21 of the 30 states with the highest life expectancy,[37] and all of the majority-white states are in the top 30 in terms of education.[38]

It is the opposite situation for many globally vulnerable groups. Taking one example, Polynesians (an ethnolinguistic group) have historically had exceedingly little power in global interactions and now face significant climate-related risks.[39] Though they certainly have a vulnerable domestic status within some states, including Australia and New Zealand, this is not true in other states and territories, such as Tuvalu, where they constitute the overwhelming majority; since vulnerability and power, as used here, are relational concepts, if there are not really any other groups in Tuvalu then Polynesians are not domestically vulnerable in Tuvalu. Still, Tuvalu's Polynesians face notable climate-related obstacles in well-being,[40] including significant health concerns,[41] as a direct result of their *global* vulnerability.[42] And if some states were to disfavor the admission of

---

[36] For an overview of which states are majority white and where the largest share of whites reside, see Kimalainen, "15 Countries." For GDP comparisons, see "Gross Domestic Product 2021," https://databank.worldbank.org/data/download/GDP.pdf.

[37] See "Life Expectancy at Birth," Knoema.com, https://knoema.com/atlas/ranks/Life-expectancy.

[38] See Legatum Institute, "Rankings," https://www.prosperity.com/rankings.

[39] On the connection between Polynesians' lack of global influence and climate change risks, see Lallemant-Moe, "Polynesian Political Awakening."

[40] The World Risk Index 2019 ranks several Polynesian-majority states among the top twenty most at-risk countries for extreme natural events (leading to water scarcity). For instance, Vanuatu and Tonga are ranked first and third respectively. Bündnis Entwicklung Hilft, *WorldRiskReport 2019*, 7, 47, 56.

[41] World Health Organization, *Human Health*.

[42] There is ample evidence that Pacific Islanders are vulnerable in nearby states such as New Zealand. Although this is a broader category than Polynesians, it is nonetheless informative to consider some of the data. For instance, Pacific Islanders constitute only about 25% of New Zealand's population but 66% of those shot by police in the last decade and are also more likely to be tasered and pepper-sprayed than white New Zealanders (Warner, "New Zealand Police"). In Australia, it seems they have faced numerous obstacles to gaining permanent visas as compared with their white counterparts (ABC News, "New Zealand Citizens"). Aside from discriminatory treatment and climate-related risks, Polynesians are among the most vulnerable people in the world in terms of health and poverty. For instance, in the Polynesian-majority states of Tuvalu, Tonga, and Samoa, roughly one-quarter (in

Polynesians, their global vulnerability would likely be worsened by being selectively denied opportunities in the excluding states.[43]

To preempt a potential misunderstanding, my aim with this discussion is *not* to attribute the differences in global (dis)advantages among groups to either past or current wrongs committed by, especially, globally secure groups. My only aim is to demonstrate how, and in what respects, global-(dis)advantage differences between secure and vulnerable groups can translate into differences in both well-being and opportunities for the individuals in those groups—sometimes mediated by domestic status, and other times more directly.

Before moving on, a final clarification is important. Though the global status of one's identity group can make a difference to the quality of one's life, global status certainly does not always matter. In particular, whether some group has a secure global status makes *no* difference in considering many kinds of discrimination its members might experience, especially identity-motivated violence, which is straightforwardly wrong. Consider Zimbabwe's minority-white farmers, subject to sometimes-extreme violence when the Mugabe-controlled government removed them from their land.[44] In such cases, discrimination concerns seem entirely symmetrical,[45] and global status seems irrelevant. Importantly, however, *domestic* status would seem just as irrelevant. For even if whites were domestically powerful in Zimbabwe, the inequality in fundamental rights and benefits they faced during that period, and especially the violence they experienced, would remain wrong.

5. Domestic Status and Differentiating among Cases

To understand how global status matters in assessing racial and ethnic immigration selection, it will be helpful to first explore a contrasting view that stresses only domestic considerations. Held by notable proponents of states' choice (and the right to exclude, discussed in Chapter 7), this alternative view suggests that racial

Tuvalu and Tonga) and 20% (in Samoa) of the populations live below the poverty line ("World Bank Puts Millions toward Literacy in Tuvalu," Borgen Project, https://borgenproject.org/world-bank-gives-14-million-to-tuvalu-for-literacy-programs; "Poverty Data: Tonga," Asian Development Bank, https://www.adb.org/offices/south-pacific/poverty/tonga; "The Main Causes of Poverty in Samoa," Borgen Project, https://borgenproject.org/causes-of-poverty-in-samoa/). In terms of health, Tonga has one of the highest populations of overweight and obese people in the world (*Healthcare Global Magazine*, "Why the Pacific Islands"; also see "Tonga Population 2021," World Population Review, https://worldpopulationreview.com/countries/tonga-population). Collectively, over 15% of the populations in these states have either type 1 or type 2 diabetes ("Diabetes Prevalence (% of Population Ages 20 to 79)—Country Ranking—Oceania," Index Mundi, https://www.indexmundi.com/facts/indicators/SH.STA.DIAB.ZS/rankings/oceania; International Diabetes Federation, *IDF Diabetes Atlas*).

[43] As will be discussed in Chapters 5 and 6, the emphasis on *selective* exclusions is central to the antidiscrimination approach and partly what distinguishes it from open-border views.

[44] See Mukeredzi, "Zimbabwe's New Land Reforms."

[45] See Lippert-Rasmussen, *Born Free and Equal*, 138.

and ethnic immigration criteria do not wrong the excluded nonmembers. Rather, such criteria only wrong the admitting state's current members whose race or ethnicity is disfavored by the criteria, and, for that reason, such criteria are impermissible. Call this the Wrong to Members view, or WM.

In the next chapter, we'll explore some of the main reasons that WM's proponents deny that excluded nonmembers can be wronged by racial and ethnic criteria—a topic much more central to this book. But by critically examining their stance that racial and ethnic criteria wrong *members* who share the disfavored race or ethnicity (or, simply "disfavored members"), we will gain an appreciation of some of the ways in which global status is morally relevant for states' admission decisions.

To motivate the idea that racial and ethnic criteria are only wrong if the admitting state has disfavored members, one of WM's two most prominent defenders, Michael Blake, provides the following hypothetical case:

Ensuring Ethnicity: "an ethnically homogenous society" that implements "an immigration policy designed to ensure and perpetuate this ethnic makeup of society."[46]

Blake suggests that this case is permissible, and he may be right. If so, however, it would not boil down to whether or not the state has disfavored members. First, WM implies that a case such as Racial Ban (from Chapter 1) in which, again, a state composed only of whites explicitly disfavors the admission of Black people, is not wrong. Racial Ban has the same structure as Ensuring Ethnicity in that there are no disfavored members, but despite that particular similarity, the cases look normatively extremely different (we'll explore some of these differences shortly).

Just as importantly, if racial or ethnic criteria are impermissible whenever the admitting state has disfavored members, we will be unable to account for even the *potential* moral permissibility of a variety of cases, some of which are, as mentioned in Chapter 1, supported by WM's proponents. For instance, recall that Michael Blake and Christopher Wellman, along with several others,[47] express support for Israel's Law of Return, which grants automatic admission to all and only Jewish people; these authors suggest that the wrong done to Israeli's disfavored members (especially Palestinians) is potentially outweighed by the Jewish experience of the Holocaust. In section 7, I will demonstrate how concerns about global status play a direct role in potentially justifying Israel's selective

---

[46] Blake, "Distributive Justice," 285.

[47] See (for example) Coleman and Harding, "Citizenship"; Miller, "Immigration," 204. Miller associates Israel's policy with religion not ethnicity, but that distinction is far from clear (see Fine, "Immigration and Discrimination," 147). Carens ("Who Should Get In?," 109, n19) suggests Israel is a "special case," though I'm not entirely clear he thinks it potentially morally permissible. Also see Carens, "Migration and Morality," 45.

immigration policies. For now, I want to focus on hypothetical cases that seem both more compelling and less controversial than Israel's: states where obviously vulnerable admitting groups favor the admission of their own group members, disfavoring members in the state who belong to secure groups.

We could examine a variety of hypothetical cases involving admitting groups with significant vulnerability, including the Kurds, Roma, Bahai'i, Uyghur, Rohingya, and Aboriginal populations throughout the world, such as the Torres Strait Islanders. But let's begin with a hypothetical case involving one of the native populations in the United States: the Navajo. As many readers may know, in the Long Walk the early US government forcibly removed the Navajo from the land they had lived on for generations, looted their homes, and forced them to walk over 300 miles to an overcrowded, desolate reservation; many died on the way. The new location required farming techniques the Navajo were not accustomed to, causing nearly one-third of their relocated population to die of starvation and disease. In light of that history, consider this hypothetical case:

Navajo: In a region of the United States inhabited only by Navajo and a small population of whites, the Navajo people establish a fully autonomous state (called Navajo), where they constitute the numerical majority and, consequently, hold the majority of political and economic power. Many of the whites choose to remain and become citizens of Navajo. Shortly after its creation, Navajo implements an immigration policy that (aside from urgent and family-reunification claims) explicitly favors the admission of Navajo.

One might raise a number of questions about this case, including how realistic it is that the Navajo would want their own state[48] or why whites would choose to remain in a majority-Navajo state. But such considerations aside, given the Navajo's history and the identity of the state's disfavored members (namely, whites), it seems that Navajo's policy may not wrong its disfavored members. Indeed, the idea that the Navajo and other native populations in North America may exclude others from their territories is something supported by nationalists and liberals alike.[49] Of course, it could turn out that, once the relevant sorts of considerations have been explored (in the next section), Navajo's policy does wrong its white members. What's important here, though, is that under a straightforward reading of WM, Navajo's white members would certainly be wronged (and simply because their race is disfavored).

---

[48] Indigenous writers argue that native groups don't seek sovereignty qua states. See (for example) Maaka and Fleras, "Engaging with Indigeneity."

[49] Though *disfavored members* are not discussed, such support may nonetheless be telling. See Carens, "Who Should Get In?," 40; Oberman, "Immigration as Human Right," 48. More generally, on self-governance rights for Indigenous people, see Kymlicka, *Multicultural Citizenship*, esp. 27–30; and Buchanan, *Justice, Legitimacy, and Self-Determination*, chap. 9.

Perhaps this conclusion is too fast however. Closer consideration of how WM's proponents describe the nature of the wrong done to disfavored members—descriptions that deeply resonate with antidiscrimination's primary concerns—could suggest that they would say that Navajo's white members are not necessarily wronged. Blake, for instance, maintains that racial and ethnic policies would amount to "implicitly treating [disfavored members] as second-class citizens"[50] and "compromise the social bases of [their] self-respect."[51] Similarly, following Blake, Wellman maintains that such policies "would wrongly disrespect those citizens in the dispreferred category" and "send a clear message that . . . they are not equally valued as partners in the political union."[52] Drawing on such reflections, it may be that WM's underlying concern is not with policies that merely disfavor the race or ethnicity of current members, but with policies that also, for instance, treat those members as second-class citizens, express a demeaning message about them, or undermine the social bases of their self-respect.

In order to assess whether Navajo's white members may not be wronged in such ways, the question then becomes when such wrongs are generally thought to occur and when they are not. For WM's proponents, the main answer is suggested by Blake. When discussing, for instance, why racial or ethnic immigration criteria are distinct from, say, height-based criteria, he writes, "Race and ethnicity represent significant cleavages within most Western societies," as they are "sites for unjust forms of domination and oppression."[53] More concretely, in considering immigration designed to protect local traditions or the local way of life, for example, he writes, "In all cases in which there are national or ethnic minorities—which is to say, the vast majority of actual cases—to restrict immigration for national or ethnic reasons is to make some citizens politically inferior to others."[54] And he stresses "the message of inferiority [ethnic and racial] policies send to citizens of minority ethnic and racial groups."[55] With such comments, Blake suggests that disfavored members are wronged in the sorts of ways described above (for example, being treated as inferior) if their group has a vulnerable status relative to other groups within the admitting state—that is, when they have a vulnerable domestic status.

This opens the possibility that disfavored members may *not* be wronged if their group is domestically secure. It should be fairly clear, however, that stressing domestic status does not help to explain why Navajo's immigration policy may not wrong its disfavored members—whites. For in the hypothetical, it is the Navajo who constitute the numerical, and thereby economic and political, majority in the Navajo state, while whites constitute the minority. Thus, it is fair to say that whites have a *vulnerable* domestic status in that state compared with the

---

[50] Blake, "Immigration," 233.   [51] Blake, "Discretionary Immigration," 284.
[52] Wellman, "Freedom of Association," 139–40.   [53] Blake, "Distributive Justice," 284.
[54] Blake, "Immigration," 232–33.   [55] Blake, "Distributive Justice," 286.

Navajo people. Despite these domestic-status differences, however, it's not obvious that the policy, say, expresses a demeaning message about Navajo's white members or compromises the social bases of their self-respect. This is because there is an important sense in which whites, as a group, do not seem vulnerable, while the Navajo do.

Before moving on to discuss this point, I must clarify that the literature engaged here primarily assesses the use of racial and ethnic immigration criteria without specifying or knowing for certain the particular attitudes or goals motivating a state's use of such criteria, such as particular beliefs or views about the disfavored race—and I will largely follow suit. This does not mean, however, that we will always be unable to interpret what attitudes or reasons seem to lie behind the criteria. Nor does it mean we will be unable to claim that a policy expresses certain attitudes. To the contrary, my claim is that global status is often key to such interpretation and expression.

6. Explaining Navajo and Other Hypothetical Cases

I will now begin to show that, as part of the antidiscrimination approach, global status is a key ingredient in explaining the potential normative differences among various kinds of selective immigration policies—both hypothetical and actual. The idea is that the global status of both the disfavored group (here, disfavored members; in Chapters 4 and 5, excluded nonmembers) and the admitting group often matter for determining whether selective immigration wrongs the disfavored group.

Let's start with Navajo's immigration policy. In the discussion of antidiscrimination within states (Chapter 2), we saw how certain domestically vulnerable groups (for example, women in many states) may be morally permitted to favor their own group in certain domestic associations while their more secure cognate groups may not. The Navajo people do not have a vulnerable status within the Navajo state. At the same time, they seem vulnerable in multiple important respects.

Already discussed are the commonly known injustices surrounding the Long Walk, but these injustices continue to plague the Navajo today in ways that bear on their self-concept and self-respect. Extensive anthropological and psychological research demonstrates how events such as the Long Walk represent significant "historical traumas" and "historical grief" for native groups, much like the Holocaust has for descendants of survivors, and documents how such trauma is transmitted across generations, affecting the mental health and overall well-being of contemporary populations.[56] In particular, there is often intergenerational grief

---

[56] For seminal work, see Brave Heart, "Oyate Ptayela."

over the destruction of land, plants, and animals (sometimes considered relatives, not property) and an intergenerational sense of shame concerning how one's group was brutally forced or incentivized by other groups to abandon their homeland, language, and significant cultural and spiritual practices.[57] In light of such issues, if the Navajo may favor the admission of their own group, this is best interpreted as reflecting a concern about securing their well-being, sense of empowerment, and self-respect, not qua members of the Navajo state, but rather qua people in a world where they once lived under conditions of abiding domination and persecution.

Before discussing the role of whites' global status, a potential objection here is that, ultimately, the Navajo's domestic status in the hypothetical case *does* matter—only, one might think, it is their *future* domestic status. For it might seem that, through selective immigration, the Navajo could protect themselves against becoming the electoral minority in their state and thereby becoming domestically vulnerable in the future.

Part of my reply to this objection is that I have not denied that a group's domestic status is often important for understanding different racial and ethnic cases. The point has been to illustrate that global status has been largely overlooked—not that domestic status is irrelevant. But what if one thinks the *only* reason the Navajo in the hypothetical may use selective criteria is to protect their future domestic status? Does that mean this case fails to illustrate the importance of global status?

Here I turn to my main reply. Insofar as the Navajo's ability to secure their future domestic status is a powerful reason for thinking Navajo's policy might be permissible, we must ask: why in that case but not necessarily others? For imagine again Racial Ban—the case of an all-white state that explicitly disfavors the admission of Black people—or imagine if the Han majority in China or the Arab majority in Qatar were to favor the admission of fellow Hans qua Hans or Arabs qua Arabs, respectively.[58] Would we be similarly concerned about these groups' ability to secure their future domestic status? It is doubtful. Given that each group—the Navajo in the hypothetical, the Han in China, and Arabs in Qatar—constitutes the domestically secure group in each case, then, what explains the difference is the Navajo's (highly) vulnerable status beyond their state. So even the explanation referring to their future domestic status seems to ultimately reflect a concern about their global status.

A similar point can be made about Blake's hypothetical case, Ensuring Ethnicity. As we saw, Blake suggests that this case is morally permissible, and that may be right. But insofar as it is, then given that we are told that the

[57] Brave Heart and DeBruyn, "American Indian Holocaust," 62; Gone, "'We Never Was Happy'"; and Beauvais, "Trends in Drug Use."
[58] For pertinent discussion, see Kotkin, "Rise of the Hans."

immigration policy is "designed to ensure and perpetuate" the state's homogenous ethnicity, the case's permissibility most likely reflects a concern that the relevant ethnic group is vulnerable in some respect—though certainly not *domestically*, since it is presumably the only group in the state. To clarify, we need not interpret Ensuring Ethnicity as centering on a vulnerable group in any sense. But the case seems much less compelling if we imagine that the admitting group has a very secure global status, as Racial Ban clearly demonstrates.

Since the immediate discussion has focused on the rationale for the Navajo favoring their own group, it might seem the suggestion above is that the Navajo's global vulnerability makes their immigration policy justified *despite* how it wrongs the disfavored members. That is certainly possible; as we'll explore with Israel's case, the admitting group's global vulnerability may sometimes justify selective immigration that wrongs members. But, additionally, in Navajo's case it seems the disfavored members might not be wronged in the first place (and, in Chapter 5, we will see that a similar point applies to excluded *nonmembers* in cases such as Navajo). This is because of the combined effect of the global vulnerability of the Navajo as the admitting group and the secure global status of whites along multiple dimensions. Not only are whites the dominant group in many other states, but, importantly, whites on the whole have historically had, and continue to have, considerable power in shaping international interactions and gaining global resources.[59]

But how might the fact that Navajo's white members belong to a larger racial group with a secure status outside their state matter for whether *their* state's policy wrongs them? Is it because there are other states in which they could live as part of the dominant group? Or is it that their larger racial group's advantages provide them a measure of security against becoming marginalized in their own state? Moreover, what is the relevance of Navajo's white members having originated in the United States, which perpetrated the massive injustices against the Navajo people? Answering such questions definitively requires a variety of considerations, not least because the answers depend on the specific antidiscrimination view of when and why differential selection is wrong. But let me say something about the major sorts of antidiscrimination concerns suggested above by Blake and Wellman.

First, consider the related idea that an action that differentiates between people on the basis of race or ethnicity may demean people or treat them in a denigrating way.[60] As discussed in Chapter 2, the sense of demeaning is objective.[61] We ask

---

[59] See, for instance, Fasulo, *Insider's Guide*; Bretton Woods Project, *IMF and World Bank*. Much of this discussion focuses on differences in *states'* power, but as explained in section 4, whites constitute the majority in many of the most powerful and wealthy states.

[60] Anderson and Pildes, "Expressive Theories of Law"; Hellman, *When Is Discrimination Wrong?*

[61] Hellman, *When Is Discrimination Wrong?* This also seems related to Glenn Loury's view on stigma and race (*Anatomy of Racial Inequality*).

whether it is plausible to interpret an action as expressing a demeaning or disrespectful message, not whether it is either intended or experienced as such. And to answer this, we primarily look at the status differences between the relevant groups and at past and current social practices to see whether, for instance, the disfavored group has been marginalized or subordinated or whether their identity has been the object of prejudice or scorn. Our hypothetical state of Navajo is newly formed and thus lacks any real history of social relations; all we know is that whites constitute the minority. But when we examine the global social context—past and current interactions outside of Navajo—we see there is little history of whites qua whites being disadvantaged that could give traction to an interpretation that whites have generally been marginalized or oppressed in the world or an interpretation that being white has generally been the object of prejudice or contempt.[62] It is not a racial identity that has historically been associated with being devalued or put down. Furthermore, we have seen that in contrast to whites the Navajo are highly globally vulnerable in multiple respects, thereby seemingly lacking the social power needed for putting others down. Given all this, it seems implausible to interpret Navajo's policy as expressing a demeaning or disrespectful message toward its white members.

As for there being other states in which whites can live as members of the dominant group, this is only incidentally relevant to the issue of demeaning actions. It provides evidence for the secure global status of whites, since territory and recognition of sovereignty are gained by comparatively powerful groups, and thus indirect evidence that whites qua whites have not generally been oppressed or marginalized.

How about whether the immigration policy would undermine the social bases of whites' self-respect, or relatedly whether they would be made to feel socially inferior?[63] As stressed in Chapter 2, a common understanding of the social requirements for one's self-respect is others' recognition of one's moral personhood and the value of one's chosen ends.[64] First, there is relatively little history of whites qua whites being marked off, shunned, excluded, or denigrated that might serve to reasonably[65] contribute to a sense that Navajo's white members are being socially devalued. Second, the Navajo's own global status suggests that their policy is plausibly interpreted more as helping to secure a vulnerable group's place in the world than as anything else. The combination of these two considerations suggests

---

[62] As the Zimbabwe example shows, there certainly are exceptions.

[63] Sunstein ("Anticaste Principle") stresses such concerns. Also see White's concerns about dignity interests ("Freedom of Association," 384–85).

[64] This is a major understanding of John Rawls's view. See (for example) Eyal, "'Most Important Primary Good.'"

[65] As Thomas Waligore argues, "What matters is not subjective fear but reasonable distrust" based on the group's experiences of injustice. See Waligore, "Rawls, Self-Respect and Assurance," 46.

that the policy lacks the normative force to weaken the social bases of white members' self-respect.

A final important issue that was suggested by Blake concerns whether Navajo's policy renders its white members second-class citizens—an idea very closely related to subordination.[66] First, that whites are the minority in the state does not mean they are, by definition, rendered second-class citizens or subordinated. As discussed in Chapter 2, these notions characterize groups that are *systematically* treated as inferiors, such as through the imposition of social and legal obstacles in multiple spheres of life or the denial of equal rights and privileges.[67] There is also a duration aspect,[68] as subordinated groups typically occupy their position for some time. Given all this, one might think there's an easy reply to the question whether Navajo's policy subordinates its white members without invoking global status: namely, it cannot subordinate them simply because it is a brand-new state.

But that reply is unsatisfactory. The likelihood of a discriminatory act causing a group's subordination or second-class status is also important.[69] And if we knew nothing about the global status of either whites or the Navajo, the fact that whites are the domestic minority would give us reason to worry about their being subordinated in the future.[70] Consider switching up the example so that a white majority favors the admission of others in that group despite the presence of a Navajo minority. Call this Reverse Navajo. We would, it seems, be quite concerned that the Navajo might become a subordinated class in Reverse Navajo. So, if we are less concerned that whites will become subordinated in the original Navajo case, it seems we have their and, just as important, the Navajo's global status in mind. Some of the ways global status is important have been discussed; for example, in most of the world, whites qua whites have not been subject to systematic injustices. But an additional factor directly relevant to subordination is whites' global economic and military power, especially compared with the Navajo's, as it plausibly provides a measure of external security against the prospect that whites will be deprived of equal rights and privileges within Navajo.[71]

To clarify, though in section 4 we saw how global status can affect domestic status, and vice versa, that is not the key idea here. Domestically, whites remain the comparatively vulnerable group, and nothing about the global status of whites

---

[66] Fiss, "Equal Protection Clause"; Ely, *Democracy and Distrust*; Sunstein, "Anticaste Principle"; and Moreau, "Discrimination and Subordination."

[67] Sunstein, "Anticaste Principle," 2429–30.   [68] Fiss, "Equal Protection Clause," 151n67.

[69] Fiss, 151n67; Khaitan, *Theory of Discrimination Law*, 35.

[70] Fiss, "Equal Protection Clause," 151–53, n67, 155–57.

[71] For instance, white-majority states (United States, United Kingdom, and France) occupy three of the five permanent seats on the United Nations Security Council, conferring them substantial influence over international-security issues and military relations, including the implementation of sanctions. (For more on how power over military engagements is distributed, see Fasulo, *Insider's Guide*.) On how being white became a transnational identity that forged significant geopolitical and military alliances, see Lake and Reynolds, *Global Colour Line*.

has altered their domestic status. The point here is that their, and the Navajo's, global status seems to bear directly on whether the state's policy will, for instance, express a demeaning message about them, compromise the social bases of their self-respect, or cause their subordination.

Importantly, although I believe—given the considerations and facts of the case presented—that Navajo's policy would not wrong its white members under the antidiscrimination approach, my goal is not to conclusively show that, since it would require examining many more considerations than are presented here, and my overall goal in the book is primarily to consider when states wrong excluded *nonmembers*.[72] Moreover, none of the discussion denies that whites could occupy a very weak economic and political position within Navajo that overshadows their secure global status; if so, and if Navajo maintained its immigration policy, I believe the policy would wrong them. For instance, given how the white population has been regarded and treated in Zimbabwe fairly recently, I believe an immigration policy disfavoring the admission of whites would wrong Zimbabwe's white members, and their global status would carry little weight. But in other existing states in which whites are in the minority, global status seems pivotal. Consider, for instance, if immigration policies were to disfavor minority populations of fully expatriated white members (that is, those who renounced their original citizenships) in states such as Costa Rica, Panama, and Uganda, where, it seems, they are not regarded or treated as inferiors. In these cases, global status seems to make an important difference, suggesting that the relevant disfavored white members would not be wronged despite their vulnerable domestic statuses.

Likewise, the point of the above discussion is that insofar as Navajo's selective immigration does not wrong its minority members in the discussed ways, it is because of considerations of global, not domestic, status. The clearest way to see the point once more is to contrast Navajo with Reverse Navajo: knowing nothing else about the two cases, global status marks an important difference and suggests that while Navajo's case may not wrong its disfavored members, Reverse Navajo likely does.

Before turning to examine some notable actual cases, one might wonder about the relevance of the fact that it was whites in the United States (where Navajo's whites originated) that committed the significant injustices against the Navajo people. Specifically, one might think that that fact plays an important role both in

---

[72] It would depend on the particular antidiscrimination view and many more details, some of which are mentioned next. More generally, a full analysis of whether a group—either disfavored members or excluded nonmembers—in some case is not wronged, or whether some case is permissible, requires understanding the significance of the various dimensions of advantage. For instance, are disadvantages in, say, access to territory and self-respect weightier than economic disadvantages? What if the admitting group is significantly globally vulnerable in only one respect but a disfavored group is vulnerable in multiple ways? These are important questions that I will discuss in Chapter 5 in the context of understanding when racial and ethnic criteria might wrong excluded nonmembers.

explaining why Navajo's white members do not seem wronged by the policy and, more generally, why the policy may be permissible. As we will see in Chapter 5, past wrongs may matter, but only insofar as they are related to the relevant groups' current global status.

7. How Global Status Explains Real Cases

In previous sections of this chapter, I demonstrated that there are often substantial differences in global (dis)advantages—in material, political, way-of-life, and self-respect terms—among various racial and ethnic groups, thus showing that race and ethnicity are socially salient in the global context. Moreover, through analyzing global status, I showed that members of different states interact in a variety of social, political, and economic relations, which operate largely through global institutions and are mediated, to varying degrees, by identity-group membership. Here I will discuss how such relations, and the notion of global status, are already implicitly invoked in some important discussions of actual cases of selective immigration.

Let's begin briefly with the case of Japan. Recall from Chapter 1 that Joseph Carens suggested that Japan's criteria may have been permissible.[73] At the time of his suggestion, Japan had just implemented a policy favoring the admission of Japanese descendants (from places such as Brazil and Peru), thereby disfavoring its tiny populations of Koreans and, to a lesser extent, Chinese—both of whose ancestors were brought to Japan during its imperial era (about 1905–45).[74] Because of the Japanese people's global material and political advantages,[75] because of how the Korean and Chinese populations arrived in Japan, and because Japan abrogated their citizenships after the Second World War, it seems likely that the Japanese did have the comparative power to, say, express a demeaning message about Japan's disfavored members. However, the point here is that we may still be able to explain the normative *pull* of the case by observing that the Japanese people are vulnerable in one potentially important respect: their population decline is one of the world's fastest.[76] If the expectation that one's group's continuation is important for sustaining one's way of life—in turn important for maintaining the background context of choice for one's conception of the good and thus one's well-being—[77] there may have been something in favor of Japan's policy. But if so, we must once again refer to global status, not domestic: the

---

[73] Carens, "Migration and Morality," 37–39.   [74] Chung, *Immigration and Citizenship*.
[75] For just one indicator, consider that Japan has one of the largest economies in the world (World Development Indicators Database, World Bank, July 1, 2021, https://databank.worldbank.org/data/download/GDP.pdf). I discuss more indicators in Chapter 5.
[76] Johnston, "Is Japan Becoming Extinct?"
[77] See Kymlicka's prominent discussion in *Multicultural Citizenship*.

Japanese people may be vulnerable (in the way-of-life sense) globally, not qua members of Japan (since their way of life is surely dominant within Japan).

Perhaps more compelling, but also more controversial, than Japan's case is Israel's Law of Return (LoR), which grants automatic admission to Jewish people only. This may be the primary example of selective immigration considered potentially permissible, including by WM's supporters.[78] Again, whether this policy, or any other, is ultimately permissible is not central here. The question is, how do we best make sense of its *potential* permissibility? While we will be examining this question in much greater detail in Chapters 4 and 5, let me make the following observations here.

First notice that exclusive reference to domestic status makes the policy clearly wrong, as it draws our attention to the policy's effects on Israel's disfavored members. In particular, Palestinians (many of whom lack full membership rights) occupy a considerably vulnerable position within Israel. LoR, then, seems to clearly wrong them by, say, sending the message that they are of marginal concern. WM's proponents seem to agree since they characterize Israel's case as a possible exception to their view, acknowledging its moral complexity.[79] More important, then, is understanding why WM's proponents think the case may nonetheless be justified. Here they refer to the lasting effects of the Holocaust and other forms of persecution and racism experienced by the Jewish people and how, against that history, LoR affirms the idea of a state where Jews are always welcomed.[80] By now, it should be unsurprising that citing substantial injustices or the lingering effects of past injustices can be an important part of explaining why some groups might be permitted to implement selective immigration. But what is significant about the present example, and not explicitly recognized, is that the relevant injustices are international and the sense of vulnerability global.

We appeal to how Jewish people were, and sometimes continue to be, subject to significant injustices in numerous states—but importantly, not to how Jewish people have experienced such injustices in the context of social, political, and economic relations within Israel. Given how the Jewish community was regarded as morally inferior in numerous states and systematically targeted and murdered in the Holocaust, it's plausible that Jewish people constitute a vulnerable group in the global sense, in terms of the social bases of their self-respect. And Jewish populations might also constitute domestically vulnerable groups within some states today, including the United States, where there has been a recent rise in hate crimes against them. But what is not plausible is that they are vulnerable qua members of Israel. If anything, they are clearly the dominant domestic group

[78] See (for example) Coleman and Harding, "Citizenship": Blake, "Discretionary Immigration"; Miller, "Immigration"; and Wellman, "Freedom of Association."
[79] Blake, "Discretionary Immigration," 286; Wellman, "Freedom of Association," 140–41.
[80] *Ibid.*

in social, economic, and political terms. So, to gain a sense of why LoR might be justified, we implicitly refer to the Jewish people's global vulnerability, not their domestic status in Israel.

More to the point, LoR's potential justification implicitly recognizes not only that there are relevant considerations of global status, but that we should care about them and take a group's global vulnerability as a reason for states to implement or avoid certain immigration criteria. For why otherwise would Jewish people's mistreatment in other states help to explain *Israel's* policy? Though I will explore potential objections to this idea in the next chapter, it seems hard to deny that global-status considerations are doing a significant amount of normative work in explaining LoR's potential justification. It's important to stress again that none of the discussion so far implies that LoR *is* justified. In Chapter 5, we will see that there are reasons why it does not seem that it is, at least in its current form.

Before moving on, one might wonder whether WM's supporters couldn't simply accept that sometimes global status, not domestic, is relevant either for whether some case is overall justified or, more importantly for WM, for whether any members are wronged by their state's criteria disfavoring them? After all, it isn't inconsistent to claim that racial and ethnic criteria are wrong only insofar as disfavored members are wronged and accept that the global status of both the admitting group and disfavored members can help determine when that is the case. However, while this amendment to WM is conceptually available, it puts pressure on the heart of the WM view: namely, that only a state's *members* can be wronged, not the excluded *nonmembers*. This issue is explored in the next chapter, where I will argue that states have (at least) certain kinds of "global antidiscrimination duties" when making admission decisions.

4

Global Antidiscrimination Duties

1. Introduction

In Chapter 2, we explored the core elements of the antidiscrimination approach, as applied domestically, and discussed how the idea of relational equality can deepen our understanding of when and why selecting against some people, but not others, is wrong. Of primary importance is that antidiscrimination accounts stress duties owed to groups with vulnerable social statuses—those either subordinated or at risk of subordination—and theories of relational equality direct us to the basis of such duties (namely, shared social, political, and economic relations). Then, in Chapter 3, we saw that there are significant shared relations at the global level and that, because of (dis)advantages with respect to those relations, identity groups have a meaningful global social status. Additionally, Chapter 3 demonstrated that differences in global status present important moral concerns in the context of immigration. In particular, it showed how such differences help to normatively explain a variety of both hypothetical and real immigration examples, such as our hypothetical Navajo example and Israel's and Japan's actual cases.

In this chapter, I begin to explore what all of this implies for the "global antidiscrimination approach," or more specifically for global antidiscrimination duties—duties owed to anyone, regardless of whether they are fellow members in our state. Building on the work of the last two chapters, this chapter is specifically focused on demonstrating what we might call global antidiscrimination's *primary duties*: duties not to exclude on the basis of identity when it degrades. Such duties are arguably antidiscrimination's most central duties since they concern exclusion on the basis of identity and so concern direct forms of discrimination; but they also seem to be fairly minimal, when considering other duties states might have. In Chapter 6, I will discuss more demanding sorts of duties, including a duty not to exclude when it contributes to global vulnerability, which pertains to indirect forms of discrimination and to non-identity groups.

The first thing I will do in this chapter is demonstrate that states resemble, in morally relevant ways, domestic associations, organizations, and communities that are subject to the primary duties. The main consideration in determining whether an association has these duties is whether it occupies a position of power over access to important opportunities—and states, especially wealthy states, control access to a significant range of life options. Then, I will show how this

Immigration and Discrimination: (Un)Welcoming Others. Sahar Akhtar, Oxford University Press. © Sahar Akhtar 2024.
DOI: 10.1093/oso/9780198898696.003.0005

analysis, when combined with concerns about global status and underlying concerns about relational inequality, supports the application of antidiscrimination duties to states' membership decisions. Along the way, I will describe and respond to two central ways of pushing back at the analogy between domestic associations and states and challenging the analysis more generally. The first challenge stresses that because identity criteria may be important for sustaining a distinct way of life found in at least certain states, those states are not morally bound by the primary duties. The second is based on the idea that a state's members have mutually contributed to the production or reproduction of the state's opportunities and argues that discretionary migrants (those lacking either urgent or special claims for admission) have no rightful claim to access those opportunities. I'll explain how each of these challenges can easily be dealt with. Finally, I'll show why the implicit acceptance of global status in prominent immigration discussions already suggests that states are bound by something like the primary duties.

2. Antidiscrimination Sites

In Chapter 2, we saw that the antidiscrimination approach stresses duties to not contribute to a group's vulnerability in order to avoid creating, sustaining, or perpetuating subordination. Having a vulnerable status with respect to some social context means that a group faces substantial disadvantages in material, political, way-of-life, or self-respect terms, in comparison with at least certain cognate group(s). Additionally, we saw that while a differentiating act can contribute to a group's vulnerability in several specific ways, we can place them into two broad categories: comparatively reduced opportunities, and degradation. While having comparatively reduced opportunities often contributes to a group's vulnerability, being degraded, we saw, does so in the particular ways that relate to moral anxieties about subordination—that is, as involving relations that treat a group as morally inferior.[1]

Armed with a description of the main aspects of the antidiscrimination approach, what we must now do is explore why certain sorts of domestic communities, organizations, and associations are morally bound by antidiscrimination duties. I will then argue that states are relevantly like these domestic associations.

To recall, there might be a range of duties generated from concerns about discrimination, including duties to not engage in certain speech acts, to provide positive assistance to groups that have experienced past discrimination, and to provide reasonable accommodations to certain groups. But our concern is mainly with the selective exclusion of people from an organization, association, or

---

[1] This difference will be especially relevant for the next chapter.

community more generally. Moreover, even within this narrower scope, there may be a number of associated duties, including favoring the admission of vulnerable groups and simply not excluding when it would contribute to a group's vulnerability. We will discuss some of these sorts of duties in Chapter 6, but we need not delve into all selection-related antidiscrimination duties here. Instead, we can start with a focus on the primary antidiscrimination duties: duties not to exclude on the basis of identity when it degrades a group.

The goal here is not to specify when the primary antidiscrimination duties are violated in any domestic context, since, again, this book is not centrally concerned with antidiscrimination within states and what particular identity groups count as domestically vulnerable in different states and in what ways. Rather, aside from illustrating a few cases in which the primary duties seem clearly violated, the question I'm interested in is: what sorts of associations and communities are generally *subject to* these primary duties when making admission decisions, and why? More specifically, the goal—which, I believe, should be fairly easy to achieve—is to uncover the broad characteristics common to the sorts of associations that generally have the primary duties and then assess whether such characteristics describe states.

But, first, since liberal societies have strong laws against discrimination in a range of activities, I should clarify that my interest is to examine the *moral* reasons that seem to best explain why certain associations are appropriately subject to antidiscrimination duties, though such reasons may well also support legal rationales.

To begin, let us assume the kind of background injustice against Black people that we find in a place such as the United States, and examine the contrast between selection decisions made in marriages and other romantic partnerships,[2] and employment decisions made by businesses. Both types of decisions confer a kind of "admission" in an association—as a fellow spouse or partner or as a fellow employee. So, for ease of discussion, I'll refer to someone making such a decision as the "admitting party."

Let's start by considering the following case. Amanda, who is white, declines to marry Evan on the basis of his being Black. It may be clear that there is something morally objectionable about Amanda's character. But it may be a little less clear whether she acts wrongly by declining to marry Evan—at least without knowing more about her reasons. If her decision not to marry someone who is Black is based on a belief that Black people are beneath others, then her action seems clearly wrong. But if her decision is based, for instance, on the worry that she would be alienated from the other people living in her parochial all-white town,

---

[2] Since states legislate marriage and divorce contracts, using marriage as a central example may address concerns about how certain associations are not morally appropriate places for antidiscrimination duties because they are not capable of being regulated.

then whether her action is wrong may be a little less clear.[3] At the very least, it may be that whether she acts wrongly depends on further issues, such as whether Amanda and Evan were in an ongoing relationship and whether she made a prior commitment to him.[4]

In contrast, imagine a large company that controls significant market share in a major industry, mainly employs white workers, and now decides to hire only white people. On that basis, Mara, who is Black, is refused a job at the company. In contrast to the marriage case, here it seems our judgments would not be tentative at all: the company's action is clearly wrong. And this is so even in the absence of any objectionable beliefs, special relationships, prior commitments, and so on. To clarify, the point of observing the contrast between these two types of examples is not to suggest that a racial criterion excluding someone in a vulnerable group is morally acceptable in the marriage case but not in the business case. It is rather that even if one has doubts about whether what Amanda does is wrong, it seems very clear that the large business acts wrongly.

One might think the important distinction between the two examples concerns the character of the relevant interests of the admitting party. There may be a variety of specific interests at stake in choosing a marriage partner, including interests in sharing a life with someone, in getting close to other human beings, and in developing one's moral personality through close relationships. What all such interests have in common is that they are best described as intimate. They answer to aspects of our lives that are personal or private, and they may be compelling enough to secure our moral entitlement to accept or decline partners based on characteristics of our choosing,[5] or at least on a wide variety of characteristics.[6] In contrast, consider the interests at stake for large businesses, which typically include the pursuit of productivity or efficiency but sometimes also include promoting a particular moral goal or advancing some social cause. Whatever the specific interests, they are not personal or intimate—at least not anything like they are in marriage. For instance, while fulfilling business and commercial goals might sometimes depend on employees' interests in having common bonds and shared values, these interests do not depend on any kind of close, personal relations. Indeed, a common culture, collegiality, and the sharing

---

[3] These points reflect the idea, described in Chapter 2, that an agent's mental state seems very important, even if not decisive, for assessing the morality of decisions in personal contexts.

[4] One might think that denying marriage on racial grounds is always morally wrong, but as we'll see momentarily, we needn't take a stand on this here.

[5] The same seems to go for polyamory. So the difference between marriages and large businesses isn't simply between individual rights (which typically have substantial strength) and (weaker) group rights.

[6] It may be wrong to marry someone who is cruel or has committed morally heinous acts, but we needn't take a stand on such examples.

of goals can emerge despite fellow employees' not engaging in social or face-to-face interactions with each other.[7]

Although the character of the relevant interests seems to matter for our moral judgments about whether an association is subject to antidiscrimination duties, its importance may ultimately be derivative. The analysis in this chapter does not hang on this point; indeed, if the character of an association does ultimately matter, this will strengthen the case that states are subject to antidiscrimination duties. But it's nonetheless worth getting clear about what is important, and the character of the relevant interests might not be doing much moral work on its own. To see this, consider a different marriage scenario. Imagine that Amanda never intends to live with or even communicate with her spouse, except through an attorney, and construes marriage as a merger akin to an economic arrangement. Perhaps she sees it as a mutually beneficial opportunity to reduce income tax burdens or to save on health care costs. In this second scenario, the character of the interests looks much more like the commercial and business sorts of interests described earlier. But though we would no longer describe the situation as involving intimate interests, this might not change our assessment of the case much, if at all.[8]

If this is right, then it suggests that a different or at least additional emphasis is needed. And this clearly seems to be the power of the admitting party (whether an individual or a collective) relative to the position of the party seeking admission.[9] Many forms of power may matter when assessing the moral permissibility of various types of differentiating decisions, but, again, we are only considering decisions to confer a kind of admission into an association—such as a fellow spouse or fellow employee. And a major source of power for the admitting parties, relative to the admission-seeking parties, is control over access to important goods, resources, and opportunities. In the absence of a prior relationship or commitment, someone who refuses to marry another person does not generally structure the latter's access to personal relationship possibilities, let alone other significant opportunities.[10] In contrast, large companies exercise considerable power over important options: they shape access to employment opportunities in the industries

---

[7] A potentially related point here concerns *reaction qualifications*—that is, qualifications that people have based on how others (for instance, customers and coworkers) react to them. If existing employees dislike members of a minority race, the latter may have difficulties adopting the company culture, and—if such reaction qualifications are morally legitimate for assessing a job candidate's qualifications—consequently have worse qualifications for the job. But discrimination theorists have provided a number of arguments against the moral legitimacy of these types of reaction qualifications (though not all). (See discussion in Wertheimer, "Jobs, Qualifications, and Preferences.")

[8] If the correct judgment in the first scenario is that Amanda's decision to refuse Evan is permissible, altering the characterization of the relevant interest might not shift her decision from being permissible to being wrong; and if the correct judgment in the first scenario is that it is wrong, it might not now be more wrong once her interests are less intimate.

[9] Khaitan, *Theory of Discrimination Law*, esp. chaps 6–7.

[10] This might not always be the case, since it seems there may sometimes be a kind of prestige or prominence even if the admitting party does not control especially important goods. For instance, if Amanda were to become a celebrity, she would still exercise very little control over Evan's marital

they occupy, and people attempting to start businesses in those industries often face significant barriers to entry, typically informal (for example, high startup costs) but also sometimes formal (for example, licenses or intellectual property rights).

The next question to ask is, why is the power of the admitting party relevant? To answer this, it's important to distinguish the powerful position that the admitting party occupies (whether in virtue of its control over opportunities and goods or otherwise[11]) from the type of power at issue in relative *social status*. In particular, I am not suggesting that what ultimately demands our moral attention is the comparative social status of the association and the admission-seeking party; it's not as if we are directly concerned with any hierarchical relations between the *company* and Mara. Rather, antidiscrimination is ultimately concerned with preventing status inequalities—subordination—between groups. To be sure, status inequalities may often be *represented* in the relationship between the admitting party and the admission-seeking party—as it is in this case, since our company is mainly composed of white employees and Mara is Black. But, from the standpoint of antidiscrimination, it is not the differences in power between the business qua business and Mara that matter.[12]

How do associations occupying positions of power potentially impact the social relations among groups? More specifically, how might an association's power contribute to the vulnerability of some group? Again, the discussion from Chapter 2 highlighted two central ways: one related to opportunities and the other to degradation.

First (again, given the background injustice against Black people), if a large company denies people employment opportunities on the basis of their being Black, this action significantly compounds the material disadvantages faced by Blacks, relative to other groups. Moreover, even beyond the particular *employment* opportunities that the company controls, it structures access to still-further material opportunities and potentially to political and way-of-life opportunities—that is, beyond the company itself. This includes facilitating the development of relationships and contacts in the industry as a whole, which can open up a variety of possibilities once the employee leaves, and providing greater access to other opportunity-shaping institutions and communities, such as banks, housing suppliers, neighborhoods, and schools.

---

opportunities. However, because of her public profile, it seems her actions would at least carry a kind of expressive power that they may have lacked before, with the result that her action would now have the power to demean. See Hellman, *Why Is Discrimination Wrong?*, esp. 35–38.

[11] See my previous note.

[12] For instance, imagine that the company's current employees are mainly Black but it puts out a statement expressing the belief that the majority of Black people would not fit into the hardworking culture of their company, and, on that basis, it refuses to hire Mara. Even though the relationship between the company and Mara does not represent power differences between different groups (though it may well *reflect* such differences), the company's refusal to hire her would still express a demeaning message about her and other Black people.

Second, and more importantly, largely because it selectively denies Black people important opportunities, the company's action clearly has the power to, say, send a demeaning message about them or reinforce social stigmas about them. And this can further worsen how they are treated and regarded across a wide range of circumstances, relative to people in secure groups. Thus, while the power of the company matters, it matters because it can affect the landscape of social relations among groups.

Most of the points just discussed apply not only to large businesses but to other sorts of associations and communities and help to explain why they too are morally bound by antidiscrimination principles when making admission decisions. First are the many kinds of associations that can also be described, along with large businesses, both as lacking a personal or intimate character and as occupying a position of power over access to significant opportunities and goods.[13] These include government agencies, colleges and universities, and housing providers. But there are also a variety of associations that can appropriately be described as having a personal, or at least strongly social, character but can nonetheless affect relations between secure and vulnerable groups. For instance, many social clubs can become important sites for antidiscrimination concerns if, and to the extent that, they shape access to significant opportunities outside of the social club, such as access to professional and political networks.[14]

3. States as Antidiscrimination Sites

We have just seen that the main considerations explaining why certain domestic associations and communities are morally bound by antidiscrimination norms seem to concern the fact that they are not organized around personal or social interactions and, more importantly, that they control, or at least structure access to, significant opportunities. With respect to these two considerations, large businesses and marriages seem to fall on opposing ends of the spectrum,[15] with a variety of other associations and communities, including small businesses and religious and cultural organizations, falling somewhere in between. But we do not need to examine all of these other types of associations in order to analyze states— that is, to understand whether states resemble the sorts of associations *clearly*

[13] Khaitan (*Theory of Discrimination Law*) suggests that, in general, determining whether some association, community, or institution bears antidiscrimination duties involves balancing concerns about power with concerns about private, personal, or intimate interests (for example, 201–12).

[14] Consider (for example) the Boy Scouts of America, Augusta National, and the Junior Chamber of Commerce. Some such organizations may be morally exempt from antidiscrimination concerns when making *leadership* decisions but not typically for ordinary membership decisions. For more examples, see Tebbe, *Religious Freedom*, esp. 97–109.

[15] Though, again, selection against people based on their vulnerable identity may sometimes be wrong even in marriage.

bound by antidiscrimination duties. It should be fairly easy to demonstrate that, for two reasons, the normative picture of states not only looks much more like that of large businesses than of marriages, but that states stand much further from associations such as marriages than large businesses do.

First, the interests at stake in state membership are not personal or necessarily social in character. In contrast, we saw that the interests of even some large businesses might require social interaction among members. To clarify, this does not mean that states are not organized around common values and shared goals; even in liberal states, the importance of a shared commitment to a set of values, including mutual respect, equality, and autonomy, should not be mini- mized. But the sharing of such values and goals does not require *socializing* or *consorting* with one another.

As to the second, far more significant, issue, a state structures access to a range of consequential life-shaping opportunities—not just employment, of course, but also broader economic opportunities as well as social, political, cultural, and geographic options.[16] Moreover, there are extraordinary, possibly insurmounta- ble, barriers to forming a state since existing states collectively occupy all the habitable territory on earth and since states restrict, often coercively, options for secession. Accordingly, states exercise enormous power over significant goods and opportunities—not the least of which is *state membership* itself. As numerous commentators have observed, the state we reside in makes an enormous difference to our life prospects.[17] Our state of residence greatly impacts our health, longevity, education, and life satisfaction. Indeed, it's difficult to overstate just how much of a difference living in one state versus another can make to our lives.[18] This does not necessarily imply that everyone should be free to live in whichever state they desire. The point is rather that, because states shape access to important life options and, especially, because these options differ *substantially* across states, states' admis- sion decisions have the potential to greatly affect the relative statuses of different groups. Any group that is selectively excluded is at least comparatively disadvan- taged by having access to fewer material, political, and way-of-life options in the admitting state, potentially making them more vulnerable. But more directly rele- vantly for antidiscrimination concerns, as we will see in section 6, (often by having access to fewer important options) their selective exclusion may also imply that they are demeaned, the social bases of their self-respect are (further) compromised, and any stigmas against them are perpetuated. Thus, we have at least initial reason to think that states are subject to a global analog of the primary duties: duties not to exclude on the basis of identity when it degrades a group.

[16] See Oberman, "Immigration as Human Right"; Akhtar, "Being at Home," 103–28.
[17] Carens, "Aliens and Citizens"; Huemer, "Right to Immigrate?"; Lomasky and Tesón, *Justice at a Distance*; Cole, "Open Borders"; Oberman, "Immigration as Human Right."
[18] See the valuable discussion in Brennan and van der Vossen, *In Defense of Openness*, esp. 19–23.

As we will see in the next chapter, the differences in potential opportunities among states will sometimes matter in determining whether a state's criteria violate the primary duties. Of particular relevance is the fact that there is often overlap between states with unstable and comparatively weak life options and states in which globally vulnerable groups comprise the majority, which implies that such states' admission decisions may be less likely to violate the primary duties. But this does not mean they are not subject to the primary duties or that their decisions are incapable of violating them.

I want to briefly address a related issue here, and I will return to it in the next chapter. Namely, many states seem to resemble what we might call "way-of-life associations," such as religious or cultural organizations, in the important role they play in imbuing meaning to, and in framing multiple facets of life for, their members. For such states, it might seem that certain identity criteria are important for sustaining their ways of life; possibilities we have already considered include Japan and Israel. Are such states somehow immune from the primary duties? Certainly, states organized around comprehensive cultures provide important background contexts for individual flourishing, and we may even think of states with public political cultures as shaping distinct ways of life for their members. But this alone does not mean that the states' admissions are not subject to the primary duties. For, even in the domestic context, many religious, social, and cultural organizations (if they are very powerful) seem to be morally bound by the relevant principles, even though such organizations may be far more integral for providing meaning and context for their members' conceptions of the good than any states might be. In short, once such organizations attain a certain power over access to important life goods, our judgments on their use of admission criteria seem to reflect discrimination norms.[19]

At the same time, this does not mean that any identity criteria that a state used would violate the primary duties, since, for starters, the state's members may constitute (part of) a group that itself faces significant disadvantages in pursuing a secure way of life. And this fact can affect whether an immigration policy contributes to the vulnerability of other groups. In the hypothetical Navajo case, the explicit favoring of other Navajo for admission didn't seem morally objectionable. In the next chapter, I will discuss why this case does not seem to violate the primary duties and more generally explore the relevance of these sorts of way-of-life issues for antidiscrimination duties.

4. Global Status and Global Relations

The discussion in the previous section does not on its own establish that states are bound by the primary antidiscrimination duties. But it does open the space for

---

[19] Tebbe, *Religious Freedom.*

thinking that they are so bound. Importantly, the analysis in the previous chapter already provided the underlying normative work needed to fill that space. Thus, it is worth summarizing here.

First, and perhaps most importantly, Chapter 3 demonstrated that, in general, racial and ethnic (and related) characteristics are socially salient on the global level, in that they shape interaction across a wide range of global and international circumstances. It did this by showing that there are substantial status differences among racial and ethnic (and related) groups and, moreover, that these status differences are often key to morally assessing different immigration criteria. As numerous examples illustrated, there are significant differences in the global (dis)advantages among groups, in material, political, way-of-life, and self-respect terms, such as those between Han Chinese and Uyghurs, whites and the Navajo, and Arabs and Kurds. Moreover, we also saw how such differences in (dis)advantage may (at least in part) be due to the lingering effects of past injustices or, more generally, objectionable moral relations, whereby some vulnerable groups were or are singled out for inferior regard or treatment. In demonstrating these issues, Chapter 3 also showed that a group's global status can have morally important effects on the lives of people in the group. Sometimes these effects arise because interactions at the global level alter the domestic status of some group within the state(s) in which the group's members live. Other times, such interactions affect the lives of a group's members directly through comparatively greater or lesser access to global economic, social, and political opportunities. Most importantly, the role of global status in explaining the moral assessment of various immigration cases, including hypothetical cases such as Navajo and actual cases such as Israel, implicitly demonstrates its moral importance.

Additionally, through exploring the significance of global status, we saw how there are important shared social, political, and economic relations and interactions at the global level, including, for instance, those that occur within international institutions (for example, the UN, IMF, and World Bank) and, more generally, through trade, climate agreements, treaty negotiations, multinational businesses, and economic associations. Before going further, I will elaborate on some of these relations and their significance.

Consider the prominence of transnational corporations and their substantial networks of suppliers, contractors, subcontractors, and subsidiaries in the global production of both final and intermediate goods.[20] By shifting production to overseas locations, these networks bring communities in vastly different parts of the world into interaction with one another. Moreover, as authors have argued for

---

[20] Trade connected to transnational corporations accounts for roughly 80% of global trade. UNCTAD, "80% of Trade." On the impact of transnational corporations on more general economic indicators, and on their political influence, see Kordos and Vojtovic, "Transnational Corporations"; Kim and Milner, "Multinational Corporations."

some time, through such interactions, people in different states routinely cooperate with one another—a point elaborated below.[21] Additionally, addressing an argument made by Michael Blake,[22] people in different states regularly impose various forms of coercion on one another. That may most obviously happen through international organizations, such as the IMF and World Bank,[23] but states also directly subject those outside their borders to coercive power in various—often ongoing—ways, not the least of which occurs through their system of coercively enforced border-control and immigration policy.[24] Other examples concern how states' domestic public law (including criminal, antitrust, and environmental law) can have extraterritorial application[25] and how states' domestic laws of intellectual property constrain outsiders, who can be tried in the domestic courts.[26] And there is certainly a long list of examples in which powerful states coerce weaker states to alter their practices through direct economic and military sanctions.[27]

Finally, people in different states are brought into relations of mutual interdependence through the global environmental commons. As Ip has effectively argued, "Human activities and increasing economic globalization exacerbate a wide range of environmental problems such as anthropogenic climate change, ozone layer depletion, marine pollution, a diminishing biodiversity, and the overexploitation of natural resources like overfishing, deforestation, and desertification...neither the causes nor the impacts of these global environmental problems are confined to any single society."[28]

In sum, we have seen that individuals around the world are connected through global institutions, organizations, and networks in variable and considerable ways.

---

[21] See Beitz, *Political Theory*; Buchanan, "Rawls' Law of Peoples"; Abizadeh, "Cooperation"; Follesdal, "Distributive Justice"; Pogge, *World Poverty* (2nd ed.).

[22] Blake ("Discretionary Immigration") argues that because of how states coerce their members, thus infringing their autonomy, fellow members have egalitarian distributive obligations to one another—obligations they do not have to nonmembers. Though I do not argue for global egalitarian distributive obligations, one could extend Blake's basic claim to my argument here concerning global antidiscrimination duties. Namely, one might argue that because of how states coerce their own members, but not nonmembers, people in different states are not obligated to create conditions of global relational equality. My reply to such an argument would highlight the same issues I elaborate in the paragraphs below, including pointing out that I am not attempting to argue that we have obligations to secure the full conditions of global relational equality but, more minimally, that we have obligations to avoid subordinating others. But, moreover, as I illustrate in this paragraph, states *do* in fact coerce people living in different states in various degrees. There is no denying there are significant differences between the extent and regularity of coercion that occurs within a shared state and the coercion that occurs across states or by international institutions. But as we will shortly see, such differences are compatible with the claim that we have duties not to subordinate nonmembers.

[23] Some critics of this latter idea have argued that one's relation to international organizations is *mediated* through one's state and that a state's membership in international organizations is voluntary. However, see Cohen and Sabel, "Extram Republicam Nulla Justitia?"

[24] Abizadeh, "Cooperation"; Christiano, "Immigration."

[25] Dogauchi, "Private International Law."   [26] Ubertazzi, *Exclusive Jurisdiction*.

[27] Julius, "Nagel's Atlas"; Cavallero, "Coercion."

[28] Ip, Egalitarianism and Global Justice, 23. See Chapter 2 in general for a more sustained discussion of global relations. Also see Nath, "Equal Standing"; Nath, "Social Equality."

But one might wonder whether these social relations are sufficiently robust for a global antidiscrimination view grounded in relational equality. Such a view, recall, stresses that we must relate to those with whom we stand in significant relations as moral equals, or, expressed negatively, avoid relating to them as moral inferiors. And one might worry that for such a view to apply *globally*, we need to demonstrate that the relations between individuals around the world are similar in nature and density to the relations between co-members.

In response to the worry, there are several things to say. As a preliminary matter, recall that my interest in this book is not in specifying or arguing for the full demands of relational equality among people in different states. Rather, my interest concerns, more narrowly, what I take to be relational equality's most central demand—to avoid subordinating others—since this is also at the heart of antidiscrimination accounts. But since this will be relevant to our discussion in section 6, it is worth pointing out that even if my goal were the more general one, this would still not imply that global relations must mimic domestic ones in central ways. In Chapter 2, I discussed how moral concerns about relational equality have relevance for a multitude of relations—all the way down to intimate relationships. Thus, they do not *only* apply between a state's co-members. And we can again invoke Elizabeth Anderson's compelling understanding that relational equality is a concern whenever some are vulnerable to oppressive relationships— that is, those relations "by which some people dominate, exploit, marginalize, demean, and inflict violence upon others."[29] Chapter 3 demonstrated that, mediated (in varying degrees) by identity groups, people do stand in relation to one another outside of a particular state in which some are vulnerable to oppressive relationships (in Anderson's broad sense).

Moreover, we saw that what relating to people as equals requires depends on the density and type of relations and interactions, so that what is required in intimate relationships is different from what is required between a state's co-members. So we can accept that there are significant differences in the density and type of relations between people globally as compared with those within a state, but this does not mean that relational equality makes *no* demands on how we treat people globally. Rather, the correct implication seems to be that what is required for relating to others as moral equals in the context of global relations is weaker than that required among a state's co-members. In particular, such moral demands likely do not require that we treat and regard nonmembers in equivalent ways to members, at least not in every respect. (I will say more about this point in Chapter 6.)

The most important response, however, particularly for the goals of this chapter and the next, is that to argue for antidiscrimination's *primary duties*, we can

---

[29] Anderson, "What Is the Point?," 313.

readily accept that there are significant differences between what is owed to fellow members and what is owed to nonmembers. For the primary duties do not imply, even in ideal circumstances and with certain exceptions, that nonmembers have a right to access the goods and benefits that members enjoy. This is, in many ways, similar to the duties that emerge in the context of many domestic-association admission decisions. Co-membership in some community or association—more specifically, the sharing of certain relations—is the basis for equal treatment and regard with respect to a particular bundle of privileges and goods, which vary across both relations of the same type and different types of relations. Thus, for instance, social clubs confer certain goods on their members but not on non-members, and these goods differ from the sorts of goods that members of a business are owed. What matters here is that people *outside* these associations are not entitled to the same rights and privileges existing members get. For instance, access to office spaces and facilities, rights to stock options and retire-ment packages, and the benefits of participating in a particular company culture are just some of the things that might be gained through employment in a particular business—not things that the business has duties to grant to none-mployees. Put differently, people applying for employment in a business are of course not entitled to *obtain* employment (even under some suitably described set of ideal circumstances); a company, even a very large and powerful one, does not have a duty to hire someone simply because they apply. But that does not mean that domestic associations do not have duties to people outside those associations, grounded in other less dense or different sorts of relations, not to contribute to subordination. In particular, as we saw above, large companies (generally[30]) have moral duties not to exclude people on the basis of identity when it degrades a group.

In section 6, I will provide further positive support for saying that states also have the primary duties when making admissions decisions. But before doing so, the analogy to domestic associations is helpful for reflecting on a potentially significant objection and for explaining why it does not damage the position here. I turn to that objection now.

5. Contributing to Collective Goods and Incurring Obligations

We have seen that states control access to a range of life options and that, in wealthy states, such opportunities are considerably valuable. However, since members in those states have, on the whole, created or at least sustained those opportunities, one might think that they have the right to deny access to others

---

[30] There might be some exceptions in cases in which, in particular, religious freedom is at stake. See Tebbe, *Religious Freedom*.

unconstrained by any moral claims of nonmembers—at least, that is, when it comes to discretionary migrants (migrants without urgent or special claims to admission). While there is something right about this concern, I believe it ultimately fails to imply that states' immigration decisions are unconstrained by nonmembers' moral claims. To see why, it will be beneficial to look at a recent expression of this concern by Ryan Pevnick.

In his book on immigration, Pevnick endorses the conventional position of states' choice, which, we saw from Chapter 1, maintains that states have a broad right to make immigration decisions in the manner they choose. His view can be characterized, more specifically, as an associational account of states' choice. Building his case from reflections on domestic associations, Pevnick argues that investing and cooperating to produce collective goods give an enterprise's insiders certain ownership rights. For states, the relevant point is that members have mutually contributed to the state's institutions, in particular through engaging in collective decision-making, upholding its laws and norms, and paying taxes, and that they thereby collectively own the state's goods. What this means, according to Pevnick, is that they have a right to make decisions about the future shape of the state's institutions and this includes decisions concerning who may access those institutions.[31] Like other advocates of states' choice, Pevnick recognizes important limits to a state's right to choose its members. Mainly, it is constrained by the claims of asylum seekers and refugees—for which he provides an expansive definition (namely, those unable to meet their basic subsistence needs)[32]—and the children of illegal immigrants.[33] But outside of such cases, outsiders cannot merely lay claim to the goods inside the state. To illustrate why, Pevnick writes, "the establishment of law and order, an effective market and basic infrastructure are hard fought accomplishments ... [Such a]ssociational benefits are the product of the coordinated collective decisions, labor and contributions of group members. When associations bring the relevant institutions into being through their collective decisions and contributions, as they often do, they may claim special entitlement to them. Such institutions are not manna, sitting waiting to be claimed by whoever happens across them."[34]

I believe Pevnick's case for the collective ownership rights of an association's members is, in general,[35] very compelling. However, such rights do not mean that members may use whatever criteria they like in their admission decisions or, more specifically, that their criteria are not constrained by the moral claims of non-members. We can see this by considering the sorts of domestic associations to which Pevnick himself appeals. Take again the case of a large business. If, through

---

[31] Pevnick, *Constraints of Justice*, chap. 2.   [32] Pevnick, esp. 84–95.
[33] Pevnick, 168–69.   [34] Pevnick, 112.
[35] In Chapter 1, we discussed what I believe are the main challenges facing any of the associational views.

their joint contributions to the goods and benefits of the business, employees have gained a right to control admission into the business, this does not mean they may use any criteria they like. Rather, their decisions are constrained by the equality demands of relations that occur *outside* the business.

Now, one might think that it's not accurate to say that the members inside the business are solely responsible for the contributions toward producing the business's goods and opportunities. Instead, one might argue, a large business is situated within a broader society, benefiting from the efforts of all who are members of the broader society, and *that* is why its admissions decisions are morally constrained in the relevant ways. More specifically, by paying taxes, abiding by the state's laws and norms, and the like, all the state's members help to provide the background conditions that enable the efforts inside the business.

However, in reply to this idea, if we scale out further, a similar point can be made about the relation between efforts inside a state and the contributions of outsiders. This implication can be drawn from points made in Chapter 3 and earlier in this chapter. Through the vast system of global capital investment, production, and trade, sometimes mediated through institutions such as the IMF and World Bank and other times through multinational corporations, individuals around the world contribute, in varying degrees, to a state's standard of living.[36] But also consider how, through states' cooperation with international norms, laws, and institutions, individuals everywhere help to sustain the *background rules* for, among other things, states entering and upholding agreements on matters of investment, trade, and currency rates. Indeed, the system of state sovereignty is a critical background condition for defining the very legal powers and immunities that enable a state not only to regulate its border, but to set its domestic policies and enter treaties, both economic and political, with other states.[37] All of this is an important, albeit less direct, way of contributing to the production of any state's collective goods.

I don't mean to suggest that there are not meaningful differences between the contributions of a state's members and outsiders in terms of the goods, resources, and opportunities created and sustained in the state. However, there can also be— and often are—substantial differences between the quality and intensity of *employees'* investments in a company's collective goods and the contributions of the state's members at large. Consider all the companies that have been constructed from the ground up, in which individual owners and employees have provided enormous time, resources, and effort toward testing and developing products and services, building the company's brand, expanding its market

---

[36] To take one example, foreign direct investment in the US increased from \$9.2 billion in 1970 to a staggering \$4.46 trillion at the end of 2019. US Bureau of Economic Analysis, "Direct Investment."

[37] See Follesdal's informed and illuminating discussion of these and related issues. Follesdal, "Distributive Justice."

share, and attracting investment.[38] In comparison with these forms of contributions, the contributions of others in the state toward producing a business's
collective goods do not seem remotely on par with the business's members. And
a similar point can be made about almost any sort of domestic association,
including schools, religious organizations, social clubs, and professional network-
ing associations. Yet despite their significant contributions to an association's
collective goods, members of these associations may not simply establish whatever
criteria for admission they choose unconstrained by outsiders' moral claims.

While domestic associations certainly do not present a perfect analogy for the
benefits of state membership and the rights of state members, the basic point is
that collective owners' rights against outsiders face greater restrictions than
Pevnick explicitly accepts (more on this shortly): if the association occupies a
position of power over valuable opportunities, then at a *minimum*, its owners are
not permitted to make admissions decisions on the basis of identity when doing so
degrades a group. And, based on the analysis in this chapter and in previous
chapters, I believe it is clear that the same goes for states. But, again, it's helpful to
observe what accepting the idea that states' immigration decisions are subject to
the primary duties does *not* imply. It does not mean that nonmembers, even in
ideal circumstances and with certain exceptions, must be allowed access to the
benefits to which members are entitled, including the economic, geographic, and
social opportunities that exist in the state. While duties to allow such access seem
implied by open-borders views and, relatedly, views that maintain that people
have a right to migrate or a right to international freedom of movement[39]—
something we will explore in greater detail in Chapter 6—the primary antidiscrimination duties are much less demanding.

Before going further, it's important to clarify that at certain points in his book,
Pevnick does suggest that racial and ethnic criteria are unjustified.[40] However, it is
not clear whether this is because he endorses a view similar to the Wrong to
Members view—whereby only the state's insiders with the disfavored characteristics are wronged—or whether he also accepts that a state's actions pertaining to
immigration are limited by the claims of outsiders. If he does accept the latter
view, his conception of when outsiders have claims against the state in this regard
may be rather limited, as best illustrated by his discussion concerning a border
wall on the United States' southern border—which, I will demonstrate in
Chapter 6, likely degrades Hispanics given the social context surrounding the
wall's proposal. To be sure, Pevnick advocates *against* building such a wall;
however, it is on pragmatic grounds, such as cost and effectiveness.[41] Indeed, he

---

[38] Fox, "Jeff Bezos."
[39] This seems to follow from the open-borders view (for example, Carens, "Aliens and Citizens";
Huemer, "Right to Immigrate?"; Oberman, "Immigration as Human Right").
[40] See Pevnick, *Constraints of Justice*, esp. 138–40, 161.   [41] Pevnick, 172–73.

maintains that despite his pragmatic concerns, US members still have the (seemingly, all-things-considered) right to construct the wall, should they democratically choose to do so. "To deny this," he writes, "is to fail to recognize the legitimate ownership claims of the citizenry."[42] But we have seen that taking the position that an association's rights are constrained by discretionary outsiders' claims does not fail to recognize the members' legitimate ownership claims. And the converse is of course also true: accepting an association's members' legitimate ownership claims does not mean that their rights face no limits from the claims of discretionary outsiders.

Here it is worth briefly exploring Michael Blake's very recent view, which can also be described as an associational account. Blake argues that the basis of states' choice is not (as Wellman maintains) members' right to refuse unwanted associations, but rather their right to refuse unwanted *obligations* toward others.[43] To establish this right, he argues that any legitimate state must protect and fulfill the human rights of all those present in the society, including those who have newly arrived.[44] This means that when people emigrate to a state, those already present incur a new obligation (to protect and fulfill the newcomers' human rights) and, he claims, we have a presumptive right to be free from obligations that others impose on us without our consent.[45] In other words, the reason that a state's current members have extensive moral rights to determine their admission as they choose is that they have a right to decide to whom, if anyone, they will enter into a relationship of obligation. To be sure, it is only a presumptive right since in some circumstances it can be overridden or outweighed—for instance, if the potential immigrant is fleeing a state in which their rights are not already adequately protected.[46] But when it comes to discretionary nonmembers, Blake maintains that we have a right not to be obligated by them.

There's much to like about Blake's view. States certainly have an obligation to protect and fulfill the basic human rights of everyone in their territory, and so it is undoubtedly correct that existing members incur new obligations when anyone enters the territory. Moreover, though others have challenged Blake's account of why incurring unchosen obligations creates moral concerns,[47] there nonetheless seems to be something right about his rationale. He argues that it is not *cost* considerations but the idea of having a standing relationship of *duty* toward someone to fulfill their rights and to care about their rights that prompts concerns.[48] Thus, he successfully argues, even if new immigrants contribute far more to the state's ability to protect and fulfill members' human rights than they cost the state, they still represent a new standing duty for those already present.[49]

---

[42] Pevnick, 170.   [43] Blake, *Justice, Migration, and Mercy*, 68–78.   [44] Blake, 70–73.
[45] Blake, 74.   [46] Blake, 82–84.
[47] Kates and Pevnick have critiqued Blake's view on several other points than those I pursue here. See Kates and Pevnick, "Immigration, Jurisdiction, and History."
[48] Blake, *Justice, Migration, and Mercy*, 78.   [49] Blake, 76–78.

But I want to discuss two concerns I have about his view.[50] First is a general comment: it does not seem to me that we have a presumptive right to be free of unchosen obligations, especially moral ones. In fact, part of what defines *moral* life is that we are decidedly not free to choose our obligations; we simply *find* ourselves in a space or in a world more generally not only with other people, but also other animals and the environment, and we must navigate our lives while heeding their interests along with their needs. And, importantly, it seems that for Blake the obligation we have to protect and fulfill other members' human rights is not merely political or legal, but also *moral*.[51] For instance, he characterizes these obligations, along with other "moral duties," as capable of being described at different levels of abstraction,[52] and he describes the burden we take on in cognitive or affective terms as much as behavioral: we must work to satisfy our obligations to protect and fulfill other members' human rights, but we must also *care* about satisfying them.[53]

All of this brings me to my second concern. It starts by observing that if the relevant obligations are (also) moral in nature, then we should again note that the current members of any domestic association also assume new obligations to newly admitted members. As we have seen, these obligations depend on the type and size of the association; for instance, members of a large business may have a moral duty to pay a certain wage and provide health and retirement benefits to new employees, and members of a small religious association may have a moral duty to provide new associates equal access to facilities and emotional support for any personal or family struggles. But that an organization's existing members must take on new obligations does not insulate them from a duty to refrain from using identity criteria when it treats or regards a group as morally inferior. Compared with a state's obligations to protect and fulfill its members' human rights, the sorts of obligations domestic associations have to their members may certainly cost less, but, as we have seen, Blake does not think that costs are the reason why new obligations prompt moral concerns; rather, it is because we incur a new standing relationship of obligation toward others. And in some cases, as perhaps with smaller, less commercial associations, acquiring a new relationship of obligation toward new members may even be more burdensome, morally speaking, than acquiring such a new relationship toward new members of a state. Thus, the fact that states must take on new obligations when they accept

---

[50]   Kates and Pevnick, "Immigration, Jurisdiction, and History."
[51]   Blake, *Justice, Migration, and Mercy*, 74.
[52]   Blake, 77–78. He also appeals here to the *moral* duty to care for children.
[53]   Blake, 78. And it certainly seems correct to think of our obligations to protect and fulfill others' human rights as, at bottom, moral: if our state were to fail to satisfy its legitimating functions and lose its right to set and enforce laws, we would not cease to have these obligations to other members—at least not those near us and with whom we interact.

new immigrants does not mean that they may make admission decisions unconstrained by discretionary nonmembers' moral claims.

Blake maintains that his argument is only the first step and that we must still figure out the moral contours of a state's right to choose its members.[54] However, as discussed in Chapters 1 and 3, he appears to maintain that any moral limits associated with using identity criteria are based in concerns about the state's character and wronging disfavored members not in how such criteria can wrong excluded nonmembers.[55] We turn to this issue next.

6. The Plausibility of the Primary Duties: Revisiting the Wrong to Members View

In this section, I will take one further step toward demonstrating the plausibility of saying that states have the primary duties. In particular, I'll show that certain criteria seem clearly wrong and, moreover, compared with the most likely alternative explanations, the global antidiscrimination approach provides the best explanation for why.

Sticking with our focus on race and ethnicity (and related categories), I believe multiple examples present clear cases, including Racial Ban (an all-white state that explicitly disfavors the admission of Black people). But let me start by considering a case that is similar to Racial Ban but directly connects to the discussion at the end of the last chapter, in which we analyzed Israel's LoR. Consider the following case:

European State: a Western European state that contains no Jewish members has an immigration policy that explicitly disfavors the admission of Jewish people.

I believe European State is an example of a clearly wrong immigration policy. There are several possible explanations for why it is wrong. For one, as in the case above in which Amanda rejects Evan's marriage proposal on the basis of his race, the use of racial criteria may reveal that an agent or association has objectionable character. In the case of European State, the criterion disfavoring Jewish people would likely indicate that the state or its members have objectionable beliefs about Jewish people, such as some sort of prejudice or contempt. If so, then by, say, failing to measure up to certain standards of a virtuous state, European State has committed a wrong. While I believe this sort of character explanation provides *one*

---

[54] For instance, he writes, "It is possible for us to have the right to exclude, after all, and still question whether or not that right is able to ground a particular exclusionary policy." Blake, *Justice, Migration, and Mercy,* 79.

[55] See discussions in Chapter 1, section 3, and Chapter 3, especially sections 5 and 7.

reason the case seems wrong, it is not the full or primary reason. For, as I will shortly demonstrate, it is not just that it seems the state has done something wrong, but the excluded nonmembers—Jewish people—seem clearly *wronged*, suggesting the state has violated an obligation or duty.

Before showing this, let me clarify that excluded nonmembers could certainly be wronged for reasons independent of antidiscrimination concerns. So even if I can show that it's plausible that Jewish nonmembers are wronged in European State, that will not necessarily provide support for saying that states have the primary duties. However, the most likely alternative candidates for explaining how Jewish nonmembers are wronged in the case are either uncompelling or easily addressed.

First, the policy could wrong Jewish nonmembers if European State has special obligations to them or to the states that they currently live in. But we could simply assume (plausibly) that there are no such special obligations in this case. Second, under a type of open-borders view, one might think the criterion goes against general obligations not to violate others' moral freedom of movement or related moral rights, and so for this reason the excluded nonmembers in the European State case are wronged. However, even if an open-borders view in the end proves correct, racial and ethnic exclusions (when they are wrong) are surely wrong in ways at least *distinctive* from or *additional* to exclusion in general. It seems woefully inadequate to say that the wrong of racial criteria is on par with the wrong of criteria based on, for instance, concerns about resource limitations or population concerns in that they all violate an individual's freedom of movement. Surely, racial and ethnic criteria are wrong in distinctive or at least additional ways. Put differently, it is not merely that Jewish nonmembers are wronged by the criterion, but that they are wronged *qua Jewish people*.

Even so, however, this doesn't mean that *antidiscrimination* duties are needed for the explanation. Another possibility is that the criterion violates anticlassification duties, which, as discussed in Chapter 2, could make any exclusion on the basis of an identity criterion wrong, whether it excludes a vulnerable or secure group. Perhaps the discussion of European State cannot alone rule out the possibility that the anticlassification interpretation of discrimination's wrongs is most appropriate for thinking about states' admissions. However, my goal in this chapter is to demonstrate that states *at least* have duties not to exclude on the basis of identity when it degrades. Whether they have duties not to exclude on the basis of identity more generally is a further and separate issue from what is being explored here (but I believe the analysis in other chapters, especially Chapter 3, provide reasons to reject the anticlassification approach to states' admissions).

More importantly, it is Jewish people's global *vulnerability*, not merely the fact that their ethnicity is the basis of the policy, that seems to account for why European State's immigration criterion clearly wrongs them. In order to see why, it will be helpful to start by looking more closely at the primary view that denies that excluded nonmembers can be wronged. Recall the Wrong to Members view (WM), endorsed for instance by Blake and Wellman, discussed in Chapter 3. Under that view, European State is permissible since there are no members sharing the disfavored immigration criterion, and so no members who could potentially be wronged by the criterion. While we discussed when and why WM's proponents believe that racial and ethnic criteria wrong disfavored members, we haven't yet explored why they deny that such criteria can wrong excluded nonmembers. Their primary reasons are in fact very much connected to our discussion of relational equality and its demands.

In particular, Wellman, who discusses the issue at some length, appeals directly to a relational theory of equality of the sort described in Chapter 2.[56] He does so first in the context of considering the luck-egalitarian case for open borders, which suggests that people should have equal access to the benefits and institutions of any state, as no one's life prospects should be affected by matters of brute luck. He claims that while the luck-egalitarian understanding of equality is compelling, it is much less important than relational equality since, he maintains, we should be much more concerned about inequalities within the same society than across societies.[57] Then, against this background, he considers the wrong of racial and ethnic criteria, and he writes, "Given the relational theory of equality detailed above it makes sense to presume that we may have responsibilities to our compatriots that we do not equally owe to foreigners. In particular, we have a special duty to respect our fellow citizens as equal partners in the political cooperative... a [racial or ethnic] policy would wrongly disrespect those citizens in the dispreferred category."[58]

On the general point that there are some important differences between what we owe members and what we owe nonmembers, as I indicated in section 4, I agree with this. But, again, saying that the excluded nonmembers are wronged by certain racial or ethnic criteria does not require that we have the same duties to nonmembers that we have to members.[59] In particular, to say that Jewish nonmembers are wronged in European State does not imply that the state must open its borders to nonmembers, whether Jewish or otherwise. Thinking that it does conflates two separate questions: "Does a state wrong a Jewish nonmember by not admitting them?" and "Does a state wrong a Jewish nonmember by not admitting them on the basis of their race or ethnicity?" Wellman addresses the first question—and argues against the luck-egalitarian case for open borders—by

---

[56] Blake ("Distributive Justice") seems to suggest something similar. In his view, what sets the boundaries of the relevant relationship is shared subjection to the state's coercive and legal power.

[57] Wellman, "Freedom of Association," 122.   [58] Wellman, 139.

[59] A preliminary point here is that a proponent of relational equality within the state certainly need not (and Wellman does not) suggest that states are incapable of wronging nonmembers altogether (in particular, see Wellman, 124) or that states have no duties to nonmembers whatsoever (for instance, he agrees that relations within the family matter for equality (124–25)).

maintaining that nonmembers are not owed equal access to the benefits of living in a state.[60] But that sort of equality with members is not needed to address the second question.

Now, Wellman may be addressing the second question when he suggests (in the quoted passage) that nonmembers are not owed the same sort of *respect* that a state's members are owed: respect "as equal partners in the political cooperative." He doesn't specify what such respect requires, but it likely demands something along the lines of viewing co-members as fellow cooperators or stakeholders in the collective decision-making affecting mutual life in the state. This affirmative form of respect might then have concrete implications for what we owe to one another as co-members, including in terms of, for instance, basic economic and political goods.[61] But we might not need to know this form of respect's precise meaning. For even to think we owe some kinds of respect only to members is compatible with the claim that we owe to nonmembers other forms of respect, namely not regarding and treating them as moral inferiors. But this is precisely how Jewish nonmembers are treated in European State. Moreover, as we will see next, they are treated this way for reasons implicitly suggested by Wellman, along with WM's other notable proponents, including Blake.

Recall that along with several other authors, WM's proponents suggest that Israel's LoR (which grants automatic admission to Jewish people only) is potentially permissible, even though it seems to clearly wrong Israel's Palestinian members.[62] They refer to the lasting effects of the Holocaust and other forms of persecution and racism experienced by the Jewish people and how, against that history, LoR affirms the idea of a state in which Jewish people are always welcomed.[63] In light of how Jewish people were, and often continue to be, subject to significant injustices in numerous states and around the world, they quite arguably have a vulnerable status in terms of the social bases of their self-respect. But Jewish people have not experienced abiding injustices in Israel, and, more generally, there is no realistic sense in which they have a vulnerable domestic status qua members of Israel. If anything, they are clearly the securest group, in material, political, and social terms. Thus, even though WM's proponents do not refer to the notion of global status, it turns out that it is the Jewish people's global vulnerability (in self-respect terms) that accounts for the policy's potential permissibility.

In the next chapter, I will explain why I do not believe LoR (in its current form) is in fact permissible. But what is relevant here is the following question: if the

---

[60]   Wellman, 119.

[61]   Anderson ("What Is the Point?," 316–31) suggests that relational equality among co-members implies that we owe fellow members the guarantee of certain basic capabilities. It's unclear whether Wellman would endorse this view, but something along these lines might be suggested.

[62]   See my discussion in Chapter 3, section 7. See (for example) Coleman and Harding, "Citizenship"; Blake, "Distributive Justice"; Miller, "Immigration"; Wellman, "Freedom of Association."

[63]   See my previous note for references.

global vulnerability of Jewish people (implicitly alluded to by LoR's defenders) potentially has enough moral significance to permit Israel to wrong its own members, why, then, would that same global vulnerability not also have enough moral significance to make it so that a state that excludes people on the basis of their being Jewish wrongs them? To clarify, the thought isn't that we can move simply from the idea that (1) members of some globally vulnerable group might be permitted to favor their own group, to the idea that (2) a state whose immigration criterion disfavors that group wrongs them. For imagine if the only reason for thinking (1) in Israel's case was a concern about the continued existence of the Jewish people as a distinct ethno-religious cultural group; that would not necessarily translate into thinking that states that exclude individuals because they are Jewish wrong them.

However, it seems highly doubtful that the only rationale for (1) is the continuation of a distinct cultural group. What (also) seems important, and likely central, is something like a concern for the individual group members' well-being, broadly construed—for instance, their sense of empowerment and self-respect in light of persecution's lingering effects. Moreover, an exclusive concern for a culture's survival carries perverse implications. It could imply that it is better for all Jewish people to remain in Israel because their living together would promote the continuation of their distinct practices and beliefs. Thus, under that line of thought, it might not only be morally permissible but morally *preferable* for states to exclude Jewish people. This highly perverse implication suggests it's far more plausible to interpret the rationale for (1) as involving a concern for the group members' self-respect in the world. But the plausibility of this concern makes it hard to avoid the conclusion that when an immigration policy like that of European State explicitly disfavors that group, the social bases of their self-respect are (further) damaged and they are indeed treated as moral inferiors.[64]

There is another, more direct, point related to the primary duties that can be drawn from the discussion of LoR. Specifically, given that LoR seems to clearly wrong Israel's disfavored members (especially Palestinians, many of whom lack full membership rights), Israel is committing a domestic injustice or wrong (wronging its members) to address Jewish people's global vulnerability. But it is difficult to see how that might even potentially be permitted from the standpoint of anything approaching *domestic* duties alone. That is, if LoR is deemed potentially permissible, it seems one implicitly has in mind some sort of *global* duties.

What I just said was fairly quick, so let me elaborate by looking at an alternative explanation that does not appeal to global duties. One might claim that I have misconstrued the relevance of Jewish people's global vulnerability to LoR's potential justification. They might claim that the fact that Jewish people are globally

---

[64] And for the same general sorts of reasons that European State's policy wrongs the excluded nonmembers, Racial Ban would also surely do so. I will discuss this policy explicitly in Chapter 5.

vulnerable is important in explaining LoR but only because of how the global vulnerability of Jewish people affects *Israeli* Jews. That is, they might accept that the global context and Jewish people's vulnerability in relation to it are salient and morally important, but only for determining Israel's duties owed to its members, not to Jewish people more generally. More specifically, they might think that the justification for LoR is that by reducing Jewish people's global disadvantages in self-respect terms, LoR promotes the social bases of self-respect for Jewish people living in Israel. According to the objection, then, the moral justification for Israel's violation of a duty to not wrong certain members (Israeli Palestinians) is that it protects the self-respect of *other* members (Israeli Jews). If so, LoR's potential justification does not demonstrate anything about global duties—only that Israel has competing duties to its different members and, thus, the policy can be entirely explained from the standpoint of domestic duties.

But though important, this objection is easy to address. First, while securing the social bases of self-respect of Israeli Jews certainly seems part of the appropriate moral rationale for LoR, much of its potential justification seems connected to the Holocaust's lingering effects on the self-respect of Jewish people *around the world* and how Jewish people in certain states (outside Israel) are still poorly treated and regarded with contempt by other members in those states (indeed, LoR seems to affirm the idea of a place where Jewish people are always *welcomed*). Given that Israeli Jews arguably have the most secure *domestic* status of Jewish people anywhere in the world, it's very unlikely that LoR's appropriate rationale only connects to a concern for them, rather than for Jewish people everywhere. Second and most importantly, Israeli Jewish people's domestic status is far more secure than Israeli Palestinians' domestic status, making it implausible that LoR's wronging of the latter can even be potentially justified on any sort of domestic-justice grounds alone.[65]

---

[65] Another worry is that the most the discussion demonstrates is that Israel has *special* duties to address Jewish people's global vulnerability when implementing immigration criteria; it does not show that states generally have such duties. I agree that this brief discussion does not, on its own, show that other states do have such obligations. Nevertheless, this implication can quickly be drawn. We know that concerns about Jewish people's global vulnerability must have fairly significant value to explain how it potentially justifies wronging members. Whether under WM or otherwise, refraining from wronging members through selective immigration is quite important, which explains why authors only highlight one or two exceptions. (See, on Japan, Carens, "Migration and Morality," and, on Israel, Blake, "Distributive Justice"; Miller, "Immigration"; Wellman, "Freedom of Association.") And, though I have questioned whether it's always true that disfavored members are wronged (for example, in the case of Navajo), I have not denied the moral importance of avoiding wronging members. So if it might be justified for Israel to wrong its members through its immigration criteria for the sake of addressing Jewish people's global vulnerability, it is because we think there are very important reasons for addressing that vulnerability. But why, then, wouldn't those same reasons suggest that *other* states have duties to reduce or at least *not contribute to* Jewish people's global vulnerability through their immigration criteria (at least in certain ways)? In fact, claiming that *Israel alone* has the moral burden of addressing Jewish people's global vulnerability seems morally distorted since the reasons for their

I have not conclusively shown that providing a potential justification for LoR requires an appeal to global antidiscrimination duties. However, the reasoning above demonstrates that something akin to such duties is needed. I have focused on the case of Israel and the world's Jewish population to make the argument that global antidiscrimination concerns seem implied in judgments about selective immigration since this case is often discussed in the literature, but we could make similar arguments for other cases.[66] After all, we have seen that many racial and ethnic groups appear to be significantly vulnerable, and along multiple dimensions.

More support for the primary duties, and the global antidiscrimination approach more generally, will come in the next chapter (by seeing how it explains normative differences among a large variety of cases) and in Chapter 6 (by assessing the advantages of the antidiscrimination approach over open-borders views). But the above discussion, in combination with the analysis of global status and global relations, gives us significant reason to claim that, while states might not have duties to treat and regard nonmembers as "equal partners in the political cooperative," they at least have duties not to exclude on the basis of identity when it treats or regards them as moral inferiors.

Cases such as European State and Racial Ban are highly unrealistic examples precisely because they explicitly disfavor the admission of one vulnerable group. In the real world, we are unlikely to see immigration policies that resemble these and are far more likely to come across policies that subtly or implicitly invoke racial or ethnic criteria. But the point of using such examples was, building on the work of previous chapters, only to demonstrate the plausibility of states' possession of the primary duties—and European State and Racial Ban both clearly violate these duties. But, beginning in the next chapter, we will also explore what these duties seem to imply for more subtle, and far more complicated, examples of racial and ethnic immigration criteria as well as for other identity criteria and non-identity criteria.

---

vulnerability relate to events and attitudes in *other* states. If anything, it might be just the opposite, especially if one thinks that what explains LoR's potential justification is both that Jewish people are globally vulnerable and that they have experienced significant *injustices*, for those injustices have occurred in other states. It's important to note here, however, that while past wrongs are often important contributors to global status, they are not necessary for the antidiscrimination approach outlined in this book. I will return to this issue in the next chapter.

[66] For instance, assume for the moment that the minority-white members in Navajo are indeed wronged by Navajo's immigration policy but that Navajo's policy is still overall justified. As in the case of LoR, it seems we are implicitly invoking the idea that there is a *duty* to address the Navajo's and other native populations' *global* vulnerability, and that duty outweighs, in this particular case, the duty not to wrong members through selective criteria.

5

The Primary Duties

1. Introduction

A major goal of the book thus far has been to develop the case that states' immigration decisions can be fruitfully viewed through the lens of antidiscrimination principles and that states are subject to at least certain antidiscrimination duties when making admissions decisions. In the remaining chapters of the book, I will explore the implications of this for a range of questions. These questions include what sorts of identity criteria are permissible and when, whether it is morally permissible for states to employ any *non*-identity criteria in their immigration policies or whether they must instead have open borders, and whether states have the moral right against interference to exclude. This exploration begins in this chapter, which is devoted to examining when criteria seem to violate the primary duties and when they do not.

I start with a focus on race, ethnicity, and related categories of nationality, religion, and ethno-religion to examine, in broad terms, what the primary duties imply for the explicit use of these sorts of criteria, distinguishing cases of disfavoring others from cases favoring one's own group. Then, by considering issues such as regional variation, the different dimensions of (dis)advantage, and immigration rates, in subsequent sections I'll explore in more detail what the duties seem to imply for a wide variety of (more complicated) cases of racial and ethnic criteria and related criteria. Then, I'll turn to discuss what the analysis seems to imply for the use of other sorts of identity criteria, including sex, gender, and disability. This chapter concludes by demonstrating how the antidiscrimination approach is not a backward-looking account stressing duties of corrective justice.

2. Recap and Terminology

Building on the groundwork lain in Chapter 2 and especially Chapter 3, the previous chapter argued that states are bound by global antidiscrimination's primary duties—duties not to exclude on the basis of identity when it degrades a group. Continuing with a focus on racial and ethnic criteria and related criteria, in the next section we will explore, in broad terms, what these duties imply for the use of such criteria.

Immigration and Discrimination: (Un)Welcoming Others. Sahar Akhtar, Oxford University Press. © Sahar Akhtar 2024.
DOI: 10.1093/oso/9780198898696.003.0006

First, some terminology will be helpful. Recall from Chapter 2 that both disfavoring and favoring certain criteria involve selecting against or selectively excluding some group (or groups). We'll begin in this chapter with the explicit use of racial, ethnic, and related criteria—that is, where criteria explicitly refer to at least one race or ethnicity (or related category, such as nationality, religion, or ethno-religion), as these are most obviously cases of selecting against or selectively excluding people on the basis of identity, and thus of direct discrimination. Though there might not always be a clear distinction between the two,[1] I will say that a state favors some criteria if it expresses a positive preference for that criterion, and it disfavors some criterion if it expresses a negative preference against it. As is likely expected, explicit disfavoring will almost always trigger greater moral concerns.

It's important to emphasize from the start that much of the analysis will be inconclusive. Particularly in instances in which a group's global status varies, whether the primary duties are violated in any specific case will depend on a variety of both empirical and normative issues, and we will only get to some of the more central ones here. More than providing definitive answers, what I hope to do is show how the conceptual resources provided by the global antidiscrimination approach can assist in thinking through complex immigration cases. In fact, the analysis of any case will proceed in a fashion similar to how the analysis of admission decisions within a specific state is undertaken, invoking related sorts of considerations. Of course, a difference is that in the domestic context, many (but certainly not all) of the relevant questions will seem to have more definitive answers, if only because such questions have been reflected on and addressed in often-systematic fashion. Aside from this point, there are certainly substantial differences between the global and domestic contexts: mainly, given the less thick and more fractured nature of global social relations as well as the size and dispersal of identity groups, our judgments about the social status of any group and about any case may be more tentative than under a similar sort of analysis within a specific state. But I hope to show that antidiscrimination norms at least provide pivotal resources for navigating the morality of complicated state-admission cases, just as they seem for admission decisions within a state.

A major result to state up front is that not all racial and ethnic criteria violate the primary duties. More relevantly, even if a state's identity criteria selectively exclude globally vulnerable groups, this does not mean that it violates its primary duties. Finally, even if such exclusion violates the state's primary duties, this does not imply that it wrongs *all* the vulnerable groups that are selectively excluded. As we will see, there are several different reasons for all of this. But a general way to

---

[1] For instance, if an immigration policy explicitly states a preference for every race in the world except for one that is not mentioned, it looks like a clear case of disfavoring the excluded race.

frame these reasons connects to the different senses in which selection might run afoul of antidiscrimination norms.

Recall that we can sort the various ways an action can contribute to a group's vulnerability into two categories: comparatively reduced opportunities and degradation. In Chapter 2 we saw that the antidiscrimination approach stresses that the reason we must not contribute to the vulnerability of groups is a fundamental concern that some groups are, or may become, subordinate. And subordinated groups are those that not only experience comparative disadvantages (in a systematic and persistent manner) but do so as a result of moral relations that have treated them as moral inferiors. Thus, ultimately, what matters from the standpoint of antidiscrimination is avoiding contributing to a group's vulnerability in the specific respects that relate to moral anxieties about treating or regarding the group as morally inferior.

Now, concerning the first category (comparatively reduced opportunities), because of the significant opportunities that a state structures, selecting against some vulnerable group might well disadvantage it relative to other groups in terms of having access to the material, political, and way-of-life options in the admitting state and, especially if the opportunities in the admitting state are significant, compound the disadvantages faced by the excluded group relative to other groups. But that does not mean the group is treated as morally inferior. If a group's exclusion expresses a demeaning message about its members, compromises the basis of their self-respect, or perpetuates stigmas against them, that directly treats them in a morally inferior way. We will see that a variety of considerations bear on whether selectively excluding a vulnerable group from a state's life options degrades it in one or more of these ways. As we saw in Chapter 2, while the three forms of degradation are closely related, which ones occur can often depend on the particular kind of action.[2] In particular, it seems it would take a higher level of act-visibility or more significant consequences for a single act to either weaken the basis of a group's self-respect or perpetuate stigmas against them; the bar for expressing a demeaning message about a group is much lower.

Some of the considerations that will matter to whether the group is degraded, and if so, in what way, include how vulnerable the group is (and in what respects), how valuable the denied opportunities are, what the group's patterns of immigration are, what the most plausible interpretation for the rationale behind the policy is, and what the historical and contemporary moral relations are, including whether there is a history of prejudice against, scorn for, or marginalization of the excluded group.

---

[2] See discussion in Chapter 2, section 3.

3. Do Racial or Ethnic Criteria Always Violate the Primary Duties?

Let's start with some relatively simple cases in which much of what I've just discussed may be obvious, examining more complicated ones after we gain an appreciation for the general approach. Consider the differences between the hypothetical Racial Ban and Navajo cases from earlier chapters—both of which explicitly referred to racial or ethnic criteria. In Racial Ban, an all-white state has an immigration policy explicitly disfavoring the admission of Black people. In Navajo, a state composed mainly of the Navajo people implements an immigration policy explicitly favoring the admission of other Navajo. Though there are a few important differences between these cases—especially that Racial Ban disfavors one group whereas Navajo favors the admission of the majority's own group (more on this soon)—one significant difference has to do with global status.

Racial Ban features an identity group with a very secure global status excluding a globally vulnerable group. Assuming the state in Racial Ban is like actual states today in which whites constitute the majority, it contains tremendous professional, educational, political, and health opportunities (to name just a few kinds).[3] Thus the policy selectively excludes a vulnerable (and arguably subordinate) group from highly valuable life options. More importantly, because of the significant global-status differences between whites and Blacks, by selectively denying the latter valuable life options, the policy would seem to clearly, say, have the power to express a demeaning message about them. Moreover, again assuming the state is like actual states containing a majority-white population, because of its global economic, political, and social power, its policy has the visibility to worsen the social bases of the excluded group's self-respect and perpetuate stigmas about them.

By contrast, the admitting group in Navajo is itself significantly globally vulnerable, casting doubt on whether its policy violates the primary duties. To clarify, Navajo's immigration policy selects against nonmembers who belong (in different ways) both to globally secure and globally vulnerable groups. That is, by favoring other Navajo people, not only white nonmembers but also, for instance, Black and Hispanic nonmembers are selected against by Navajo's criterion. However, similar considerations are relevant for understanding why selecting against either type of group—secure or vulnerable—does not seem to violate the primary duties. For, aside from the fact that the policy would not even contribute to the vulnerability of groups such as whites—since such groups have a very secure

---

[3] For instance, as we saw in Chapter 3, roughly half of the states ranked in the top thirty for largest GDP, highest life expectancy, and strongest educational systems are majority white. See "Gross Domestic Product 2021," World Bank, https://databank.worldbank.org/data/download/GDP.pdf; "Life Expectancy at Birth," Knoema.com, https://knoema.com/atlas/ranks/Life-expectancy; "Rankings," Legatum Institute, https://www.prosperity.com/rankings.

global status—the Navajo's own global status as the admitting group is important. First, generally speaking, the Navajo have little power to put others down, say, or further compromise the social bases of others' self-respect—whether considering nonmembers in secure or vulnerable groups. Moreover, in favoring other Navajo, the policy is far more plausibly interpreted as aiming to secure their own global status and not as motivated by prejudice or animosity toward other groups. Finally, consider which group is relatively advantaged by Navajo's immigration policy by having greater access to the opportunities in the admitting state: it is mainly other Navajo. Thus, because it is a highly vulnerable group, not a group with a secure status, that is primarily advantaged, the policy seems unlikely to contribute to the vulnerability of any groups that are selected against, let alone do so in a way that ranks them as inferior. Thus, while the case of Racial Ban clearly violates the primary duties, the Navajo case seems to clearly not do so.

Of course, there is another important difference between Racial Ban and Navajo. Racial Ban disfavors a single group, whereas Navajo favors the admission of the majority's own group. As might be expected, there is assuredly a difference between criteria explicitly disfavoring another group and criteria explicitly favoring one's own group.[4] So, to isolate the impact that global status has on the primary duties, let's consider a variant of each case that has the same structure as the other.

First, imagine that if instead of favoring other Navajo, Navajo's immigration policy explicitly disfavors the admission of, say, Arabs. Here, the Navajo's own significant global vulnerability bears little on the moral status of the immigration policy. First, unlike the Navajo's policy favoring their own group, with respect to the life options in the state the present policy specifically singles out one group for a disadvantage. Second, recall from Chapter 2 that in order to understand whether an action degrades people in one of the central ways, we must not only look at the status differences between the admitting and excluded groups but also consider past and current social practices to see whether, for instance, the excluded group has been marginalized or exploited or whether its identity has been the object of prejudice or scorn. We saw in Chapter 3 that Arabs are fairly advantaged in global economic and political terms—something we will revisit in section 4.2 below. At the same time, as predominantly Muslims, it is plausible that Arabs have been comparatively vulnerable in self-respect terms, especially since September 11, 2001. For as we also saw in Chapter 3, Muslims, taken as a group, have experienced varying forms of marginalization and prejudice, with the terrorist acts committed in the United States having contributed to fear and suspicion of Muslims as well as violence and attacks against them in multiple states around

---

[4] However, shortly we'll see that this doesn't mean that all instances of either disfavoring or favoring are normatively equivalent.

the world.[5] Third, despite the Navajo's own significant global vulnerability, it seems implausible to interpret an immigration policy explicitly disfavoring Arabs as aiming to secure the Navajo people's self-respect or way of life—for instance, it seems there are other groups that could pose an even larger threat to the Navajo's way of life—suggesting that there is a kind of prejudice or unwarranted fear behind the policy. Taking all of these considerations in combination, then, it is more than fair to say that past and current social practices support interpreting criteria that single them out for a disadvantage as expressing a demeaning message about them and, very likely, again because they are singled out, that such criteria further compromise the social bases of their self-respect and perpetuate stigmas against them. Thus, it seems clear that the immigration policy degrades Arabs, thereby violating the primary duties—and this even though the Navajo people, as the admitting group, are significantly vulnerable.

The preceding analysis makes it tempting to conclude that whenever a group that is disadvantaged in any sense is explicitly disfavored by an immigration policy, no matter the global status of the admitting group, the policy violates the state's primary duties. Now, there may be some rare exceptions. Consider a group that is significantly vulnerable with respect to its distinct way of life and some other vulnerable group that is an existential threat to it because of an entrenched pattern of violent conflict between the groups; if the first group were to explicitly exclude the second group (or vice versa), such a policy might not degrade the excluded group.[6] Aside from such rare cases, though, it does seem that explicitly excluding a group that is disadvantaged along any dimension is always wrong, if for no other reason than it is hard to interpret such a policy as not expressing disdain or malice.[7] At the very least, it seems to suggest a kind of failure to consider the interests of the members of the excluded group, or, put differently, an "absence of appropriate recognition of someone's personhood, whether that absence comes about willfully or by neglect."[8]

In fact, for similar reasons, it's hard to see how *any* instance of explicitly disfavoring some group could not generally be wrong. And this seems to largely hold symmetrically. That is, it is difficult to see how even the case of a globally vulnerable group explicitly disfavoring the admission of a globally secure group could not generally be wrong. As with the type of case in the previous paragraph, there are of course possible exceptions. For instance, it could be that explicitly disfavoring some secure group is a vulnerable group's response to its concern

---

[5] Stahnke et al., "Violence against Muslims; Carr, *Experiences of Islamophobia*; Ma, "Anti-Islamic Movement in China."

[6] But notice that this seems tentative and, in any case, is likely a rare scenario.

[7] Though (again) we may be unable to know for sure whether any such attitude is behind an immigration policy, it is nevertheless hard to imagine any case of explicitly disfavoring a vulnerable group as not involving some such attitude.

[8] Eidelson, *Discrimination and Disrespect*, 75.

about being subjugated by that group (because of recent history, for instance). Or imagine a Navajo state that has no white members (to sidestep concerns about potentially wronging members) and explicitly excludes whites because that is viewed as an important step to shoring up the Navajo way of life against what is perceived as the biggest threat to that way of life. Moreover, even without knowledge of some such rationale, given the history of relations between whites and the Navajo, it may not be implausible to infer that such a rationale is behind the hypothetical policy and not necessarily, for instance, prejudice about or malice toward whites. Under such circumstances, it's possible that explicitly disfavoring the secure group would not be wrong.

More important here, however, is that even when wrong, explicitly disfavoring a secure group would not typically violate the primary duties. Before elaborating on this point, let me first observe that there could again be exceptions, but ultimately any exceptions would be due to concerns about vulnerable groups. As I briefly discussed in Chapter 2, selecting against members of a secure group can exacerbate the disadvantages experienced by a vulnerable group by, for instance, causing retaliation against the latter group's members or further damage to the social bases of their self-respect. Moreover, it is possible that selecting against a relatively secure group could by itself cause that group to become vulnerable, depending on whether its relative advantages are unstable, not especially significant, or only pertain to particular dimensions of disadvantage. This will depend on various kinds of empirical facts and comparative judgments about different groups that we will begin to explore in the following section. Aside from such cases, though, explicitly disfavoring secure groups would not typically violate the primary duties since it would not typically contribute to (or cause) any group's vulnerability and especially not in a way that treats it as inferior. In contrast, in cases of admitting groups (whether vulnerable or secure) explicitly disfavoring globally vulnerable groups, we've seen that the action has the power to express a demeaning message about the excluded group and may weaken the basis of its self-respect and perpetuate stigmas against it. But this is all very unlikely to occur when secure groups are explicitly disfavored.

One might think that that what I've just said provides reason to reject the antidiscrimination approach, with its built-in asymmetry. But I don't believe it does. First, as was suggested in the previous paragraph, to say that explicitly disfavoring a secure group would not typically violate the primary duties (or any potential further antidiscrimination duties) is not to say that it is not wrong. I certainly believe that this sort of case would typically be wrong even if it is not the wrong of antidiscrimination. One possibility is that, as in the domestic context, explicitly disfavoring a group, whether vulnerable or secure, always violates an important sort of anticlassification duty. If so, one option is to accept that antidiscrimination duties do not capture the full extent of our state-admission duties associated with discrimination concerns. But there is also another option, which is to maintain that discrimination concerns do not exhaust all the ways in which a state's immigration decisions may be wrong. For starters, in the next chapter, we will see that excluding people who have urgent or special claims for admission is wrong for reasons quite independent of discrimination concerns. More relevant to the present discussion is the suggestion from the previous chapter, which will be discussed far more in Chapter 7, that immigration criteria are wrong when they imply that a state's members have poor character or that the state, as a whole, fails to live up to certain standards of a virtuous state—something that can (and does) certainly apply to states largely composed of vulnerable groups in addition to those composed mainly of secure groups.

But, importantly, none of what I have just discussed means that the converse is true—that explicitly *favoring* one's group is always morally permissible. Indeed, it is in such cases that antidiscrimination's built-in asymmetry seems most compelling (again, at least for states' admission decisions). Consider again Reverse Navajo from Chapter 3. That case involved a state in which whites (of European descent) are the economic, political, and social majority, with the Navajo comprising the minority, and the state explicitly favors the admission of other whites. Unlike Navajo explicitly favoring the admission of other Navajo people, the favoring of other whites in Reverse Navajo seems clearly wrong. The antidiscrimination approach accounts for this difference. And having just seen what the Navajo's global status implies for the original Navajo case, we can now run a similar analysis, but in the opposite direction, to see what the global status of whites implies for Reverse Navajo.

To start, we know that actual states in which whites constitute the majority are very wealthy and contain tremendous professional, educational, political, and health opportunities.[9] And it would mainly be other whites who are relatively advantaged by Reverse Navajo's criterion in terms of these sorts of opportunities in the admitting state. Thus, with respect to immensely valuable life options, an immigration policy that favors the admission of whites might contribute to the relative material, political, and way-of-life disadvantages of at least some groups. More importantly, whites, as a group, have the global power to express a demeaning message about vulnerable groups and (further) compromise the social bases of their self-respect (as well as potentially causing a vulnerable group's subordination). Relatedly, because of whites' secure global status along multiple dimensions of advantage, the policy cannot plausibly be interpreted as aiming to secure their status in any sense. Rather, it likely reflects some sort of vainglory or belief in their superiority over other races, perhaps masquerading as either pride or a desire to live with others with whom they mutually identify. More directly, it might simply reflect hostility toward other racial groups. Taking all of the above considerations

---

[9] See discussion in Chapter 3, section 4.

in combination, even though the state's policy does not explicitly disfavor any vulnerable group, but rather explicitly favors a secure group, the policy seems to clearly violate the primary duties. Indeed, any time a secure group explicitly favors the admission of its own group (or even another such group[10]), it is frankly hard to see how the primary duties would not be violated—at least, that is, with respect to *some* vulnerable group or groups.

The previous qualification is crucial. As we will see in the next section, to say that the primary duties are violated does not mean that a policy degrades all disadvantaged groups that are selected against. This issue will be instrumental when we discuss groups not considered identity groups, such as the global poor, and when we discuss indirect forms of discrimination (both of which are discussed in the next chapter). But it will also be very useful in the next section for understanding why a secure group explicitly favoring its own group might not degrade all of the vulnerable groups that are selected against.

Conversely, we will also see in the next section that in some cases in which the admitting group is itself vulnerable (at least in certain respects), favoring other members of its group for admission may in fact violate the primary duties. All of this will largely depend on the *sense*(s) in which a group is vulnerable or secure and to what *extent*. Let's turn to these issues now.

4. Role of Region and Type of Disadvantage

In Chapter 3 we saw that, as is the case with domestic statuses, having either a vulnerable or secure global status does not mean that a group's status is constant under all types of international institutions or in all types of interactions or social relations. Relatedly, it does not mean that a group is either disadvantaged or advantaged in all the relevant respects—that is, in material, political, way-of-life, and self-respect terms. A general way to categorize these differences is to say that a group's status can vary according to both region and dimension of (dis)advantage, and often both. Here, we'll explore what all of this might mean for favoring one's own group and, especially, for whether doing so wrongs a given selectively excluded group.

4.1 The Excluded Group(s)

Let's begin by examining this issue from the standpoint of excluded groups whose vulnerability might vary, starting with a focus on regional variability. Consider

---

[10] Imagine, for instance, that a state's Han Chinese were to favor the admission of whites. Depending (of course) on the particular circumstances, it seems this would express a demeaning message about at least certain vulnerable groups. Which groups is a matter I will explore in the next section.

again Christians living in the Middle and Near East, who seem vulnerable in relation to interactions in that region (and North Africa[11]) but not in relation to other regions and states, including Europe, North and South America, and parts of Asia. An implication of the fact that their vulnerability is primarily regional is that while it would seem to clearly degrade Christians if, say, Jordan, Bahrain, or Pakistan were to favor the admission of their dominant religious group (namely, Muslims), it's plausible that it would not degrade Christians if, say, Japan were to favor the admission of practitioners of Shinto or Buddhism.[12] In large part this is because there do not seem to be any sustained patterns of viewing Christians with prejudice or disdain in the latter region, and so there is little if anything to support interpreting their selective exclusion as treating them as inferior. But that is not true of the Middle East and nearby regions.[13]

For a group whose status varies in terms of dimension of (dis)advantage, to some extent we have already seen that Jewish people seem like a good example. For while Jewish people face a substantial disadvantage in terms of the global social bases of their self-respect, they have considerable advantages in global economic, political, and military terms,[14] and, relatedly, they have access to valuable life opportunities in a variety of wealthy states, including Israel.[15] Because of these kinds of significant advantages, many cases of an admitting group favoring its own

[11] For a recent overview of some of these issues, see Wintour, "Persecution of Christians." Also see discussion in Chapter 3, section 3.

[12] Antidiscrimination norms in some domestic contexts also seem responsive to regional differences. For instance, recall the considerably vulnerable status of Appalachian whites in the United States. Importantly, their vulnerability is mainly regional, as many outside the relevant area may even be unable to identify them on the basis of their perceived characteristics. Because much of their vulnerability seems to depend on their salience as a social group, and this, in turn, is mostly regional, there are laws forbidding discrimination against Appalachian whites in the region, such as in the city of Cincinnati, but not in other areas of the United States. I'm not suggesting that laws should determine the way we think about antidiscrimination duties, but it's worth noting that regional variation seems to make the application of antidiscrimination duties less straightforward even domestically. For valuable discussion, see Rhee and Scott, "Geographic Discrimination."

[13] See relevant data in Chapter 3, especially footnote 10.

[14] Since the majority of the world's Jewish population lives in Israel (which is 73.9% Jewish), measures of Israel's advantages in these terms may be sufficient to illustrate the point. For instance, it has about the 30th largest economy in the world. Considering its size of less than eight million people, this ranking is significant. And it is ranked 30th for its overall prosperity. Additionally, it ranks tenth for longest lifespan. According to one ranking that compiles information based on sources such as the *CIA World Factbook*, Israel is among the top 20 states worldwide in terms of the military's strength and size. See "Vital Statistics: Latest Population Statistics for Israel," Jewish Virtual Library, https://www.jewishvirtuallibrary.org/latest-population-statistics-for-israel; "Gross Domestic Product 2021," World Bank, https://databank.worldbank.org/data/download/GDP.pdf; "Israel Population," Worldometer, https://www.worldometers.info/world-population/israel-population/; "Israel," Legatum Institute, https://www.prosperity.com/globe/israel; "Life Expectancy at Birth," Knoema.com, https://knoema.com/atlas/ranks/Life-expectancy; "2021 Military Strength," GlobalFirepower.com, https://www.globalfirepower.com/country-military-strength-detail.php?country_id=israel.

[15] See my previous note. Outside of Israel, the vast majority of the world's Jewish population lives in the United States (38.8%), followed distantly by France (3.1%), Canada (2.7%), and the UK (2.0%). See "Vital Statistics: Jewish Population of the World," Jewish Virtual Library, https://www.jewishvirtuallibrary.org/jewish-population-of-the-world#region. And, as Chapter 3, section 4 demonstrated, these states contain a significant range of valuable material, political, and way-of life options.

identity-group members and thereby selecting against Jewish people (among others) would likely not degrade them.

A clear example might be if India were to favor the admission of Hindu Indians. Hindu Indians enjoy a relatively secure status around the world, including in terms of how they are regarded by others. India's economic growth may certainly be either an indication or part cause of this.[16] But, in addition, note that outside of India, many Hindu Indians occupy leadership roles in both business and politics in wealthy states (including the United States, the UK, and Australia) and generally seem to enjoy a considerably higher social status in comparison with many other racial or ethnic minorities in those states.[17] Because of their global status, and because of the comparatively valuable life options in India, especially in comparison with other states in the region,[18] India's favoring the admission of Hindus qua Hindus would likely contribute to the relative vulnerability of groups that already face, say, significant material or political disadvantages, particularly within the shared region (more on this soon). More importantly, it would also likely degrade certain vulnerable groups, such as the Bengalis, because of the history and current context of Hindu-Muslim relations—more specifically,

---

[16] For instance, India is one of the fastest-growing economies in the world. As of 2018, it ranked seventh among states globally in share of world GDP and thirteenth in share of total world exports. Its 2019 GDP was calculated to be US$2.871 trillion, and, in recent years, it has enjoyed a roughly 7–8% rate of growth. Additionally, it has made substantial progress in combatting absolute poverty, lifting more than 90 million people out of extreme poverty during the period 2011–15 and shrinking the extremely poor's population share from 21.6% in 2011 to 13.4% in 2015. See "Percent of World GDP—Country Rankings," GlobalEconomy.com, https://www.theglobaleconomy.com/rankings/gdp_share/; GlobalEconomy.com. "Percent of World Exports - Country Rankings," GlobalEconomy.com, https:// www.theglobaleconomy.com/rankings/share_world_exports/; "GDP Growth (Annual %)—India," World Bank, https://data.worldbank.org/indicator/NY.GDP.MKTP.KD.ZG?locations=IN; "India Overview," World Bank, https://www.worldbank.org/en/country/india/overview.

[17] Consider their success in the USA, for instance. In 2021, the most popular and successful startups are Robinhood, Clubhouse, and Instacart, all of which were founded by Indian Americans. The number of billion-dollar startups founded by Indian Americans is considerably higher than that for any other non-native group (14 in comparison to eight for Canadian Americans, the next highest-ranked group). Their economic success is discussed further in Chapter 3, note 8, which also discusses comparative measures concerning their educational success. Dash, "Meet This Successful Bunch"; "Nation of Origin for Immigrant Founders of Billion Dollar Startups," Atlas, https://theatlas.com/charts/Hy3DRvRwg; Aleem, "These Statistics." Also see Vucetic, *Anglosphere*, chap. 3, 147–48; Stokes, "How Indians See."

[18] In addition to its economic success (see note 16), its literacy rate for youth (15 to 24 years of age) is considered successful for a country of its diversity and size (the literacy rate in 2018 was 92%). It also has a stable business environment that facilitates new enterprises and has a relatively effective government, with fairly substantial checks on power that inhibit corruption. In contrast, nearby Pakistan's youth literacy rate is much lower; Pakistan also has far less stable business and government environments, and it is ranked 140th out of 167 states in terms of its economy's potential to generate wealth. Though not as stark, similar comparisons can be seen with Bangladesh. See "Literacy Rate, Youth Total (% of People Ages 15–24)—India," World Bank, https://data.worldbank.org/indicator/SE. ADT.1524.LT.ZS?locations=IN&view=chart; "India," Legatum Institute, https://www.prosperity.com/ globe/india; "Literacy Rate, Youth Total (% of People Ages 15–24)—Pakistan," World Bank, https:// data.worldbank.org/indicator/SE.ADT.1524.LT.ZS?locations=PK&view=chart; "Pakistan," Legatum Institute, https://www.prosperity.com/globe/pakistan; "Bangladesh," Legatum Institute, https://www. prosperity.com/globe/bangladesh.

hostility toward the Bengali population living in India.[19] Thus, a policy favoring Hindus would almost certainly violate the primary duties with respect to certain groups. But, in the absence of any objectionable relations between Hindus and Jewish people, India's policy would not degrade Jewish people.[20] In contrast, if some European state were to favor the admission of Christians, then given the history and social context of massive injustices toward Jewish people in certain parts of Europe, that policy would most likely express a demeaning message about Jewish people and further compromise the social bases of their self-respect.

Often, as in the previous example, region and dimension of (dis)advantage can interact in ways that have consequences for antidiscrimination duties. Polynesians provide another example. Consider again the history of policies such as White Australia, which, rooted in the belief that whites were superior to other races, was designed to exclude nonwhites from Australia.[21] Against this sort of background, Polynesians' disadvantages in terms of self-respect are likely considerably amplified in the context of social relations in the South Pacific area.[22] Since Polynesians are also extremely vulnerable in material, political, and way-of-life terms,[23] the implication might not be that Polynesians are only further disadvantaged when secure admitting groups in that region favor their own groups. But the fact that Polynesians' disadvantages in self-respect terms may be largely dependent on the social context in one region of the world does plausibly suggest that an admitting group explicitly favoring the admission of others in their group degrades Polynesians if it is done by, say, Australia or New Zealand, but not if done by, say, Italy or Germany. More generally, the bar for establishing that the relevant Australian or New Zealand policy degrades Polynesians may be much lower and, as we'll see in the next chapter, carries implications for less direct immigration policies that might affect Polynesians.

4.2 The Admitting Group

What if the admitting group's vulnerability varies either across region or across the dimension of (dis)advantage or both? How might this affect whether an immigration policy favoring the admission of its own group violates the primary

---

[19] On the recent citizenship tests implemented in India's Assam state, which is heavily populated by Bengali Muslims, see, for instance, Raj and Gettleman, "Mass Citizenship Check"; BBC, "What's Happening in Assam?"

[20] Moreover, while Jewish people (along with all other non-Hindu groups) would be disadvantaged in life-option terms by the policy, that in itself would not be likely to even contribute to their global vulnerability since their global vulnerability specifically pertains to the social bases of their self-respect and not to material or political disadvantages.

[21] See Wellman, "Freedom of Association," 140.   [22] See Chapter 3, section 4.

[23] As demonstrated in Chapter 3, section 4 (especially notes 40–43), they face considerable climate change-related obstacles and risks and are among the most vulnerable people in the world in terms of health and poverty.

duties? Let's first consider the dimension of (dis)advantage. Though it may depend on further empirical research, it is not clear how, on their own, material disadvantages would be reduced or meaningfully addressed by selective immigration favoring one's group.[24] At the very least, there are likely numerous alternative strategies for bolstering a group's material position in the world, including cultivating (more) avenues for global trade, developing the sorts of domestic institutions that reduce poverty (stable property rights, legally enforced trade, and commerce[25]), and perhaps also gaining greater representation, voting power, and agenda-setting power in international organizations.[26] These are not easy strategies, but they represent meaningful, and likely far more effective, alternatives to selective immigration. And because of these potentially better routes for remedying a group's material disadvantages, the rationale for immigration favoring the group is likely unsupported and thus most plausibly reflects efforts on the part of the admitting group to selectively exclude a particular group or groups—especially those with high emigration rates to the state (an issue I discuss below). None of this means, however, that material disadvantages are irrelevant to understanding whether the primary duties are violated, for as numerous examples in this chapter show, they can certainly impact whether an *excluded* group is degraded in some instance.

In contrast to material disadvantages, disadvantages in the social bases of self-respect and in way-of-life terms, especially in combination, appear to present the clearest rationales for selective immigration. In Chapter 3, we saw that selective immigration favoring other Navajo seems important for securing their cultural and spiritual practices and sense of empowerment in the world, and we saw that Israel's favoring of the admission of Jewish people supports the idea of a place where Jews always have secure membership. Moreover, it isn't obvious that there are plausible alternative routes to selective immigration for effectively addressing these disadvantages. These are again largely empirical matters. But consider Israel's LoR. Under the rationale that it bolsters the self-respect of Jewish people by providing them assurance that there will always be a place where they can feel at home, it's unclear how an alternative to an immigration policy could achieve this. It's certainly not obvious how economic or political measures alone could do this. But even with respect to the idea of secure membership in a state, the sense that they might have a home in multiple states or in another state is not, it seems, primarily achievable by Jewish people as a group; rather, it involves action mainly by other groups.

However, that there is a clear rationale supporting immigration favoring one's group does not mean that *any* immigration policy doing so avoids violating the

---

[24] However, it may be unlikely that many groups are vulnerable *only* in this sense.
[25] North, *Institutions*; Acemoglu and Robinson, "Unbundling Institutions"; Acemoglu and Robinson, *Why Nations Fail*.
[26] See Fasulo, *Insider's Guide*; Bretton Woods Project, *IMF and World Bank*.

primary duties. In the case of LoR, for the same reasons (discussed in Chapter 3) that it seems to degrade Israel's Palestinian members—namely, they are highly globally and (in Israel) domestically vulnerable along multiple dimensions, they themselves lack secure membership, and there has been a contentious and violent history between Jewish people and Palestinians—it seems that it degrades Palestinian *nonmembers*. But there are two additional reasons, one of which— Palestinians' emigration rates to Israel—will be discussed shortly. The other reason is that there seem to be suitable alternative immigration policies that would protect the idea of a place where Jewish people are always welcomed and yet contribute far less to the vulnerability of Palestinians (whether Israel's members or nonmembers). Consider, for instance, a policy that grants Jewish people automatic membership but also does the same for a limited number of Palestinians. Since Israel's retaining of its status as a Jewish-majority state may be important for the idea of secure membership for Jewish people, perhaps Israel does not have a duty to implement a policy granting any and *all* Palestinians the right of return. But we could imagine numerous other policy designs, such as numerical limits on automatic Palestinian membership or prioritizing membership to either Palestinians who have urgent needs or those living in East Jerusalem.[27] Such policies could protect LoR's original rationale while also signaling to Palestinian members and nonmembers alike that they are not *unwelcome* in Israel and that addressing their vulnerable status is important to Israel's Jewish members, diminishing the policy's potential to wrong Palestinians (both Israel's members and nonmembers). Thus, both because Palestinians in the region are vulnerable along multiple dimensions and because such alternative policies seem available to Israel, LoR (in its current form) seems in violation of the primary duties.

I've just discussed how disadvantages in self-respect terms combined with disadvantages in way-of-life terms can present a clear rationale for immigration favoring one's group (though not necessarily any policy designed to do so). To see the importance of the combination of these disadvantages, consider Arabs: again, as (predominantly) Muslims, they have been comparatively vulnerable in self-respect terms, but we also saw in Chapter 3 that Arabs undoubtedly have significant global economic and political power and access to numerous important opportunities in a variety of states.[28] So if, say, the United Arab Emirates were to implement a policy favoring the admission of Arabs qua Arabs, the policy would disadvantage many vulnerable groups—compared with a fairly powerful group— with respect to valuable life options. More relevantly, because Arabs are domestically dominant in a number of (wealthy) states,[29] and thus do not have a vulnerable

---

[27] See Baskin, "Israel Should Give."   [28] See my discussion in Chapter 3, especially section 3.
[29] For instance, six Arab-majority states count among the 30 richest states in the world in per capita terms, with Qatar the single richest. And, in total, Arabs constitute the majority in 22 states around the world. See Ventura, "Richest Countries"; "Population Total—Arab World," World Bank, https://data.worldbank.org/indicator/SP.POP.TOTL?locations=1A&most_recent_value_desc=false.

way of life, it would be implausible to interpret the policy as aiming to secure their status in any sense. Because any rationale for securing their status would seem unsupported, the policy is more likely to degrade certain vulnerable groups, especially those who have experienced a history of tremendous injustice within the region, such as the Kurds,[30] and those with high emigration to Arab states (more soon).

Finally, consider again the case of Japan's policy, discussed in Chapter 3, that favored the admission of other Japanese people that applied for immigration. While the Japanese people may be globally disadvantaged in the sense of facing a rapidly declining population and thus potentially in terms of a compromised way of life, they are quite advantaged in global economic terms and do not seem disadvantaged in self-respect terms,[31] and, relatedly, have access to valuable life options in the state of Japan.[32] In such a case, even if it is plausible to interpret the immigration policy as aiming to secure their way of life, the policy would likely still serve to contribute to the comparative disadvantages of at least *certain* excluded vulnerable groups—for starters, those groups that have far less access to important life options. But more importantly, as suggested in the previous case involving Arabs, the question of which groups of nonmembers may be degraded might turn on whether they are located in the same region.[33] In Japan's case, the immigration policy may well degrade certain groups, including Filipinos, because of the historical and current context of Japanese-Filipino relations, especially Japan's previous wartime crimes and atrocities committed against Filipinos.[34]

---

[30] As in the case of Polynesians, it's likely that Kurds' disadvantages in terms of self-respect are considerably more compromised in the region, considering the background of injustice against Kurds by other groups in the region. Additionally, though Kurds make up the fourth-largest ethnic group in the Middle East, they do not have their own state. See Human Rights Watch, *Group Denial*; Reuters, "Factbox"; BBC News, "Who Are the Kurds?"

[31] For instance, Japan's per capita wealth is among the top 30 in the world, making the average Japanese person relatively prosperous. After the United States and China, Japan has the largest share of millionaires in the world. Japanese people enjoy success in many wealthy states apart from Japan. For instance, the 2018 annual median income for Japanese Americans was $74,000 while the national average was $63,100. And in 2018, Asians had the highest SAT scores. (Although this education data also includes Han Chinese and Indians, we saw [in Chapter 3] that Han Chinese and [above] that Indians are similarly globally advantaged.) See "Projected GDP Ranking," *Statistics Times*, https://statisticstimes.com/economy/projected-world-gdp-ranking.php; "Population Distribution in Japan in 2018, by Wealth Range," Statista, https://www.statista.com/statistics/684329/japan-population-distribution-by-wealth-range/; *Economist*, "Millions of Millionaires"; National Community Reinvestment Coalition, *Racial Wealth Snapshot*; "Fast Facts: SAT Scores," National Center for Education Statistics, https://nces.ed.gov/fastfacts/display.asp?id=171.

[32] For instance, Japan has the third-largest economy in the world, one of the best health care systems in the world (second best, according to one ranking) and the second- or third-longest lifespan. It also has an equitable and highly respectable education system. See FocusEconomics, "Top 5 Largest Economies"; "GDP Ranked by Country 2021," World Population Review, https://worldpopulationreview.com/countries/countries-by-gdp; Legatum Institute, https://docs.prosperity.com/9016/0508/7373/Japan_2020_PIcountryprofile.pdf, esp. 13; "Japan Life Expectancy 1950–2021," Macrotrends, https://www.macrotrends.net/countries/JPN/japan/life-expectancy.

[33] Note that in terms of wealth and economic freedom, Japan is ranked sixth among 40 countries in the Asia-Pacific region. Heritage Foundation, "Japan."

[34] See Mydans, "Japanese Veteran Writes"; McCarthy, "World War II Sex Slaves."

4.3 The Role of Shared Region

Prompted by many of the previous examples, it might seem that the admitting and excluded groups' being in the same region is almost always morally relevant when considering policies in which the admitting group favors its own racial or ethnic group. In particular, shared region might always seem relevant for understanding whether some excluded group is degraded. For instance, to take a different example, it does seem that a policy favoring the admission of whites in the United States would very likely degrade say, Hispanics, but it is much less obvious that it would do so to, say, the Uyghurs, an ethnic Turkic group predominantly living in Northwest China, or the Bahai, adherents of a faith with strong roots in Iran and parts of the Middle East. The short answer is that shared region does often make a difference—whether directly or indirectly—and so it is likely true that the hypothetical US policy would more obviously degrade Hispanics than other groups. Indeed, it might not do so at all for such groups as the Uyghurs. But there are several issues to unpack here.

First, as seems the case for Polynesians under a New Zealand policy and Kurds under an Arab policy, a group's disadvantages may be more pronounced in a particular region, especially in self-respect terms. Unjust historical relations can be critical for determining this, as can power differences over regional institutions, organizations, and partnerships. But second, sometimes shared region tracks a different important issue: where a group's members tend to emigrate to or at least apply for admission. Before discussing the relevance of emigration rates, it seems fairly apparent why shared region is often important to where people do emigrate to. For starters, costs of travel and relocation may be appreciably lower within the shared region. Additionally, typically as a result of lower travel costs, cultural and familial ties might be considerably easier to maintain, and familiarity with the admitting state's cultural norms and practices may be greater. All of this can reduce the emotional and psychological tolls of moving to a different state.[35] Thus, given the United States' proximity to Hispanic-majority states, especially Central American states, it's not surprising that Hispanics' emigration rate to the country, compared with that of other groups, is very high.[36] But regional proximity is not always a key factor for this. Consider, for instance, the high emigration rates to the UK among people located in the Indian subcontinent, including Pakistanis,

[35] See Akhtar, "Being at Home"; Somerville, "Strategic Migrant Network Building."
[36] Between 1965 and 2015, immigration from Latin America accounted for about 51% of all immigration to the United States (Pew Research Center, "Modern Immigration Wave"), with about 25–30% coming from Mexico alone during the period 2000–2019 (Batalova, Hanna, and Levesque, "Frequently Requested Statistics"). In a 2019 Gallup poll, about 42 million people in Latin America indicated that they desired to migrate to the United States (Harper, "Gallup Research Estimate"). Since 2009, however, Asians, and not Hispanics, have represented the single largest new-migrant group in the United States (Budiman, "Key Findings").

Indians, and Bangladeshis:[37] historical relations and (often as a result) existing communities in the admitting state can be important factors apart from region for determining where people migrate to.

So why do emigration rates matter for assessing whether a state's immigration policy wrongs a particular excluded group or groups? A central reason they may appear to matter is that when numerous people in a group seek admission in the same state, any (dis)advantage differences between them and the admitting group are likely to be far more pronounced. Because of Hispanics' high emigration rates to the United States, if the United States were to have a policy favoring the admission of whites, we may be much more likely to notice and be concerned about the disadvantages of Hispanics relative to whites[38] than about any comparable differences between whites and, say, the Uyghurs. But that doesn't of course mean that there are not even more considerable (dis)advantage differences between whites and the Uyghurs.[39]

It is rather a different reason that emigration rates matter for whether a policy degrades a group. To see this, let's set aside any history of objectionable relations between the admitting and excluded groups by considering white populations and the Uyghurs (as discussed in section 6 below, there do not appear to be any objectionable social contexts concerning the two groups' interactions). If the Uyghurs are unlikely to apply for admission to, say, the United States, and subsequently there are relatively few Uyghurs present as a result, a US policy explicitly favoring other whites would not seem to, for instance, signal much, if *anything*, about the Uyghurs. However, given that Hispanics apply for admission and emigrate to the United States at a high rate, the policy would very plausibly,

---

[37] Between 2006 and 2020, migrants from South Asia (which mainly consists of the Indian subcontinent) made up roughly 95,000 to 192,000 of the roughly 248,000 to 343,000 total long-term immigrants arriving to the UK outside the EU. Kierans, *Who Migrates to UK?*

[38] A variety of measures demonstrate Hispanics' global vulnerability. For instance, Mexico, the second-largest economy in Latin America, has very poor business, government, and legal infrastructure and lacks a stable economy. Additionally, it has very little global economic and political power (*US News & World Report*, "Mexico," "Entrepreneurship" and "Power" categories). Moreover, according to the World Health Organization, its health care system, while one of the largest in Latin America, is much smaller than the developed world's (Paxson, "How Healthcare in Mexico"). Taken collectively, Central American states have an average poverty rate of 34.2% ("10 Facts about Economic Development in Central America," Borgen Project, https://borgenproject.org/10-facts-about-economic-development-in-central-america/). Collectively, Honduras, Guatemala, El Salvador, and Nicaragua have a global wealth-share of only *0.13%*, whereas (for comparison) the United States' global share of wealth is almost 21% ("Percent of World GDP—Country Rankings," GlobalEconomy. com, https://www.theglobaleconomy.com/rankings/gdp_share/). In 2019, South America, excluding Uruguay, Argentina, and Paraguay (all typically considered majority white or at least majority European descent; see, for instance, "Argentina vs. Uruguay," Index Mundi, https://www.indexmundi.com/factbook/compare/argentina.uruguay/demographics) and excluding Brazil (not considered Hispanic since its primary language is Portuguese), had a share of the world's purchasing-power-parity-adjusted GDP of only 0.541% (International Monetary Fund, *World Economic Outlook Database*).

[39] The latter are arguably some of the most vulnerable people in the world. For recent discussions, see Chan, "'I Never Thought China'"; Wong and Buckley, "U.S. Says China's Repression"; *Economist*, "Persecution of Uyghurs"; Serhan, "Saving Uighur Culture."

say, express a disparaging message about Hispanics—again, even aside from any known negative stereotypes about them and animosity toward them. Indeed, it might not be unreasonable to interpret a policy favoring whites as being motivated, at least in part, by some kind of aversion or hostility toward Hispanics or their (perceived) cultural norms and practices, further contributing to the ways in which it may degrade them.[40] Thus, while it is unlikely that the policy would degrade the Uyghurs, it would seem to clearly do this to Hispanics. And the point generalizes to other cases. Policies favoring the dominant group in the UK, India, and France, for instance, are far more likely to, say, express a demeaning message about, or further compromise the social bases of self-respect for, respectively, South Asians, Bengalis, and Berbers, compared with other groups, since these groups tend to emigrate to those states at very high rates.[41]

Before turning to discuss the implications of the analysis for other sorts of identity categories, as well as non-identity criteria (in the next chapter), I want to note again that what I have just discussed is not exhaustive or conclusive. For many of the cases examined, there may be other morally and empirically relevant issues that, if considered, would alter the normative evaluation of the case. Again, more than providing definitive answers, I hope to have provided a general framework, employing the resources of antidiscrimination norms, for examining racial and ethnic (and related) immigration policies. It may seem that the inability to conclusively evaluate cases is a flaw of the antidiscrimination approach, but I believe it is a virtue. It would be far less messy to say that racial and ethnic criteria either always wrong the excluded group(s) or never do so, but those stances seem unappealing when we consider the full range of potential cases. It certainly seems, for instance, that the original Navajo policy (in which Navajo are explicitly favored in admission) would not wrong excluded nonmembers but a version of the policy in which Arabs are explicitly disfavored would. And in many other types of cases, such as whether a policy favoring the admission of the state's dominant racial, ethnic, or religious group would wrong, say, Polynesians or Jewish people, there are numerous relevant issues to consider. Thus, it is hard to see why it would

---

[40] It may also be that if high numbers of a group apply for admission to a state and, because of the state's immigration criteria, high numbers are subsequently *rejected*, that increases the likelihood that the policy degrades them.

[41] According to the 2001 Indian Census, Bangladeshis form the largest group of migrants in India, with a population of about 3 million, beating the next-largest category of migrants (from Pakistan) by more than 2 million (Government of India, *Census of India 2001*). (Also see notes 18 and 19.) In 2018, people born in Algeria and Morocco represented roughly 25% of the total immigrant population in France ("Immigrants by Country of Birth," French Institute for Demographic Studies, https://www.ined.fr/en/everything_about_population/data/france/immigrants-foreigners/countries-birth-immigrants/#r152; "How Many Immigrants Are There in France?," French Institute for Demographic Studies, https://www.ined.fr/en/everything_about_population/demographic-facts-sheets/faq/how-many-immigrants-france/). And Algeria's and Morocco's populations are overwhelmingly of Berber origin ("Morocco Demographics Profile," Index Mundi, https://www.indexmundi.com/morocco/demographics_profile.html; "Algeria Demographics Profile," Index Mundi, https://www.indexmundi.com/algeria/demographics_profile.html).

be preferable to have one single answer in all (or even most) cases rather than an approach that stresses attention to the specific details of a case, including any potential variability in the statuses of the relevant groups, historical relations, present social contexts, and empirical facts concerning emigration rates.

5. The Primary Duties and Other Identities

In this section, we'll expand the discussion to the other central categories of identity groups—in particular, groups based on gender, sex, sexual orientation, and disability. Given the above analysis of racial and ethnic (and related) groups, I believe it should be fairly easy to see both how the new categories of groups have a global social status and why, under the antidiscrimination approach, states' admission decisions are morally constrained by the groups' statuses.

To begin with, it appears undeniable that there are global-status differences when it comes to these identity categories. Women have a vulnerable global status,[42] as do members of the LGBTQ+ community and people with disabilities,[43] especially visible disabilities. For each of these types of groups, their vulnerability is very widespread—without a doubt, not limited to a single state or even single region of the world. Women, for instance, make up more than two-thirds of the people in the world who lack literacy[44] and, in comparison with men, have far less access to both schooling (and education in general[45]) and a variety of medical services (often because of stigmas associated with their provision[46]), have higher rates of depression,[47] experience wide income gaps around the world (earning only about half of the annual income of men),[48] and represent only 25% of national-parliament members around the globe.[49] Similar, and often *far*-larger, disparities characterize members of the LGBTQ+ community compared with people who are cisgender, straight, or both. For instance, globally, members of

---

[42]   Also see Haslanger ('Gender and Race," 38), who makes this point.

[43]   The same might also be said of the elderly in contrast to people of working age, but I won't explore the category of age here.

[44]   See "Facts and Figures," UN Women, https://www.unwomen.org/en/news/in-focus/commission-on-the-status-of-women-2012/facts-and-figures, in section titled "Education."

[45]   See UNICEF, "Girls' Education," under section titled "Why Are Girls Out of School?"

[46]   These include abortions and infections associated with women's reproductive organs. See World Health Organization, "Maternal Mortality," under "Why Do Women Die?"; Harvard Medical School, "Urinary Tract Infection."

[47]   The rate for women is 8.7%, as compared with 5.3% for men. See "Women and Mental Health," US Department of Health and Human Services, National Institute of Mental Health, https://www.nimh.nih.gov/health/topics/women-and-mental-health/index.shtml, in section titled "Prevalence of Major Depressive Episode Among Adults."

[48]   See Hutt, "Equal Pay at Work," in section titled "A Small Step Back."

[49]   See "Facts and Figures: Women's Leadership and Political Participation," UN Women, https://www.unwomen.org/en/what-we-do/leadership-and-political-participation/facts-and-figures, in section titled "Women in National Parliaments."

the LGBTQ+ community are more than twice as likely to have mental health disorders[50] and four times more likely to commit suicide.[51] Of those who identify as lesbian, gay, or bisexual, it is estimated that more than 80% do not disclose their orientation at all, which can lead to significant mental health issues.[52] According to the World Bank, the LGBTQ+ community is overrepresented in the bottom of the world's population in measures such as unemployment, education, and health.[53] Finally, members of that community are far more likely to suffer from violence and various forms of hostility and discrimination.[54] State-sanctioned violence against them is not uncommon, as seventy-six states criminalize same-sex sexual relations with penalties that can include fines, several years of imprisonment, and even execution.[55] Last but not least, as we will see, people with disabilities are also substantially globally disadvantaged along important dimensions.

Let me clarify that these categories are highly heterogeneous. This applies most obviously to disability and LGBTQ+. For instance, people with physical disabilities face different sorts of obstacles from those with cognitive disabilities, and even within these subgroups there is of course substantial variation depending on the specific type of disability one has, the challenges one might face, and how others interact with and respond to them. And a similar point certainly applies to members of the LGBTQ+ community. Thus, I don't mean to suggest that people in these identity categories are all disadvantaged in the same way or to the same extent. My only point is to observe that all the above types of groups are globally vulnerable in significant ways, as compared to their cognate groups. And because of these status-differences, we can straightforwardly see how the primary duties can be extended to these identity groups—though, as we will see soon, what this means for whether, and when, states may exclude some group is a complicated matter. Let's start by continuing the previous section's focus on explicit *favoring* of a cognate group in immigration decisions.

---

[50] American Psychiatric Association, "Lesbian, Gay, Bisexual, Transgender."

[51] American Psychiatric Association, *Mental Health Disparities*, under "Mental Health Status and Disparities."

[52] See Poitras, "'Global Closet' Is Huge." Revealing their identities can often harm their educational prospects. For instance, it's estimated that between about half and two-thirds of LGBTIQ+ youth experience bullying in childhood, causing one in three students to skip school days or leave school altogether. See Plan International, "LGBTIQ+ Inclusion."

[53] See Hammond, "We Need to Fight Homophobia," in section titled "Tears and Dollars: The Many Repercussions of Homophobia and Transphobia."

[54] For instance, according to the Organization of American States' Inter-American Commission on Human Rights ("IACHR Expresses Concern"), LGBTQ+ members suffer significant harm and violence. And, across 62 states, 1,612 transgender people were murdered between 2008 and 2014. See Plan International, "LGBTIQ+ Inclusion." It's hard to know the significance of this, given that so many LGBTQ+ members do not disclose their identities. To read more about the numerous tragic examples of violence and murder against, especially, trans people, see "Transgender," Human Rights Campaign, https://www.hrc.org/news?topic=transgender; "LGBT Rights," Human Rights Campaign, https://www.hrw.org/topic/lgbt-rights.

[55] See Moagi, "Mental Health Challenges," in "Introduction."

The clearest implications seem to concern women and members of the LGBTQ+ community. It appears obvious that if a state were to explicitly favor people in a cognate group—such as a state that explicitly favors either men or cisgender people—this would almost always violate the primary duties. Importantly, the analysis in the previous section can help us understand why, aside from rare circumstances,[56] it makes little to no difference whether the admitting group is itself vulnerable, even significantly so, along any of the relevant dimensions (material, political, way of life, or self-respect). For instance, imagine that a Kurdish-majority state explicitly favors the admission of men. If we imagine that the value of the life options in this state is reflective of the Kurdish people's current material and political disadvantages, this policy might not do much to exacerbate any material or political disadvantages faced by women globally. But since the policy is likely not best interpreted as an attempt by Kurds to secure their way of life or bolster the social bases of their self-respect (barring rare circumstances[57])—and given historical and current widespread practices treating women in inferior ways to men around the world and, more narrowly, in the region—the policy would degrade women (and maybe others[58]).

The most difficult and complicated questions, however, concern people who have disabilities since this category prompts questions related to what costs a state is required to bear. In particular, one might think that because of concerns about the costs of providing adequate health resources and social or economic services, a state is permitted to explicitly favor people who do not have (at least certain) disabilities. I should state up front that I do not have a fully formed view on this issue given what I believe to be its deep complexities—many of which we will discuss. But even for considering the question, it's important to unbundle a variety of factors.

First, although there can undoubtedly be overlap, we should distinguish between people who have a disability from those who have a deleterious health condition, such as diabetes, lower respiratory infections, lung disease, heart or liver disease, or cancer. As this is a very complicated issue that has garnered considerable debate,[59] I can only briefly touch on it here, and much of what I say is liable to revision. But it is important to dwell on this issue for a moment—for its

---

[56] For instance, imagine if for some reason the vast majority of births over an extended period were female, and the state wanted to attract males to keep the population from rapidly declining so as to perpetuate its vulnerable way of life. Given this particular context, the policy may not degrade women.

[57] See previous note.

[58] Depending on other factors and the social context, it could also do these things to LGBTQ+ individuals.

[59] For some of this work, see Shakespeare, *Disability Rights and Wrongs*; Wasserman, et al., "Disability"; Wendell, "Unhealthy Disabled"; Murphy, "Concepts of Disease"; Boorse, "Concepts of Health"; Amundson, "Disability, Handicap, and Environment"; Becker, *Habilitation, Health, and Agency*; Howard and Aas, "On Valuing Impairment." Even in the domestic context of antidiscrimination, determining whether someone has a health condition or (also) has a disability is a very complicated matter. See Khaitan, *Theory of Discrimination Law*, 173.

own sake and for its implications for topics discussed in the next chapter. One general observation is that it seems intuitive that while people with disabilities often (though not always) constitute identity groups, people who have the types of diseases or illnesses mentioned above typically do not. As we saw in Chapter 2, two central factors determine what counts as an identity characteristic versus a mere (ascribed) trait or characteristic: the characteristic is socially salient, or shapes interaction across a wide range of social contexts; and it is important to how one develops values and a conception of the good (and often to one's self-understanding).

Health conditions might not typically be like this, especially when considering the global context. To clarify, many health conditions make the people who have them significantly globally vulnerable along certain dimensions, perhaps especially in material terms (which, recall, are broadly construed and include resources such as health care). However, they might not generally constitute identity groups. Consider, for instance, how those with cancer seem to typically view it with detachment; notably, they seem to regard it as something to overcome. More importantly, the types of illnesses mentioned above are not visible in the ways that many disabilities are, since their occurrence does not typically provoke (especially, negative) reactive attitudes from others, such as the perception that the individual is "deformed," flawed, or subhuman, and, relatedly, might not prompt feelings like shame. For these sorts of reasons, many illnesses might not be relevant to the structure of our global social interactions across a wide spectrum of relations. Thus, to say that a state's primary duties extend to people with disabilities does not necessarily mean that it applies to all health conditions.[60] The result is that the range of potential morally prohibited criteria is likely restricted a great deal.

What I've just said concerns the primary duties and, more broadly, any duties to not exclude identity groups. But it may seem that this discussion reveals a deep flaw within the antidiscrimination approach. In particular, one might wonder why, if the people who have health conditions are significantly disadvantaged, it matters that those conditions might not qualify as identity characteristics. Put differently, why does it make a difference whether disadvantage attaches to identity-group membership rather than to any individual as such? To answer this question, we need to briefly return to several issues discussed in Chapter 2 and alluded to at the beginning of this chapter. I believe it's worth doing this, not only for its relevance for analyzing disabilities and health conditions, but also for thinking about topics such as disproportionate disadvantage, taken up in the next chapter.

In Chapter 2, we saw that what ultimately matters from the standpoint of antidiscrimination is avoiding contributing to a group's vulnerability in the specific senses that relate to the moral relations involved in subordination—namely, treating or regarding the group as morally inferior. This is mainly why

---

[60] Whether it does so depends on whether such groups form identity groups and, moreover, have *global* social salience as identity groups.

degradation and not comparably reduced opportunities seems central to whether selective exclusion wrongs a group. While comparatively denying important opportunities to a group that is relatively disadvantaged in, say, significant material terms might further contribute to its disadvantages, it does not necessarily treat the group in ways resembling, or prompting concerns about, treating or regarding the group as morally inferior. In contrast, if a group's selective exclusion also expresses a demeaning message about it, (further) compromises the social bases of its self-respect, or perpetuates any stigmas against it, the exclusion directly involves such relations.

And here is where the emphasis on identity groups matters. We have seen that if it is a vulnerable identity group that is comparatively denied options, this can often degrade it,[61] especially if there is a past or current practice of marginalizing the group or a history of scorn or prejudice against them. Indeed, as discussed in Chapter 2, these are central reasons that particular characteristics *become* socially salient and important to the way individuals who have them form and pursue values in the first place. However, insofar as an illness such as cancer or heart disease is not relevant to the structure of our global social interactions across a wide spectrum of relations, it may not generally influence how others perceive people with the illness or serve as the basis for attributing certain qualities to the people who have it and for responding to them in particular ways. If so, then while being selectively excluded from valuable life options on the basis of having such an illness can certainly exacerbate a person's disadvantages (especially material disadvantages such as access to health care), it may not typically do so in a way that ranks them as morally inferior.

Moreover, at this point it will be useful to note that in the next chapter, I will discuss why states have independent obligations—independent, that is, from any antidiscrimination duties—to assist a substantial number of people, either in their current locations or, if this is not feasible, by admitting them. This includes any person whose basic human rights are not being protected in their home states— that is, not only those who are persecuted or oppressed but also those who are disadvantaged by such conditions as institutional incapacity or deep poverty. And this applies to people with health conditions as well as disabilities. If someone with either an illness or disability is deprived of their basic human rights, other states have an obligation to assist them. Focusing only on disabilities, a variety of indicators show that people who have them experience persecution, violence, and death at a disproportionate rate.[62] And of people living below the international poverty line, the percentage of people with disabilities is higher than—in

---

[61] See Khaitan's related discussion on expressive salience, *Theory of Discrimination Law*, 171–76.

[62] See the following informative resources: World Health Organization, *State of the Art*; United Nations, *Toolkit on Disability*; "Developmental Disability across Cultures," Caring for Kids New to Canada, https://www.kidsnewtocanada.ca/mental-health/developmental-disability; American Civil Liberties Union, "Solitary Confinement's Devastating Harm"; Maqbool, "Don't Shoot, I'm Disabled."

some states, double—that of those without disabilities.[63] Thus, states will have obligations toward a good many people with either an illness or disability independently of antidiscrimination concerns.

What I have just said does not of course have any bearing on the issue of discretionary migrants—which again refers to migrants who do not have urgent or special claims for admission—and so there may be a variety of lingering concerns about discretionary migrants with either health conditions or disabilities as well as about such migrants who face disadvantages more generally. I will examine, in broad outline, whether states have admissions-related obligations with respect to health and other disadvantages in the next chapter, but for now I will continue with the discussion of disabilities.

So, setting aside nondiscretionary migrants who have disabilities, we still face the question whether states may exclude people with disabilities on that basis because of cost and resource considerations. To address this question, we must first get clear on whether, and to what extent, disabilities in fact raise significant concerns about costs and resources. For starters, a crucial point is that many disabilities do *not* impose heavy costs on the state. Assuming that deafness, blindness, and dwarfism, for instance, count as disabilities,[64] people with those conditions live autonomous and independent lives without requiring much, if any, particular state support.[65] Second, once we restrict the scope of disabilities to include only those that compromise independent living, we must still recognize that it is far from obvious that people with (the restricted set of) disabilities would impose *net* costs on the admitting state—that is, costs over and above what they contribute through their productivity and payment of taxes. Third, it is relevant to consider whether any of the admitting state's current members have a disability that requires similar accommodations—but not just because of concerns about wronging disfavored members. From a relational-equality perspective it is easy to justify the idea that states have duties to accommodate their current members who have disabilities, such as by investing in certain infrastructure (for instance, wheelchair ramps) and by offering a range of supportive health and social services.[66] Not doing so may treat someone with a disability as not capable of being a participating member of society. So, either the infrastructure and services

---

[63] https://documents-dds-ny.un.org/doc/UNDOC/GEN/N20/188/87/PDF/N2018887.pdf? OpenElement. The problem is not limited to developing nations. For instance, in the United States, about 26% of people with disabilities lived in poverty, while 10.7% of people without disabilities lived in poverty (Institute on Disability, "Power of Statistics"). In general, according to the World Bank, about 20% of the poorest people in the world have a disability (Disabled World, "Disability Statistics"). But this figure may greatly underestimate the true percentage since people in many states are reluctant to admit that they have a disability because of stigma and fear of shame being brought upon their families.

[64] For instance, the deaf community might not describe itself as being disabled, but the relevant point is to distinguish traits such as deafness that figure prominently (and positively) in one's identity from traits such as cancer that typically don't.

[65] See, for instance, European Parliament, "Assistive Technologies."

[66] See Anderson, "What Is the Point?" esp. 334–35.

are already in place, or the state may have an obligation to incur the costs to provide them for existing members.[67] Either way, the point here is that in many cases it might not impose *additional* (or marginal) costs if a state accepts people with a particular disability.

The general idea of the previous three points is that if admitting people with some disability does *not* impose a net marginal cost on the state, selecting against people with that disability on the basis of their disability would straightforwardly violate the primary duties. For the immigration policy may then be interpreted as motivated by disparaging attitudes, or at the very least it may suggest that the state or its members have failed to adequately and honestly consider the relevant concerns about costs, signaling dismissiveness or disregard toward people with the disability.

But what if there *are* legitimate and significant costs a state would have to incur by admitting people with a disability? One might think that the situation would resemble that of selecting against particular health conditions: selecting against people with the disability (on that basis) would likely contribute to their comparative disadvantages in terms of the life options in the admitting state, but it would not typically violate the primary duties. The thinking here is similar to that in evaluating cases in which a vulnerable racial or ethnic group excludes others on the basis of race or ethnicity; if the rationale can be reasonably interpreted as, for instance, protecting a vulnerable way of life or as important for helping restore the group's self-respect, then it is far less likely to degrade any excluded groups. Similarly, if it is plausible to interpret the rationale for excluding people on the basis of certain disabilities as a concern about the significant costs of admitting them, then, one might think, excluding them might not, say, express a demeaning message about them or further compromise the social bases of their self-respect.

As with the more general topic of how to think about selectively excluding people with disabilities, I'm very uncertain about this suggestion. First of all, much depends on how significant is the proportion of a state's resources (or budget) that would be employed as a result of admitting a person (or people) with the particular disability, and here the difference between rich and poor states may be critical. Consider, for instance, Liberia which has an admission policy that explicitly excludes people with disabilities.[68] Since it is a developing state, and arguably still recovering, both politically and financially, from a second civil war, the policy can readily be interpreted as indicating that the state lacks the capacity to accommodate the health needs of many with disabilities. In general, members of states that are already at, or, especially, far beyond, resource and institutional capacity may well be globally vulnerable in material terms themselves. If so, the

---

[67] For a more detailed and systematic argument along these lines, see MacKay, "Immigration Selection."

[68] For discussion of its policy, see Tannenbaum et al., "Aliens and Nationality Law," 9.

scenario may resemble that of a state whose members' self-respect, say, is significantly disadvantaged in the sense of plausibly constituting a rationale (for the relevant immigration criteria) that would not signal that the excluded nonmembers are considered or regarded as inferior in any sense.

On the other hand, one of the central stigmas attached to people with disabilities is that they are burdens on others.[69] This is, I believe, especially relevant for considering wealthy states' immigration policies. Take Canada. In addition to restrictions based on safety and public health concerns, a relatively recent act in Canada restricts the permanent admission of people with health conditions (including disabilities) who "might reasonably be expected to cause excessive demand on health or social services."[70] And Australia and New Zealand have similar restrictions. In Canada, as of 2022, the cost limit applied for admitting someone with a disability was $24,057 per year, and this figure included all expected health care costs.[71] It's hard to know just how large of a percentage of the state's resources the corresponding figure would represent for the total number of people with disabilities who annually apply for admission to Canada.[72] Given Canada's overall wealth, it may be the case that the annual figure does not represent a relatively large demand on the state's budget and, moreover, that that portion of the budget would not otherwise be devoted to helping to satisfy the basic rights of people (in Canada or outside it), to security or defense, to addressing environmental concerns, or to providing the needed resources for securing the conditions of relational equality among the state's members. These are speculations, not least because it's difficult to get a complete financial picture. But something that is less speculative is that Canada's annual cost limit for admitting a person with a disability does not seem to take into consideration an individual's contributions to the state, whether economic or otherwise.[73] In this and other cases involving very wealthy states when the immigration policy does not consider a disabled person's contributions, explicit criteria selecting against people with disabilities—one of the most vulnerable groups around the world—would seem to perpetuate highly damaging stigmas about them, clearly violating the states' primary duties.

6. Antidiscrimination, Not Corrective Justice

Before ending this chapter, this is a good place to discuss how the approach in this book is not fundamentally a response to past injustice or one that stresses duties to

---

[69] United Nations, *Toolkit on Disability*; World Health Organization, *State of the Art.*
[70] Immigration and Refugee Protection Act, Provision 38 (1)(C), https://laws.justice.gc.ca/eng/acts/i-2.5/page-9.html#docCont; Government of Canada, "Program Delivery Update."
[71] Government of Canada, *Excessive Demand.*
[72] In part, this is because I am unable to find data on how many people with disabilities are admitted annually.
[73] See note 67.

correct for past wrongs. There are several reasons for this. For starters, efforts to establish duties to correct for past wrongs encounter deep theoretical difficulties. For instance, if the position is that only responsible parties have corrective duties to groups wronged in the past to, say, admit them, then the various methods of identifying responsibility—for example, by establishing who is culpable or who benefits—encounter significant challenges,[74] as do the different ways of determining the relevant baseline for assessing harm or loss or for assessing benefit.[75] Even if these issues can be worked out, corrective duties might not suggest any particular form of remedy, or, perhaps more accurately, they may imply that any number of potential remedies are morally appropriate responses to the injustices committed against some group. If so, then as long as the relevant corrective duties are being discharged in some way, we may have significant difficulty explaining why the *selective exclusion* of some group is wrong.[76] For example, consider again Racial Ban, where an all-white state explicitly disfavors the admission of Black people. Even if we were to establish that the state's members shoulder the relevant corrective duties to (at least some subgroups of) Black people, we would need to determine the best way to discharge those duties. And it is at least possible that, say, fostering trade relationships on terms that are favorable to them or helping to bolster institutions in their home states would be viable options (maybe preferable ones). But if the corrective duties are discharged in those ways, it's not obvious that it would be wrong for that state to simultaneously block Black people from admission—a very unsettling result.[77] Moreover, as we saw with multiple examples in sections 3 and 4, it's not just that when some particular state explicitly disfavors some vulnerable group that it wrongs the excluded nonmembers, but that if virtually any state were to explicitly disfavor a vulnerable group, it would likely wrong that group—i.e., even states that bear no responsibility for past injustices against that group or otherwise have corrective duties toward them. For instance, we saw that if an all-Navajo state were to explicitly disfavor Arabs,

---

[74] For some of these challenges, see Lippert-Rasmussen, "Affirmative Action," 75.

[75] Though he argues that many such issues can be resolved, see the view outlined in Butt, *Rectifying International Injustice*, esp. chap. 4.

[76] An exception might be if the excluding state illegitimately acquired territory from the ancestors of those they wish to exclude. For then it would look more plausible that the *particular* means of addressing past wrongs would be related to admission to the territory. However, given the other challenges facing corrective accounts that I discuss in the next paragraph, especially moral concerns about current claims to property, it still seems a strong case could be made that the state should rectify the illegitimate property acquisition through distributing resources rather than attempting to distribute the territory in question to the descendants of those wronged. If so, then under such accounts, it seems plausible that as long as the state is making good on past wrongs in other ways, selectively excluding the descendants might not wrong them.

[77] Butt (*Rectifying International Injustice*) suggests there are two primary sorts of corrective duties (which he calls "rectificatory" duties): seeking to undo or reverse the act (as with giving back stolen property) and paying compensation (for example, see 176–77). It seems both sorts of duties could be satisfied and a state (such as that in Racial Ban) could retain its objectionable immigration policy.

that would almost certainly wrong Arabs, but the explanation for why would not have anything to do with the Navajo having wronged Arabs.

Aside from determining the responsibility for and content of any corrective duties, attempting to correct for past injustices encounters concerns stemming from the passage of time regarding whether, and if so how, we should attach a sort of discount rate to past injustices.[78] If it is appropriate to discount past wrongs, then it looks more difficult to justify, say, the hypothetical Navajo policy since many of the primary injustices against the Navajo people were committed some time ago.

In contrast, antidiscrimination based in the idea of relational equality does not face these same difficulties. The reason—and this is the key point—is that it is not a purely backward-looking framework that aims to repair past wrongs but is instead concerned with current social status. If anything, it is particularly forward looking, as it focuses not only on groups that presently have a subordinate status but also those that might become subordinate in the future.[79]

To be sure, determining which groups are vulnerable, in what ways and to what extent they are vulnerable, and which are at risk of becoming subordinate is very tricky, and in Chapter 3 as well as this chapter I have highlighted various complexities of this approach. Thus, one might think that at the end of the day, it is a toss-up between the two strategies. But there is another reason to favor the forward-looking approach, which is that it seems to better explain the concerns, or conversely lack thereof, we might have about many kinds of immigration policies. In addition to the few examples just recalled, this can be appreciated through returning to two further examples.

First, recall that in Chapter 3 we briefly pondered the relevance of the fact that it was whites in the United States (where Navajo's white members originated) that committed the significant injustices against the Navajo, since that might have seemed important for explaining why Navajo's white members may not be wronged by the admission policy disfavoring them. For instance, one might think that their collective responsibility for those injustices forfeited their moral standing to be wronged by the Navajo (at least in certain ways) for some time.

In contrast, under the framework here, past injustices only matter incidentally—only insofar as they are related to the relevant groups' current global statuses. Imagine that instead of forming the minority in a majority-Navajo state, whites constitute the minority in a majority-Uyghur state. The Uyghurs have experienced a long history of exclusion and persecution by the Han Chinese. If the

---

[78] See the prominent discussion in Waldron, "Superseding Historic Injustice." Waldron is mainly concerned with the illegitimate taking of property and whether past claims to property should be discounted. He argues that current populations' life plans built around the expectation of continued holdings matter morally. But since we are not considering any group's right to reclaim territory, Waldron's particular focus can be set aside.

[79] See Fiss, "Equal Protection Clause," 144–46, esp. 150–51; Sunstein, "Anticaste Principle," 2433.

newly formed Uyghur state implemented an immigration policy akin to Navajo's—favoring the Uyghurs over the white minority—it would again seem that the white members would not be wronged. But their culpability in past injustices can't explain this since whites were not the offenders. Nor is it plausible that whites have benefited from the injustices committed against the Uyghurs[80] and now owe them a kind of moral compensation.[81] The explanation for why whites may not be wronged by the immigration policy instead draws on their current secure global status and, more importantly, the Uyghurs' current vulnerable status and lack of security in the world.

In general, though it may be hard to distinguish past injustices from social status since the former can contribute to the latter,[82] that past injustices are part of, or even primarily, the cause of a group's global disadvantages seems to be merely an incidental part of the explanation. The easiest way to see this is if an admitting group experienced significant injustices but is now globally secure in all or most of the relevant ways: it seems much more likely that both any disfavored members and selectively excluded nonmembers would be wronged. One possible example is Hindu Indians, who were once subjugated by the British and treated with enormous contempt but, as we saw in section 4, now enjoy a relatively secure status around the world, including in terms of how others regard them.[83] We saw that their comparative global power means that certain groups of nonmembers, such as Bengalis, would likely be wronged if Hindu-majority India favored the admission of Hindus qua Hindus. But additionally, the admission policy would also seem to clearly wrong disfavored members (especially if the latter are also globally vulnerable),[84] despite the past wrongs committed against Hindus themselves.

For a final illustration of the benefits of the antidiscrimination approach over corrective-justice accounts, imagine that a remote island nation experiences an entirely unpredictable natural disaster. As a result, its dominant ethnic group, some of whose members long ago left the island, is now vulnerable in the sense of not being able to sustain its distinct way of life. Though their vulnerability was not caused by any past injustices, it looks as if an immigration policy explicitly favoring the return of their fellow ethnics would not be wrong. But this would be very difficult to explain under a corrective-justice approach to immigration.

---

[80] See Butt (*Rectifying International Injustice*), who argues that agents can acquire duties by involuntarily benefiting from the injustices committed by others.

[81] This is so under both primary understandings: benefiting either relative to others or relative to one's condition absent the relevant wrong(s). See Lippert-Rasmussen, "Affirmative Action," 75.

[82] Past injustices may certainly account for at least part of a group's current disadvantages. For instance, on the relationship between colonialism and economic development, see Acemoglu, Johnson, and Robinson, "Colonial Origins."

[83] See Vucetic, *Anglosphere*, chap. 3, 147–48; Stokes, "How Indians See."

[84] This would be similar to the recent Citizenship Amendment Act (fast-tracking citizenship to India's non-Muslim immigrants from neighboring countries).

6

Between the Primary Duties and Open Borders

1. Introduction

In the last few chapters, I argued that states have global antidiscrimination duties not to exclude on the basis of identity when such exclusion degrades a group. As we saw in the previous chapter, these primary duties do not imply that states may never use identity criteria in their immigration decisions, even when the criteria disfavor a globally vulnerable group. In this chapter, I will turn to examine whether *non*-identity criteria, including preferences based in health, professional, and language qualifications, can violate the primary duties. This discussion will have implications for actions related to immigration beyond admission policies or criteria, such as the proposal to build a wall along the USA's southern border.

Then, I will consider whether states have antidiscrimination duties exceeding the primary duties. I will focus on two possibilities: duties not to selectively exclude when it contributes to a group's global disadvantages, with implications for both identity and non-identity criteria; and duties not to exclude anyone who faces significant disadvantage (material, political, or otherwise), with implications for non-identity groups such as the global poor and people with significant health conditions. A final goal of this chapter is to highlight the distinctions between the antidiscrimination approach and the open-borders view, while critically evaluating the main deontological arguments for the latter.

2. Non-identity Criteria

The analysis in the previous chapter, especially section 5, is helpful for thinking about whether, and, if so, when, states' use of *non*-identity criteria in their admissions policies violates the primary duties. Here I have in mind criteria such as language proficiency, education, skill, and professional requirements. There are at least two general, related questions relevant for considering these. First, does the social context or the unevenness of the impact of a state's non-identity criteria, or both, suggest that the criteria are being used to selectively exclude a particular group or groups? Second, to what extent are the non-identity

Immigration and Discrimination: (Un)Welcoming Others. Sahar Akhtar, Oxford University Press. © Sahar Akhtar 2024.
DOI: 10.1093/oso/9780198898696.003.0007

criteria accessible—specifically, can one satisfy the criteria in a way that doesn't require them to change a significant component of who they are?

To begin, let me explain why non-identity criteria can violate the primary duties even though they do not explicitly involve selection on the basis of identity. In particular, non-identity criteria, especially when certain criteria are strongly *dis*favored, sometimes constitute proxies designed to select against particular groups and so, as we will see shortly, amount to a (less direct) form of selection on the basis of identity. Accordingly, they are subject to the same sorts of considerations used to determine when direct discrimination violates the primary duties.

In practice, it is often tricky to determine when non-identity criteria are being employed as proxies, but there are some fairly clear examples. The best recent example may be the United States' 2017 executive order temporarily banning nonrefugee immigration from seven predominantly Muslim states purportedly for security reasons.[1] As many critics observed, the security rationale was highly implausible and, ultimately, unjustified. For the law only singled out risks from Islamic terrorists, not other sorts of security risks, and the risks posed by foreign terrorism are extremely low.[2] These issues, in combination with the fact that the executive order gave priority to non-Muslim refugees (such as Christians) from Muslim-majority states more generally, seemed to clearly render the law nothing more than a thinly veiled attempt to exclude (some number of) Muslims; that is, it constituted a proxy for excluding on the basis of identity. And, as when criteria explicitly disfavor a vulnerable group (in one of the relevant senses), this case certainly involved treating the group as inferior.

What does it mean that proxies exclude on the basis of identity? Importantly, it does not mean that they do so at the level of the criteria themselves. Rather, proxies select on the basis of identity at a remove—at the level of *choosing* the criteria.[3] In the case of the United States' executive order, at least regarding nonrefugee prospective immigrants applying from one of the seven banned states, the relevant criterion (namely, not being from one of the seven banned states) excluded not only Muslims but also non-Muslims. Thus, the law's *criterion* did not exclude Muslims on the basis of their identity. Nevertheless, the social context surrounding the law indicates that at the level of choosing the criterion, Muslims qua Muslims were excluded.[4]

---

[1] The states were Iraq, Syria, Iran, Sudan, Libya, Somalia, and Yemen. Shear and Cooper, "Trump Bars Refugees."

[2] For relevant criticisms, see Nowrasteh, "Terrorism and Immigration"; Shane, "Immigration Ban."

[3] I have benefited here from Eidelson's discussion on the issue of proxies, which he terms "second-order discrimination." See *Discrimination and Disrespect*, 40–44.

[4] In addition to the issues discussed in the previous paragraph, note that in a 2015 press release, Donald Trump—who signed the executive order very shortly after becoming the President of the United States—called for "a total and complete shutdown of Muslims entering the United States." *BBC News*, "Trump Travel Ban."

Certain non-identity criteria constitute proxies; and when they do, they at least have the potential to violate the primary duties. But many other criteria are not like this and so do not qualify as proxies. The analysis from the previous chapter (especially sections 3–5), as well as the brief discussion of the 2017 executive order above, reveal many sorts of considerations relevant for determining when non-identity criteria are being used as proxies to screen against a vulnerable group or groups. Such factors include whether the admitting group now or in the recent past treated or regarded the excluded group(s) as inferior, what is the most plausible interpretation of the criteria, and whether the admitting group is itself vulnerable in certain ways (thus shaping the appropriate way to interpret the criteria's rationale).

But there is an additional factor, and it is related to the concern that non-identity criteria can often impose a disproportionate disadvantage on certain groups. Recall from Chapter 2 that practices and patterns that disproportionately disadvantage people may constitute wrongful indirect discrimination. It should be clear that from the standpoint of whether the primary duties are violated, what matters is not simply disadvantage. Rather, what matters is whether the criteria select against the group on the basis of identity and treat its members as morally inferior. Consider, for instance, a state that implements skill-based or education criteria, such as preferences for workers in the high-tech field or a ban on admitting adults who have less than a high school-equivalent education. Such criteria may well impose a disadvantage on a vulnerable group or groups by limiting access to valuable life options in the admitting state, but that does not mean that anyone is treated as morally inferior and so does not mean that the primary duties are violated.[5] Of course, there does seem to be a difference between incurring a disadvantage relative to other groups and incurring a disproportionate disadvantage relative to other groups. I think the latter may sometimes be very important, but its importance for the primary duties ties into whether some non-identity criteria constitute proxies; and this depends on just *how* disproportionate the disadvantage is to any particular group.

There are different ways to measure disproportionate disadvantage, one of which concerns whether a large percentage of people in a given group is impacted. But another important measure is the impact on one group relative to the impact on another group. It is the latter understanding of disproportionate disadvantage that partly explains why the US executive order amounted to a proxy. For the executive order certainly did not ban a significant proportion of the total world Muslim population. Nevertheless, since the banned states' populations were between 90% and 99% Muslim, it virtually *only* disfavored Muslims and thus virtually only singled out the identity of being Muslim. In general, if a state's

---

[5] This follows from the discussions in section 3.2 below and in Chapter 5, especially section 3.

disfavored non-identity criteria closely track a particular identity group, this seems to constitute an important sense in which the group is significantly disproportionately disadvantaged and so suggests the use of a proxy (though it might not conclusively mean this). Consider a case more extreme than the US executive order. Imagine a state that has a policy of not admitting people whose primary language is Tagalog. Because it virtually only excludes Filipinos, even in the absence of any past or present objectionable relations, the policy would seem to be used as a proxy designed to select against Filipinos.

However, in the absence of any morally objectionable social context, cases of *favoring* non-identity criteria, including education, skills, and language, are not like this, even when the favoring takes the form of a requirement. Consider a state that requires that any newcomers be proficient in the state's dominant language. This may be unlikely to disproportionately impact any particular group or groups, let alone significantly so.[6] This does not mean that such criteria can never be interpreted as proxies. For instance, imagine that New Zealand implements a policy favoring English speakers. If the policy were implemented in the context of strong public sentiment against a vulnerable group that primarily speaks a different language, such as Polynesians, it would not be implausible to interpret it as aiming to select against people with that identity even if it does not disadvantage them disproportionately. But on its own, or in the absence of such a social context, states' favoring of particular non-identity criteria does not generally seem to amount to the use of proxies.

There is a related issue that seems relevant when considering why non-identity criteria in cases of favoring would not on their own constitute proxies. Namely, they might not be inaccessible. This simple point is important for noting the distinction between, say, favoring a particular religion and favoring a particular language. In Chapter 5, section 4.3, I gave the example of the United States having an immigration policy explicitly favoring the admission of whites. Setting aside the social context of, among other things, disparaging treatment toward Hispanics, I argued that simply in virtue of Hispanics' high rate of emigration to the United States, such a policy would seem to, say, express a demeaning message about Hispanics, thus degrading them (but might not have the same meaning with respect to other vulnerable groups that are unlikely to emigrate to the United States). Based on the reasoning there, it might be natural to think that if the United States were to explicitly require that new immigrants speak English, this criterion also would degrade Hispanics—again, simply because of Hispanics' high emigration rate to the United States.

---

[6] My concern here is whether non-identity criteria violate the state's global antidiscrimination duties, not whether they are wrong from the standpoint of domestic antidiscrimination duties or domestic justice considerations more broadly. For discussion on how language (and related) immigration criteria wrongly treat current members of a society who do not speak the language, see Hosein, '"Where Are You Really From?"'

However, a critical difference between the two kinds of criteria is that for many kinds of non-identity criteria, it is very possible for members of the group to overcome the relative disadvantage in a way that doesn't require them to change a significant component of who they are. That is, the criteria are relatively accessible, loosening the connection between the criterion and some particular identity. Now, depending on economic circumstances and educational background, the hypothetical US language policy might of course not be very accessible to every Hispanic person (or every person in any particular group). But it is not an *in*accessible requirement for Hispanics as a group; moreover, as a language, English is not (today) necessarily tied to any distinct identity. Because of that consideration (and again, assuming away any social context of hostility, disparagement, and the like), the language requirement would not seem to signal anything about Hispanics as such—or, alternatively, compromise the bases of their self-respect or perpetuate stigmas against them—and so would not seem to treat them as morally inferior.[7]

What I have just discussed seems to square with the perhaps widely shared intuition that accessible criteria for admission are morally permissible. Examples include not only language proficiency or training, but also history tests or other demonstrations of familiarity with the political background, and professional and educational requirements. Indeed, as we will see in section 4, even advocates of open borders sometimes allow for such criteria as departures from the ideal or, put differently, as being pro tanto wrong (or wrong absent justification) but overall justified.[8] Under the primary duties, accessible criteria are not typically wrong in any sense. Again, the former sorts of criteria might not be accessible to every individual in some group. What's important is whether they are inaccessible to the group as a whole. And to the extent that they are not, and if there is no associated morally objectionable social context, the relevant criteria would not mark the group out as morally inferior.

In considering the hypothetical US language criteria, I momentarily set aside the social context concerning the United States' members and Hispanics. But, of course, there is a recent context in the USA of prejudice toward and disparaging treatment of Hispanics, especially those from Central America, and this bears not only on the hypothetical US criteria but the proposed wall along the US southern border. One only need recall the statements made by Trump during his presidential campaign in 2015: "When Mexico sends its people, they're not sending their best. They're bringing drugs. They're bringing crime. They're rapists. And some, I assume, are good people."[9] In the midst of comments such as these, large crowds

---

[7] Again, for the moment I am putting aside objectionable attitudes and social practices and only considering the role of Hispanics' immigration rate to the United States.

[8] Compare Carens's (*Ethics of Immigration*) stance regarding "personal abilities and job prospects" (251).

[9] Korte and Gomez, "Trump Ramps Up Rhetoric."

shouted, "Build that wall." Moreover, there was no similar call for a wall along the northern border. For such reasons, it seems obvious that the proposed wall would have degraded Hispanics had it been built during that time (or perhaps now). What this brief example demonstrates is that even actions that do not amount to admission criteria or policies can violate the primary duties.

3. Further Antidiscrimination Duties

I have thus far argued that states have duties not to exclude on the basis of identity when such exclusion treats a group as morally inferior, or degrades it, and I have argued that the concern about degradation typically only applies to globally vulnerable groups. In the previous section, we saw that many cases of non-identity criteria, and other types of actions related to immigration, can violate the primary duties. However, we have also seen that even when a state's identity criteria selectively exclude a globally vulnerable group, this does not yet mean that it wrongs that group or violates its primary duties. In short, although criteria that select against a group would comparatively reduce their access to the admitting state's opportunities, this might not entail treating the group's members as morally inferior.

Before going further, it's worth restressing several reasons for this book's emphasis on duties not to exclude when excluding degrades as opposed to when it contributes to a group's global economic or material disadvantages. As discussed in the book's introduction, it might seem odd not to pay greater attention to concerns about vulnerable groups' economic opportunities or material interests, given that the latter sorts of issues might be considered much more significant and pressing to the excluded migrants themselves. One reason for the emphasis on degradation is that, as discussed in Chapter 2, it is conceptually connected to subordination, whereas there is no such connection between subordination and comparatively reduced opportunities. Another reason, however, is that economic and philosophical work on migration primarily focuses on the material and economic concerns associated with exclusion,[10] whereas there has been little to no sustained analysis of the idea that a state's immigration policies can express a demeaning message about, undermine the self-respect of, and perpetuate stigmas against excluded migrants.[11] But we should not take that to mean that such

---

[10] For some of these, again see Caplan and Weinersmith, *Open Borders*; Carens, *Ethics of Immigration*; Brennan and van der Vossen, *In Defense of Openness*; Clemens and Bazzi, "Golden Door"; Clemens, "Economics and Emigration"; Huemer, "Right to Immigrate?"; Kukathas, "Case for Open Immigration"; Miller, *National Responsibility*; Oberman, "Immigration as Human Right"; Wellman, "Freedom of Association."

[11] There are very few such treatments. For examples, see Fine, "Immigration and Discrimination"; Lim, "Selecting Immigrants by Skill." Also see Hosein, *Ethics of Migration*, chap. 4, esp. 91–92.

degradation concerns are not important nor that such degradation's impact on people's lives is minimal. Though research on the subject does not always distinguish causation from correlation, many studies in different societies suggest a clear connection between (changing) attitudes toward vulnerable groups and the groups' access to opportunities.[12] Moreover, in a variety of examined cases, especially those in which the relevant disadvantages are based mainly in the social bases of a group's self-respect or way of life, such as in the case of Jewish people, selectively excluding some vulnerable group might not meaningfully alter the landscape of material opportunities for the group but remains morally troubling nonetheless.

At the same time, however, there is no denying the significance of material and economic concerns to most vulnerable groups. And if the opportunities that the state provides are significant, selective exclusion can greatly compound the disadvantages they face relative to other groups. Thus, in this section, I want to consider whether states might also have duties not to selectively exclude (whether on the basis of identity or otherwise) when it contributes to a group's disadvantages more generally—that is, simply in virtue of comparatively denying them access to the material, political, and way-of-life opportunities in the admitting state and not only when excluding them degrades them. A related issue I will explore is whether we should only be concerned with identity groups, rather than any class of people that face disadvantages—especially the poor and those with significant health conditions.

3.1 Duties Not to Selectively Exclude When It Contributes to Disadvantages

Starting with the first issue, a strong case can be made that if some group faces substantial disadvantages, then further contributing to those disadvantages in any (nondegrading) way could place it at significant risk of becoming subordinated. Moreover, we have seen that a great number of globally vulnerable groups are already subordinated, and it is plausible that actions that further contribute to their disadvantages perpetuate their subordination. If so, then even in the absence of concerns about degradation, an identity criterion selecting against certain groups that simply further contributes to their disadvantages could very well be wrong from the standpoint of the antidiscrimination framework—for what

---

[12] See for instance, US Council of Economic Advisers, *Changing America*; Desai and Kulkarni, "Changing Educational Inequalities"; Johnson-Ahorlu, "The Academic Opportunity Gap." Using research found in two sources, we calculated that there is a −0.38% correlation between racism against Black Americans and their job participation. In other words, there is a moderate correlation between declining racism and job participation. See Lynch, Bond, and Sachs, *In the Red*; US Department of Labor, "Four States and D.C."

ultimately matters from this standpoint is avoiding and not contributing to subordination. In fact, a similar point can be made even about non-identity criteria that selectively exclude certain groups, such as educational and professional preferences that cannot be interpreted as proxies to exclude any group. I have not argued for these positions in the book, but they seem to be straightforward extensions of the primary duties I have argued for. For there does not seem to be any reason to limit our concern only to identity criteria that degrade or to identity criteria at all if other sorts of criteria or admission policies more generally prompt the same underlying anxieties.

Now, as compared with identity criteria that degrade, in considering whether other types of, or reasons for, exclusion wrong a group, we would likely need to attend far more closely to a number of empirical issues, especially the likelihood that some vulnerable group would become subordinated by an immigration policy and the rate at which a group seeks to emigrate to the admitting state to examine the extent to which they would be disadvantaged by the state's policy. But such practical hurdles do not seem to count against the idea that states may have a greater variety of duties beyond the primary ones. However, there would also be limits to such duties—at least under the antidiscrimination approach as opposed to the broader theory of relational equality (more on this soon). As we saw in section 2—setting aside the use of proxies to exclude a group—non-identity criteria may certainly disadvantage globally vulnerable groups, but that does not always raise concerns about (the potential for) subordination.

But, of course, we also saw that there is a distinction between criteria that disadvantage and those that *disproportionately* disadvantage but nonetheless fall short of proxies ("indirect discrimination"). As observed in Chapter 2, in the domestic context, there are often duties to avoid using criteria that disproportionately disadvantage vulnerable groups even when the criteria cannot be interpreted as proxies designed to exclude those groups. More precisely, cases of indirect discrimination are often thought to stand in need of some sort of special justification, such as the discrimination's relevance to an association's legitimate aims, and if it does not meet some such suitable standard of justification, then it may be wrong (and prohibited by law). Might there also be a similar presumptive stance against the use of immigration criteria that indirectly discriminate against vulnerable groups? There are a few things to say about this idea.

The first point is that the presumption against indirect discrimination might be best understood as reflecting general distributive goals pertaining to, for instance, equality of opportunity[13] and not necessarily (as I have argued is the central emphasis under antidiscrimination) avoiding treating or regarding others as moral inferiors. In the domestic context, given the density of relations between

---

[13] See discussion in Eidelson, *Discrimination and Disrespect*, 51–56, 58–67. In contrast to his focus, however, I am not concerned with whether indirect discrimination counts as a form of discrimination.

co-members, it is highly plausible that a presumption against at least certain forms of indirect discrimination is part of the correct standard of distributive equality that is born of the broader ideal of relational equality among co-members. But we should not expect that the appropriate ideal of relational equality among *non-members* is equivalent to the ideal applied among a state's fellow members, just as the latter does not seem equivalent to the appropriate ideal applied in personal relationships.[14] We simply do not interact with nonmembers or on a global level in the ways that we interact inside a state. To clarify, the point is not that a state's fellow members interact in face-to face contexts whereas members of different states only interact anonymously; on the contrary, relations among co-members also predominantly occur anonymously and indirectly through social, political, and economic institutions. The point is rather that by living in the same state, there is a far more developed network of shared and overlapping institutions, norms, social patterns, social meanings, attitudes, and media that connect co-members.[15]

This isn't to say that once the appropriate ideal of relational equality among members of different states is worked out, there is not a case for a presumption against indirect discrimination in states' admission decisions.[16] Moreover, because of the considerable density of, say, cultural, political, or trade relations between certain states and particular vulnerable groups, whether mediated through regional institutions or more direct, it seems plausible that those states have presumptive duties to those groups not to implement immigration criteria that disproportionately disadvantage them (again, even aside from avoiding the use of proxies). For instance, the discussions in Chapters 3 and 5 of the relevant institutional connections support the idea that Australia and New Zealand have such duties to Polynesians and other indigenous groups in the South Pacific and that the UK has such duties to groups from the Indian subcontinent. Rather than being based on general global relations, such duties would depend on the specific

---

[14] To take one example, Viehoff ("Power and Equality") argues that in order to fulfill the demands of relational equality in some close relationships, including friendships, there must be equal power among the parties but that equality of power is not needed to satisfy the demands of relational equality among a state's co-members.

[15] For a recent and useful discussion of social equality at the global level, see Nath, "Social Equality." Nath appears to concede that the demands of social equality across societies may be less weighty, and perhaps even of a different nature, than those between co-members. Her project is different from mine. For instance, she seems fundamentally concerned with relations between different states (see, for example, 186) (or at times, individuals in those states), not between social groups, and she is concerned with broader issues including inequality of opportunity between societies (see, for example, 199), while my concern is restricted to immigration.

[16] Indeed, this ideal would likely also have numerous implications beyond immigration. For instance, would addressing global disadvantages require something akin to a global basic income? And what requirements would it entail for the design and structure of international organizations and trade agreements? While I believe that we have weighty obligations to nonmembers in all these regards, arguing for and articulating the ideal of relational equality at the global level is far beyond the scope of this book.

relations between these particular states (or their admitting groups) and the particular vulnerable groups. Additionally, it is important to once again note that while there is certainly overlap between many of the relevant economic, political, and cultural relations, on the one hand, and injustices committed against the particular vulnerable groups, on the other, under the antidiscrimination approach any presumptive duties not to disproportionately disadvantage a group are not ultimately based on correcting past wrongs.[17]

Returning to whether, under a fleshed-out ideal of relational equality among people of different states, there might be a *general* presumptive duty against disproportionately disadvantaging vulnerable groups—that is, a duty applying to any state in relation to any vulnerable group—it is worth pointing out that a variety of immigration policies would remain unobjectionable under that ideal. For starters, this includes the use of all sorts of criteria that disadvantage many groups but do not disproportionately disadvantage any group. Examples might include caps on admission, as in the following type of case, which we considered in Chapter 1.

Population Limits:

A state accepts everyone on a first-come-first-serve basis, but with numerical caps.

Instead of imposing a particular burden on any specific group or groups, an immigration policy such as this might disadvantage all groups in a more or less uniform manner. Additionally, there may be many types of criteria that disproportionately *benefit* certain vulnerable groups. Recall the following cases from Chapter 1 in which permissibility seemed to depend on the details.

Occupational Preference:

A state's immigration policy prioritizes workers in one industry, disfavoring other occupations.

and

Language Criteria:

A state excludes people who fail its language criteria.

---

[17] Under the suggested alternative approach of corrective justice, it seems plausible that certain states have a duty to the vulnerable groups they have wronged in the past not to implement immigration criteria that further disadvantage them. More broadly, states might have a positive duty to favor the admission of members of groups they have wronged in the past, akin to a kind of global affirmative action. Since the disadvantages experienced by many groups may be the result of past injustices committed by other groups, this strategy would likely have wide-ranging results. But, again, such a strategy would be separate from the antidiscrimination approach, for reasons expressed in Chapter 5.

In the first case, if the prioritized industry is predominantly populated by workers belonging to vulnerable groups—a possible example is the agricultural industry— the policy would not only likely not be wrong but may be laudable. And for Language Criteria, consider the following actual examples: new immigrants to Laos must be able to speak, read, and write in Lao,[18] and for admission to Cambodia, one must be able to speak Khmer.[19] As in these cases, if the state's dominant language is primarily spoken by a vulnerable group or groups—other examples include Samoan, Kiribati, or even in many cases Spanish—a policy insisting that immigrants must speak the dominant language would likely benefit a vulnerable group or groups.

3.2 Antidiscrimination Duties to the Poor

We can now turn to similar points in relation to the issue of *general* disadvantage mentioned above. Specifically, one might wonder whether there are global anti-discrimination duties owed to anyone who faces disadvantage more generally, including the relatively poor and those with significant health conditions such as cancer, or heart, liver, or lung disease. In short, what, if anything, is distinctive about identity groups? As with the first question about disproportionate disad-vantage, this is a very important issue, but to address it fully would require far more investigation than I'm able to undertake in this book. At the same time, there are several things to say about how such an investigation would proceed based in this book's central analysis.

First, recall that we are setting aside those whose basic human rights are at stake (the main type of nondiscretionary nonmembers). As I will discuss later in this chapter, I believe that all states (and, more generally, all people) have separate duties to help secure the rights of any person who faces basic human rights deprivations, whether by admitting them or by assisting them in other ways.

Second, in considering people who face relative disadvantage but whose basic human rights are not threatened—that is, discretionary nonmembers—as a gen-eral matter I certainly do not believe that there is anything especially morally significant about *identity* characteristics. I have focused on these characteristics because, as discussed in the introductory chapter, they have often taken center stage in debates about immigration. But any group that is subordinated or at risk of becoming subordinated should concern us not only in general but also from the standpoint of global antidiscrimination duties. It may be that subordination more frequently *attaches* to, or more closely tracks, identity rather than other charac-teristics, such as poverty and health, but there does not seem to be any reason to

---

[18] "Law on Lao Nationality," Refworld, https://www.refworld.org/docid/3ae6b4f014.html.
[19] "Law on Nationality," Refworld, https://www.refworld.org/docid/3ae6b5210.html.

otherwise privilege groups sharing a common identity in contrast to shared characteristics such as poverty or poor health.

But while there might not ultimately be anything distinctive about identity groups, the emphasis would likely remain on the subordination of different *groups* of individuals, not, in the first instance, subordination that attaches to individuals as such. If we consider again a conception of relational equality among a state's co-members, it is arguable that certain conditions of status equality must obtain among individuals as such, or at least among individuals occupying certain roles, especially when such roles entail personal interaction, such as that between customers and clerks or between parents and teachers. And even when roles appear in the context of anonymous and indirect relations, such as those between public officials and voters or between large firms' executives and employees, those roles need not always track group membership but may nonetheless be apt sites for concerns about subordination. Because a state's co-members are often enmeshed in a number of overlapping relations with one another—including political organizations, the workplace, schools, neighborhoods and communities, places of worship, and social clubs—the idea of securing certain conditions of equal social status among individuals as such seems compelling.[20] However, this idea seems far less likely to get traction globally since individuals qua individuals do not interact under global and international institutions and arrangements in anything like the way individuals may interact within a state.[21] At the same time, we have seen that interaction and relations mediated by group membership have been and continue to be common on the global scale.

Now, returning to the issue of whether states' admission decisions are plausibly constrained by antidiscrimination duties to anyone who faces disadvantages, perhaps especially when it comes to the relatively poor, it is highly plausible that such people have a vulnerable global status *qua poor people*—that is, apart from any other characteristics they have. For in addition to experiencing material and political disadvantages, the relatively poor qua poor are treated or regarded in inferior ways in numerous states around the world, including by being regarded as lazy or as less moral than others,[22] and facing residential segregation and limits on occupational choice.[23] (Indeed, the same may well be true of people who do not count as poor but have visible health conditions.) We would of course need to specify what is meant by "relatively poor" and whether that meaning is constant across the globe or, more likely, varies according to type of state, region, and so on (excluding for the moment, again, people so poor their basic human rights are

---

[20] See Anderson (*Imperative of Integration*, 89–95), for a discussion of the moral importance of interacting as people with equal social status in civil society. Her focus is mainly social status between identity groups, especially racial groups, but similar points can be applied, it seems, to different roles.

[21] See Fourie, Schuppert, and Wallimann-Helmer, *Social Equality*, 193.

[22] Lichter and Crowley, *Poverty in America*; Lauter, "How Do Americans View Poverty?"

[23] Jodhka and Shah, "Comparative Contexts of Discrimination."

violated). If all of this can be established and worked out, then what we would need to consider is whether, and if so under what circumstances, states' admission decisions have the potential to degrade the relatively poor (suitably defined) or otherwise contribute to their disadvantages in ways that place them at substantial risk of becoming subordinated.

As I stressed above, these questions would take far greater empirical and normative exploration than I can engage in here. But if it turns out that it is often or even always wrong for states to exclude the relatively poor, rather than constituting one implication of a view that claims that (aside from migrants posing security and safety threats) it is wrong to exclude *anyone*, this implication would emerge ultimately because of a concern about significant disadvantage and subordination in the world. To highlight the relevant point, in contrast to the open-borders position, under the antidiscrimination approach it would not be wrong for states to exclude relatively wealthy people as a group—that is, outside of potential duties to identity groups to which any wealthy individuals might belong—by applying a wide range of admission criteria.

To see this, let's return to Occupational Preference and imagine that the prioritized industry is one that is typically populated by the relatively poor around the world—such as the textile, service, or agricultural industries.[24] Even under a wider understanding of global antidiscrimination duties that includes duties to the relatively poor, then, controlling for the role of identity factors, this sort of immigration criterion (qua criterion[25]) might not be wrong under most circumstances.

4. Antidiscrimination Versus Open Borders

In various places throughout the book, I have provided a variety of examples to illustrate the advantages of the antidiscrimination approach over other approaches, including, in the previous section, the open-borders position. Additionally, in Chapter 4, we saw that the antidiscrimination approach's background normative commitments are more minimal than those needed for at least certain arguments for the open-borders position, such as the luck-egalitarian case. What I want to do in this section is summarize and elaborate on the distinctions between the antidiscrimination approach and the idea of open borders. In doing so, I believe we will have a greater appreciation for the antidiscrimination approach.

---

[24] "Agriculture Overview," World Bank, https://www.worldbank.org/en/topic/agriculture/overview; International Labour Organization, "Agricultural Wage Workers."
[25] To be sure, there are often concerns about the working conditions and pay in these industries, but these sorts of concerns can be set aside in evaluating whether the immigration criteria on their own are wrong. If anything, immigration criteria favoring these industries would likely place upward pressure on wages and working conditions in workers' home states.

Though it is not always clear what is meant by open borders, it's safe to say that the dominant philosophical idea is outlined by Joseph Carens. His conception mirrors the idea of domestic open borders in that he suggests that restrictions on immigration are morally wrong just as restrictions on moving within a state are morally wrong.[26] It implies, for instance, that just as one has a moral right to move from Virginia to California without requesting permission from California, qualifying for residence in California, or passing any tests for admission, one has a moral right to move from Pakistan to the United States. In short, Carens suggests there is something like a moral right to international freedom of movement (or a moral right to migrate).

Carens does consider some reasons for excluding people potentially justifiable. The idea seems to be that in the case of any prospective immigrant, there is a presumption in favor of international free movement—a presumption that must be overcome to justify free movement's violation.[27] To understand what sorts of exclusions might qualify as justifiable, we need to distinguish what the view suggests for our actual world from what it suggests for an ideal, or just, world.

In the actual/nonideal world, Carens implies that some grounds for exclusion—especially concerns based in culture and public order (which seem to include infrastructure and population concerns)—may be allowable in an all-things-considered or overall sense; however, they would at least count as pro tanto wrong, or, again, wrong absent justification.[28] National security may be the exception to all of this, and, accordingly, exclusions grounded in national security might not even be pro tanto wrong[29] (however, this is not fully clear[30]). Turning to an ideal (or just) world, Carens describes it as a world in which there exists "roughly the same level of economic development and basic freedoms protected in each state."[31] Aside from national security, it seems that the grounds for exclusion mentioned above, such as those based in cultural, infrastructure, and population concerns, are not just pro tanto wrong, but all-things-considered

[26] To clarify, authors maintain that just as within a state, movement can be legitimately curtailed for certain important reasons (such as protecting property rights and public safety), so too can international movement. But there is a moral presumption in favor of free movement in both instances. Carens, "Migration and Morality," 36–37; Carens, *Ethics of Immigration*, 246–48 and, for analog domestic scenarios, 251.

[27] Concerning national security, public order, and culture, Carens (*Ethics of Immigration*) writes, "they justify restrictions on freedom of movement only if and to the extent that these restrictions are necessary to prevent harmful consequences that outweigh the moral claims to freedom of movement" (276). Given that such grounds for exclusion must "*outweigh* the moral claims to freedom of movement," it seems plausible to interpret such restrictions on freedom of movement as pro tanto wrong. For additional views concerning a right to freedom of movement or a right to migrate, see Huemer, "Right to Immigrate?"; Oberman, "Immigration as Human Right."

[28] For Carens's discussion regarding such grounds (and national security), see 2013, 276–87.

[29] He writes that "a principled use of national security as a criterion of exclusion is morally permissible." Carens, *Ethics of Immigration*, 176.

[30] The meaning of Carens's (176n23) claim is unclear given his comments elsewhere (see my note 27). Also see Kukathas, "Case for Open Immigration," esp. 211.

[31] See Carens, *Ethics of Immigration*, 311.

wrong.[32] In other words, under ideal circumstances, it seems the only sorts of exclusions that would *not* violate someone's right to freedom of movement are based in national-security considerations.

Apart from textual support for this understanding of a right to international free movement, support is provided through the analog understanding of domestic freedom of movement—something often appealed to by proponents when making the moral case for international freedom of movement. For instance, Carens suggests (rightly, of course) that in the domestic context, if some domestic sub-unit (for example, California) were permitted to weigh considerations such as "its current unemployment level" or the "overall number of requests to enter" that it receives, and if it were permitted to deny someone entry on such bases, this would illustrate what lacking the right to freedom of movement looks like.[33]

Things are a little more complicated because Carens also suggests that even in an ideal (or just) world, certain hurdles to international movement may be permissible. For instance, he maintains that obstacles to one's freedom to move are justified if they increase overall free movement. Though it is not entirely clear what sorts of obstacles would count as enhancing overall free movement, plausible candidates include limits related to traffic efficiency and traffic safety.[34] Moreover, he maintains that the boundary of one's right to free movement is shaped by respect for other important freedoms and rights, especially property rights; consequently, traffic- and property rights-based constraints on free movement might not be wrong in any sense. However, it is important to note that when Carens provides the analogous picture of domestic freedom of movement, he discusses traffic restrictions and constraints arising from obligations to respect property not in terms of being permissible grounds for excluding people, but rather as speed bumps, so to speak, that merely permissibly decrease the *speed* and *ease* of moving or that permissibly affect its timing.[35] Thus, while such constraints on one's freedom of movement might not be considered wrong, it is far from clear that they amount to morally permissible grounds for *exclusion*.

In contrast, under the antidiscrimination approach, there is not a presumption in favor of free movement. To see what the implications of this are, let us begin by considering the actual/nonideal world. First, in addition to security grounds, exclusions based in infrastructure, population, and resource concerns would not

---

[32] Though Carens writes, "in principle, borders should *generally* be open and people should *normally* be free to [move]" (225, emphasis mine), when he examines various exclusion grounds, he suggests most (if not all) would be wrong in ideal circumstances (see chaps 11–12, esp. 285–87). Also see Huemer, "Right to Immigrate?"; and Oberman, "Immigration as Human Right."

[33] Carens, *Ethics of Immigration*, 251. He writes about such a scenario that "you don't enjoy a right to move" since the authorities "are entitled to balance your desire to move from New York to California against various other considerations which might make it seem better from a public policy perspective if you are not allowed to make the move."

[34] Carens, esp. 246–48.

[35] Carens, 246–48. Also see the first scenario described at the top of 251.

necessarily be even pro tanto wrong—"not necessarily" because, like any criteria, they might be abused in order to exclude certain (for example) racial or religious groups. But primarily apart from their potential use as proxies,[36] infrastructure-, population-, and resource-based immigration exclusions often have similarly unobjectionable domestic analogs. Consider, for example, a church, college, or social club that refuses applicants because its facilities have reached their capacities or even because it wishes not to grow too large. Such considerations do not ordinarily violate antidiscrimination norms. Second, we saw in section 2 that there are a range of criteria, such as language, educational, and professional criteria, whose permissibility depends on further facts.[37] Third, the previous chapter demonstrated that certain states—in particular, those that consist primarily of a vulnerable group—may be permitted to exclude on identity grounds when other states are not. Though particular open-borders proponents might agree with some of these results,[38] they are at odds with the general construals of the view.

Now considering ideal circumstances (or a just world), however defined,[39] let us assume that one condition is that groups have more or less equal global social status. In such circumstances, it would presumably no longer be plausible to explain the rationale behind a group favoring the admission of its own group members in terms of mitigating the group's disadvantages or securing their status in the world. However, this does not necessarily mean that identity criteria would be more likely to conflict with antidiscrimination duties. On the contrary, it may be possible that a greater variety of groups may be permitted to favor their own group members—not just vulnerable groups (since these would, by assumption, not exist) but any groups. Indeed, a whole host of groups currently having a secure status may, in certain circumstances, favor the admission of their own group members without violating antidiscrimination duties. It may be difficult to imagine such a result now because the world is far from just, and I don't wish to speculate as to what the possible alternative circumstances might look like since much would depend on what exactly we mean by an ideal (or just) world. But if we were to achieve a world in which there were minimal to no social-status differences between groups, then outside of explicitly disfavoring certain identities, using identity criteria in immigration decisions might nearly cease to be wrong from the standpoint of the antidiscrimination approach. More obviously, all sorts

[36] Few such grounds for exclusion used by actual states today might be justified under antidiscrimination, but if the grounds mentioned here are not abused as proxies, they would not typically be wrong (contrary to Open Borders).

[37] For instance, if conducted with genuine effort to make them accessible, certain language- and skill-based requirements might not be objectionable. (See Akhtar, "Being at Home." For a critique, see Hosein, "Where Are You Really From?") But if a secure group imposes those requirements as a way to exclude certain vulnerable races or ethnicities, then they would clearly be wrong.

[38] Carens ("Migration and Morality," 37–39) suggests that Japan might be such a case. Also see Carens, *Ethics of Immigration*, 286.

[39] I don't believe we need to delve into the various ways of differentiating between ideal and nonideal, or just and unjust, to see the basic differences stressed here.

of non-identity criteria—language proficiency, history tests, educational, and professional requirements—would stand an even better chance of being permissible. To be clear, this discussion says nothing about whether it is wise or overall good for states to use such criteria. Some, such as professional qualifications, may be counterproductive to a state's economic or political goals and, from a consequentialist perspective (discussed below in section 5), states having significantly more open borders than they currently do might contribute to enormous gains in global wealth. The point is rather that a wide range of criteria would not typically violate antidiscrimination duties.

I believe that the above sorts of implications of the antidiscrimination approach count in its favor and present some intuitive advantages over the open-borders position. While open-borders proponents might agree with some of these implications (such as certain vulnerable groups' being permitted to exclude on identity grounds), they would almost certainly disagree with others (such as the result that many non-identity exclusions may be permissible for a variety of states). At the end of the day, my goal is not to convince anyone that the open-borders position should be rejected. As I will explain in the next section, I am deeply drawn to this position for a variety of reasons. However, I'll discuss some significant concerns about the primary attempts at arguing for a right to international freedom of movement.

5. Why Not Open Borders?

The idea of open borders is highly alluring, especially to any fan of individual liberty. Why should boundaries that were forged often long ago—and just as often, under highly unjust circumstances—play a decisive role in determining where we can visit, whom we can encounter, what jobs we may take, and in what places we may settle? More significantly, why should morally arbitrary factors such as where we were born so deeply impact our prospects for a good life? As numerous researchers have demonstrated, our life prospects are substantially shaped by where we happen to be born; one's chances of having a good life are vastly different if they are born in, say, Portugal versus Pakistan or in Sweden versus Sudan.

Despite the power of these questions, though, I am unsure that the open-borders position is correct. I have already suggested that it cannot account for the permissibility of a variety of types of exclusions that, I believe, are highly plausible, but there are additional reasons for being skeptical having to do with its proposed rationales, or at least a certain type of rationale.

Broadly speaking, there are two types of cases made in favor of open borders. The first is largely an economic, consequentialist argument, observing how total world product would increase dramatically, mainly because it would increase the productivity of migrants from developing countries, leading to enormous material gains in overall well-being around the world.[40] I'll leave this sort of case aside, but not because it is not very compelling. Rather, assessing it properly requires assessing a good deal of empirical and moral issues concerning what sorts of potential trade-offs, if any, would need to be accepted; whether any potential trade-offs morally outweigh the income gains;[41] whether states with highly stable political and welfare institutions and networks would receive unsustainable levels of migrants, compromising those very institutions and networks;[42] and what sorts of conditions would need to be in place to mitigate any costs of open borders, including the possibility of various special taxes levied on new migrants.[43]

Since this book, beginning with the discussion of the idea of states'-choice, has explored the issue of immigration from a deontological or rights-based perspective, I wish to focus on the second sort of moral case for open borders, which argues, in different ways, for a right to international freedom of movement (or right to migrate). Let's start with the most important reason one might claim there is such a moral right: it would permit people and their families to flee political or religious persecution in their current states or escape conditions of extreme poverty by securing employment in other states, thus securing their most morally significant interests, including interests in being free from oppression and in avoiding extreme poverty.[44]

There is no doubt that millions of people around the world bear significant burdens in pursuing a minimally decent life and, I believe, that their circumstances place moral demands on others.[45] Though the question of what exactly are the conditions needed for a good life is complex and far from settled, it is widely thought that we have duties to assist people to attain the conditions of a *minimally decent life*, including, for instance, food, shelter, clean water, vaccinations against preventable disease, and various political and security conditions such as safety against aggressors and freedom from persecution.[46] And there are at least a couple

[40] Clemens, "Economics and Emigration"; Also see Clemens and Bazzi, "Golden Door."

[41] On the (mis)conception that migrants lower domestic workers' wages, however, see Friedberg and Hunt, "Impact of Immigrants."

[42] See, for example, Jones, *Culture Transplant*; Collier, *Exodus*.

[43] For a very recent paper on this subject, see Guerreiro, Rebelo, and Teles, "Optimal Immigration Policy?" Also see Smith, "Open Borders."

[44] Walzer, who's given significant attention to immigration, identifies the central question as "Can a political community exclude destitute and hungry, persecuted and stateless . . . men and women"? See *Spheres of Justice*, 45.

[45] Considering the number of refugees and asylum seekers alone, it is estimated to be anywhere between about 30 and 80 million worldwide. "Figures at a Glance," United Nations, UN Refugee Agency, https://www.unhcr.org/en-us/figures-at-a-glance.html; "World's Refugees," Amnesty International, https://www.amnesty.org/en/what-we-do/refugees-asylum-seekers-and-migrants/global-refugee-crisis-statistics-and-facts/. The variance is due mainly to morally irrelevant definitional issues. See note 42 in the introductory chapter.

[46] For important discussions, see Buchanan, *Justice, Legitimacy, and Self-Determination*, esp. chap. 3; Nickel, *Making Sense*, chaps 4 and 5; Miller, *Strangers in Our Midst*, 30–34.

of broad strategies for arguing for such duties. For instance, we might argue that such duties are the most minimal requirements entailed by a conception of global justice, which is generated by a global basic structure in which we engage in mutual cooperation with others around the world.[47] Or we might maintain that such duties emerge from a more general obligation to treat and regard all persons as moral equals, regardless of our interaction or relations with them.[48] But, however these duties are best justified, there are several related things to say about whether our relevant interests (to which such duties correspond) support a moral right to free *movement*.

The main thing to note is that the sorts of interests at stake plausibly ground *independent* moral rights of different sorts—basic human rights—which has certain practical implications. For instance, the interest in avoiding extreme poverty grounds something like a right to (attain) subsistence or basic welfare, the interest in avoiding religious persecution grounds something like a right to religious freedom, and the interest in avoiding political oppression grounds rights such as the rights to free expression and political participation.[49] Sometimes these interests can be more effectively protected in one's current state through assistance from other states or their members—for instance, by helping to secure economic opportunities or stable political conditions,[50] by eliminating barriers to trade, and by helping to promote the sorts of institutions that reduce poverty: stable property rights, legally enforced trade, and commerce.[51] If such steps are effective, they may also be preferable to moving since most people don't wish to uproot their lives and move to new states and since moving to a new state is cost prohibitive to many, *especially* the very poorest.[52] A similar response is sometimes available regarding victims of genocide and other tyrannies: our obligation to help them may at times be satisfied in better ways than through migration, such as through armed humanitarian intervention or by securing temporary safe zones until they can return to their homes.[53]

That said, however, they cannot always return to their homes and it may be very difficult or ineffective to assist in these sorts of ways, and so it's often not an option to help people living in extreme poverty in their home states. In such cases, I believe people have a moral right to be granted admission into other states. Similarly, many who reject open borders accept (as I do) an understanding of *refugee* that is broad enough to include not only the persecuted and oppressed, but

---

[47] For an argument along these lines, see Beitz, *Political Theory*, part III; Pogge, *Realizing Rawls*.
[48] See, for instance, Buchanan, *Justice, Legitimacy, and Self-Determination*, esp. 85–98.
[49] Miller, "Immigration."   [50] Pogge, *World Poverty and Human Rights*.
[51] For excellent work on these issues, see the early work by Douglass North and Hernando de Soto. North, *Institutions*; de Soto, *Mystery of Capital*. Also see the following more recent work: Acemoglu and Robinson, "Unbundling Institutions"; Acemoglu and Robinson, *Why Nations Fail*.
[52] Clemens, "Emigration Life Cycle."   [53] See Miller, "Immigration."

anyone whose basic human rights are significantly and urgently jeopardized,[54] and in Chapter 1 we saw that they maintain that states have at least some moral obligation to admit such persons. But admission into another state would be a means for remedying basic human rights violations or deprivations in their current states.[55] Thus, I believe it is more accurate to say that people have a remedial right to migrate in these cases since migration would be the "appropriate remedy of last resort."[56] This is distinct from a primary right, or a right to migrate that is not conditional on violations of independently characterizable rights, and certain pragmatic consequences may follow from this distinction. For instance, a remedial right might often support entry into *some* other state, but not necessarily into any specific state or the state of one's choice, and sometimes on a temporary rather than permanent basis.[57] At the same time, this does not mean that the decision to accept someone with urgent needs is at the sole discretion of an individual state. In fact, I will argue in the next chapter that a state is *not* morally entitled to unilaterally determine whether to admit people with urgent needs.

At this point, however, a reader might think what I have just suggested misses the point. They might insist that *how* one's morally significant interests or one's basic human rights are satisfied is up to oneself—that these should be satisfied in the manner of one's *choosing*, which may often include migrating to a particular other state. I certainly agree with the general stance that we should have the (presumptive) freedom to choose for ourselves whatever courses of action improve our lives, but in order to assess what its implications are for migration, we need to consider the broader sort of position arguing that a right to free movement is grounded in a presumption in favor of liberty or, perhaps more specifically, in the value of being free to choose, for instance, where one lives, what job to take, and where to go to school. But before turning to this sort of argument, let's consider another important rationale for migration that is often given, one based in the significance of family (re)unification.[58]

The interest in family (re)unification (where, again, this is construed broadly, including, for instance, unmarried partners) does seem to ground a moral claim to

---

[54] Pevnick extends the idea of refugee to people who are unable to meet their basic subsistence needs. Pevnick, *Constraints of Justice*, esp. 139–58. Wellman also suggests that the traditional understanding of refugee as someone fleeing persecution may be too narrow. Wellman, "Right to Exclude," 119.

[55] Others claim states can satisfy their duties to nonmembers without admitting them: Miller, "Immigration"; Wellman, "Freedom of Association." My claim is instead that the situation of nonmembers living under burdened conditions does not seem to ground primary migration rights, not that states do not have obligations nonetheless to admit them.

[56] Buchanan makes this distinction in the context of a right to secede. Buchanan, "Theories of Secession."

[57] In *Whiteshift* (236–37), political theorist Eric Kaufmann argues that if the goal is to help refugees, settlement may be a wrongheaded strategy as it might make the domestic populace more hostile to accepting refugees, resulting in weakened political will to accept them.

[58] On the weight given to family reunification in US policy, see Clark, Hatton, and Williamson, "Where Do U.S. Immigrants Come From?," esp. 5–7.

enter a specific state—namely, the state in which one's family is located—and perhaps on a permanent basis. But it's not clear why this interest is not secured by moral rights we claim against the states in which we currently have membership. Given the significance of preserving family and intimate relationships to one's ability to lead a meaningful life, it's highly plausible that one has a right to be joined by their loved ones without having to exit their current state. That is, the preservation of relationships seems to support rights that belong to us as current members (whether citizens or residents)—rights we mainly claim against our *current* states rather than against other states. We might wonder which state has the obligation to admit if each party in a relationship has such a right. But it seems the answer is clear: *both* states would have the moral obligation toward their members to admit their members' family, and the parties could in turn choose between the states. Structurally, this would be similar to the rights of dual citizens, where both states have the obligation to admit the bearer of dual citizenship, who can often simply choose which of the two states to live in.

Both types of rationales presented above—basic human rights and family (re)unification—point to cases of what I have thus far referred to as nondiscretionary nonmembers. But once we have bracketed nondiscretionary admissions, how strong is the case for a right to international free movement? It seems the most compelling argument in its favor is liberty based and rather straightforward. It typically starts by demonstrating the intuitive appeal of thinking that coercive interference with our movement ordinarily stands in need of justification, especially perhaps when it prevents such significant choices as where we live, what jobs we take, with whom we associate, and where we go to school. Proponents of this argument concede that for any type of movement, it's an open question whether justification can be given; but they argue that it *must* be given.[59]

I entirely agree with the stance that there is a moral presumption in favor of free movement. It is hard to overstate the values served by freedom of movement, including freedom of association, freedom of religion, and freedom of occupation.[60] At the same time, I'm not convinced by existing arguments that states lack justification to coercively interfere with, and hence defeat the presumption in favor of, nonmembers' movement. To clarify, it's not that I'm convinced that states are so justified; rather, it seems the central issue that would decide the matter one way or another, especially from the standpoint of liberty arguments, has yet to be addressed. This issue is whether states, or their members jointly, own the relevant territory, goods, or institutions.

---

[59] For instance, see Brennan and van der Vossen, *In Defense of Openness*, esp. 28–30.

[60] For discussion of these and related interests, see Carens, "Migration and Morality"; Kukathas, "Case for Open Immigration"; Cole, "Open Borders"; and Oberman, "Immigration as Human Right."

To see what I mean, let's look at a very recent defense of the liberty-based argument.[61] In their compelling and empirically informed book, *In Defense of Openness*, Jason Brennan and Bas van der Vossen accept that if a state has the moral right to determine who can gain admission—as under the states'-choice position—it thereby also has the moral right to coercively interfere with non-members' (attempted) movement onto its territory. However, focusing on Wellman's associational-freedom view of the states'-choice position, Brennan and van der Vossen argue that states do not have such a right. To briefly recall, Wellman's view maintains that, along with other groups such as clubs, states have a moral right to decide their potential associates, one grounded in their freedom of association. While Brennan and van der Vossen find the central intuition behind such accounts compelling, they maintain that the idea as applied to states ultimately fails.

Their reasoning is as follows.[62] If we understand a group's rights to decide associates in individualist terms, then the group's right is the aggregate of its individual members' rights, and individuals who disagree with the aggregate decision are bound by it if they have freely accepted being subject to it. But, according to Brennan and van der Vossen, the latter understanding only seems to make sense for voluntary associations, such as clubs, which states are not. States impose their rules on members, and the only exit option (to leave the state) is extremely costly, in both material and personal terms. On the other hand, if we understand a group's rights to decide associates in collectivist terms, as Wellman explicitly suggests we should,[63] then the group as a whole has a right to choose its associates. The problem with this interpretation for these authors, however, is that immigrants do not seek to *associate* with the *state as a whole*; rather, they claim it makes more sense to say that immigrants seek to either associate with *individuals* in the state or *join* the state. Thus, they argue, the very idea that the state as a whole has a right to choose its associates does not apply to the decision to admit immigrants, though it may apply to, say, the decision to sign treaties with other states.[64]

Let's begin with their argument about the individualist interpretation of moral rights to associate. It's certainly true that states are not voluntary in any meaningful sense. But it's not clear this matters. Imagine that the current generation of members of a large religious community have simply been born into it, with all of its benefits, such as use of numerous facilities and extremely affordable housing that members gain access to through their membership fees. Also imagine that the community is located hundreds of miles away from the next town and that leaving

---

[61] For the case that there is a presumption in favor of liberty, see Brennan and van der Vossen, *In Defense of Openness*, 23–30.

[62] Brennan and van der Vossen, 49–52.   [63] Wellman, "Freedom of Association," 41–42.

[64] It does apply, they argue, to treaties and agreements with other states and international organizations. See Brennan and van der Vossen, *In Defense of Openness*, 51–52.

is very costly, both because there are strong norms against leaving and ex-members are shunned and because one would have to give up the affordable housing, friends, and close bonds with the community. Does the fact that none of the current members joined voluntarily and that leaving is costly imply that members lack the individual moral right, exercised jointly, to decide who else can gain admission? It's far from obvious that it does. If half of the members wish to accept new members but half of them do not, that may present legitimate concerns about how membership is decided within the group. But that doesn't suggest that the individuals in the group must cede membership control or that they lack the right to jointly decide the community's membership. Something that would suggest the latter is if they lack moral rights over the relevant territory, facilities, or institutions. But nothing in the argument purports to show that.

We can see the same point from the standpoint of the collectivist understanding of a state's right to choose its associates. I agree that it is odd to say that potential members wish to associate with the state as a whole; rather, they wish to join it or perhaps associate with individual members. But recall from Chapter 1 that associational accounts need not interpret "associate" in the narrow terms of consorting, socializing, or interacting with others, despite the worry that some authors raised. Instead, the collectivist understanding of the state's right to choose its associates can simply be interpreted as its moral freedom to structure the shape and nature of the association, or more specifically, to decide its membership, relationships, affiliations, partnerships, and the like.

There's certainly a significant distinction between a state associating with parties external to the state, such as other states, and a state associating with those wishing to join it: the state can subject the latter to a far wider set of rules, institutions, and laws. Among the other things states can do, they can implement formal institutions and rules regarding education requirements and language policies; use noncoercive measures such as positive incentives for higher education, homeownership, and entrepreneurship, whether universal or tailored to specific groups; influence informal norms and values and enact a wide variety of policies pertaining to individual behavior in, for instance, marriage, euthanasia, sexual activity, and drug use; and define the content and scope of the freedoms of expression, assembly, and association in particular ways.[65] In contrast, outsiderassociates would presumably not have to accept a state's self-governing rules and laws. This means that a state's ability to shape the common association when it is with another state or states is greatly limited compared with its power to shape the internal association. This difference may, at the end of the day, support states'

---

[65] Sarah Fine ("Freedom of Association," 353) suggests that control over the collective self is only one way in which a state can be self-determining and that another important element is the freedom "to set its own internal policy agenda without external interference." While this is a good point, my goal here is to emphasize that there are ways in which a state retains control over itself even in the absence of the right to deny membership.

having considerably more freedom to deny potential external associations than to exclude those seeking membership. But it seems we cannot know this until the prior issue of moral rights over the territory, goods, or resources has been settled. To see this, consider a large club with thousands of members. Those wishing to join the club would likely be subject to the range of club rules and bylaws shaping the club's culture and patterns of norms in ways that the club's outsider-associates, such as other clubs and nonmembers, would not be. But the question remains: does the club as a whole have the right to decide who is admitted? If it possesses the requisite moral rights to its facilities and grounds, it appears it would have that right even if it can control the shape of the club with other, non-membership-related decisions. Applying this reasoning to states doesn't mean that there are no moral constraints on states' right to decide membership; it has been a goal of this book to demonstrate that states, along with associations such as large clubs, are constrained by certain antidiscrimination duties. But constraints do not imply that some group lacks the right to decide membership altogether.

Though the case for a right to international free movement based in liberty is powerful, it seems the central question, especially from a liberty standpoint, must still be addressed: whether states, or their members jointly, are morally entitled to control access to their territories or the goods or institutions within the territories. For no one seems to doubt that there are legitimate moral limits on our domestic freedom of movement stemming from property rights, including joint or collective property rights:[66] unless perhaps our basic human rights are compromised, we are morally restricted from accessing and settling in, among other things, privately owned facilities and land, such as those owned by businesses and clubs, and we face legitimate limits in accessing religious spaces and temples.

Moreover, while some might argue that individual members have the moral right to accept immigrants to live or work on their own private property, this stance also requires determining whether members jointly have a moral right to the relevant territory, goods, or institutions. For unless the immigrants would be forced to remain within the boundaries of someone's private property, they would require, at a minimum, use of the roadways and collective land surrounding and between private property parcels. Given all of this, arguments from liberty cannot really be assessed without considering whether states, or their members jointly, have morally justified property rights to the relevant territory, collective goods, or public institutions, and if so, what this implies for the idea of a right to international free movement; for as we saw in Chapter 4, there are some very compelling arguments for such state property rights.[67]

---

[66] Onora O'Neill ("Commentary") raised similar concerns along these lines, especially regarding the libertarian justification for open borders.

[67] Cara Nine ("Do Territorial Rights Include?") argues that most Lockean conceptions of states' territorial rights do not support a state's right to exclude nonmembers from its public spaces. However, see Chapter 4 on Pevnick's argument that a state's members collectively own its public institutions.

7

Rejecting the Right to Exclude

1. Introduction

Most scholars of international ethics accept that there are limits to state sovereignty, especially those issuing from basic human rights. But many of the same people who think that states lack the right against interference in the realm of human rights-related wrongs nonetheless think that states have the right against interference when they commit the immigration-related wrongs of using wrongful immigration criteria (in particular, for most authors, any time race or ethnicity is used) and—as we saw in the introductory chapter, relatedly[1]—failing to admit people with urgent claims for admission (such as refugees).[2]

More generally, a variety of prominent defenders of states' choice (the idea that states have extensive moral rights to make membership decisions as they choose), including David Miller, Christopher Wellman, and Andrew Altman, maintain the conventional position that despite some immigration decisions being morally wrong, states nonetheless have the moral right to unilaterally determine their memberships, or the "right to exclude." And although Joseph Carens is arguably the leading philosophical *opponent* of states' choice, in his latest book he presupposes (and ultimately seems to accept) that states have the right to exclude. I will explain in this chapter how the right to exclude is distinct from states' choice; the right to exclude amounts to claiming that states have the moral right even to do something that is morally wrong (that is, the right to do wrong[3]) in the context

---

[1] See again the following: the valuable discussion in Song, *Immigration and Democracy*, chap. 7. See also "UNHCR Guidance on Racism and Xenophobia," UN Office of the High Commissioner for Human Rights, https://www.unhcr.org/en-us/protection/operations/5f7c860f4/unhcr-guidance-on-racism-and-xenophobia.html; International Labour Office, International Organization for Migration, and Office of the United Nations High Commissioner for Human Rights. *International Migration*; Espova, Ray, and Pugliese, "Syrian Refugees Not Welcome"; "Are Some EU Countries Wrong to Only Want Christian Refugees?", Debating Europe, September 8, 2015, https://www.debatingeurope.eu/2015/09/08/are-some-eu-countries-wrong-to-only-want-christian-refugees/#.Y-v4tXbMLEY; Alexander et al., "How Race and Religion"; Watson, "United States' Hollow Commitment"; Lipka, "Most Americans Express Support."

[2] See (for example) Walzer, *Spheres of Justice*, e.g., 61; Wellman, "Freedom of Association," esp. 112–14, 137; Blake, "Immigration and Political Equality," e.g., 970; Altman and Wellman, *Liberal Theory*, esp. 4–7, chap. 7; Miller, *Strangers in Our Midst*, esp. 33, 57, 62–63, 104–5, chap. 6.

[3] While numerous scholars have examined the idea of individuals' having a right to do wrong, the idea applied to states has received very little attention; this chapter examines the idea in the context—immigration—where it seems the most widely accepted or at least implied. The only other sustained analysis concerning states seems to be Gerhard Øverland and Christian Barry's valuable paper,

Immigration and Discrimination: (Un)Welcoming Others. Sahar Akhtar, Oxford University Press. © Sahar Akhtar 2024.
DOI: 10.1093/oso/9780198898696.003.0008

of their admission decisions. Importantly, this position does not merely entail the reasonable idea that because making wrongful admission decisions is often nothing like committing human rights abuses, outside intervention might do more harm than good and thus might often be wrong. The position assessed here has a much stronger implication for outside interference: outsiders are seemingly under an *all-things-considered duty* not to interfere with a state's wrongful exclusion decisions, even if interference takes the form of only economic, political, or diplomatic sanctions or penalties.

This is a deeply troubling position, however, considering the millions of people with urgent needs for admission. Even construed narrowly, there are over 35 million refugees and asylum seekers (and, more generally, over 100 million forcibly displaced persons)[4] in need of admission worldwide. This number increases *significantly* under the broader understanding of *refugee* that many (including me) accept, which again includes not only the persecuted and oppressed but anyone whose basic human rights are significantly and urgently jeopardized.[5] In Chapter 1 we saw that a variety of immigration theorists maintain that states have moral obligations to admit such persons if they are unable to be helped in their home state. Moreover, it is widely accepted that the needs of people experiencing significant and urgent basic human rights threats are unlikely to be met without substantial international coordination, including through the use of economic, political and diplomatic sanctions or penalties.[6] Finally, since a significant share of refugees, about 85% construed in the narrow sense and likely far more when construed in the broader sense, are hosted in already-burdened developing states, prominent immigration theorists readily accept that wealthier states have moral obligations to admit a *much* greater share than they currently do.[7]

"Do Democratic Societies Have a Right to Do Wrong?", but its focus is different. It concerns whether a majority has the right to have its democratically produced, morally wrong decisions complied with/not interfered with by other *members*, and is thus perhaps more related to issues of democratic authority and political obligation than the right to do wrong as held against outsiders. Relatedly, it does not discuss immigration decisions, which (as section 7 will highlight) are considered perhaps the most central domain for states' rights against outside interference.

    [4] "Refugee Data Finder," UNHCR, last modified October 27, 2022, https://www.unhcr.org/refugee-statistics/. The traditional conception of a refugee refers to someone who has departed their original state. But about 53 million forcibly displaced people remain in their original states, and their conditions and circumstances typically mirror those of traditional refugees. For more, see "About Internally Displaced Persons," UN Office of the High Commissioner for Human Rights, https://www.ohchr.org/en/issues/idpersons/pages/issues.aspx.

    [5] Pevnick extends the idea of refugee to people who are unable to meet their basic subsistence needs. Pevnick, *Constraints of Justice*, esp. 139–58. Wellman also suggests that the traditional understanding of refugee, as someone fleeing persecution, may be too narrow (2011). "Right to Exclude," 119.

    [6] See Cole, *Philosophies of Exclusion*; Carens, *Ethics of Immigration*, chap. 10; Gibney, "Refugees and Justice"; Owen, "Refugees, Fairness"; Miller, *Strangers in Our Midst*, 162–63; Bertram, *Do States Have the Right to Exclude Immigrants*; Song, *Immigration and Democracy*, esp. 121–27; Brock, *Justice for People on the Move*; and Owen, *What Do We Owe to Refugees*.

    [7] "World's Refugees," Amnesty International, https://www.amnesty.org/en/what-we-do/refugees-asylum-seekers-and-migrants/global-refugee-crisis-statistics-and-facts/. In addition to the references in my previous note, see (for example) Carens, *Ethics of Immigration*, chap. 10; Miller, *Strangers in Our*

However, if the conventional position is correct and states have the right to exclude, or the right against interference to unilaterally determine whom, if anyone, to admit, then outsiders, whether other states or international organizations, are under a duty not to impose any kind of sanction or penalty on the states that either fail in their moral duty to take in people with urgent needs or that, again often relatedly, use wrongful identity criteria. Thus, if this position is accepted, the prospect of meaningfully addressing the refugee crisis through international coordination would be significantly compromised.

In this (final) chapter, I will argue against the conventional position of the right to exclude by showing that it is morally implausible that states have the right to *wrongfully* exclude. My arguments do not depend on the claim that collective agents are different from individuals. I will argue that even if one thinks that individuals sometimes have the right against interference to do wrong, the corresponding view about states is implausible, at least when it comes to immigration related wrongs.

My argument takes the form of a reductio argument. Specifically, I will demonstrate that a plausible moral defense for the right to wrongfully exclude in the central cases of using identity and excluding people with urgent needs can only be given for states with morally *objectionable* character—protecting the very states whose immigration policies we should be most concerned with, which is surely morally counterintuitive. A major implication of my argument is that it is implausible to think that states are unilaterally entitled to make their membership decisions.

2. The Right to Exclude: What Exactly Is It?

Throughout this book we have discussed the conventional position of states' choice, which maintains that, when it comes to discretionary immigration, states have extensive moral rights to make membership decisions as they choose. But there is another aspect of the conventional position that, as I will demonstrate shortly, is distinct from states' choice: the right to exclude. The right to exclude refers to a state's moral claim-right to unilaterally decide to whom (if anyone) it will grant admission,[8] absent explicit agreements between states (for example, in the case of EU states) or agreements between states and international organizations.[9]

Midst, chap. 5. Andrew Altman and Christopher Wellman maintain that wealthy states have moral duties to rescue refugees, which can often only be satisfied by admitting them. Altman and Wellman, *Liberal Theory*, esp. 181–82.

[8] See (for example) Walzer, *Spheres of Justice*, esp. 112–14, 137; Altman and Wellman, *Liberal Theory*; Miller, *Strangers in Our Midst*, 33, 57, 62–63, chap. 6; Blake, "Immigration and Political Equality," e.g., 970. Sometimes the idea of a right to exclude pertains to a state's entitlement to exclude people from gaining *citizenship*, but my interest here is the state's right to exclude nonmembers from gaining admission. See Fine, "Freedom of Association," 342–43.

[9] See (for example) Blake, "Immigration, Jurisdiction, and Exclusion," 122–25.

The reasons given for maintaining that states have the right to exclude vary, but they appeal largely to the same sorts of rationales for states'-choice views we have considered in previous chapters. These range from arguments based on the value of protecting the dominant culture, to arguments based on members' collective freedom to associate with whomever they choose, to claims that members collectively own the institutions to which they have contributed.[10] A different sort of common rationale we have yet to discuss is a methodological one that claims that we can make progress on a variety of ethical questions regarding immigration even if we treat the right to exclude as a kind of realistic background assumption. As we will see, Carens adopts this perspective in at least the first part of his most recent book, and perhaps throughout.[11] My interest in this chapter is in examining and critiquing the right to exclude apart from any of the particular arguments in its favor.[12]

The most important aspect of the right to exclude is that it is understood as states' *sole discretion* or *unilateral control* to decide their memberships, or, put differently, that states are entitled to decide their memberships free from any (even in-principle) interference by outsiders (whether other states, the excluded migrants, or international organizations).[13,14] Interference can mean many things, including persuasion, social pressure, or even moral guidance, but the sort of interference at issue in the discussion of the right to exclude (and the right to wrongfully exclude, discussed in section 3) is coercive interference or enforcement. Though the exact meanings of these terms might be disputed, we can use the terms to refer to either the use of physical force or the issuing of economic, political, or diplomatic sanctions or penalties as well as credible threats to employ any such measures.

Given my arguments in preceding chapters, one might think that it is odd to devote an entire chapter to arguing against the right to exclude. After all, since I have already argued that exclusion on many grounds can violate global

---

[10] It's unclear whether Pevnick (*Constraints of Justice*) endorses the right to exclude. See my discussion in Chapter 4 concerning the United States' southern border wall.

[11] At several points, Carens (*Ethics of Immigration*) discusses how states' "discretionary authority" is limited by duties not to use (for example) race (see, for instance, 174). But at those moments, he seems to be suggesting that states lack the liberty-right to choose whatever criteria they want (making choosing such criteria morally wrong) not the claim-right against interference. In fact, he quite explicitly seems to maintain that states have the claim-right to choose morally wrong options (6–7), including about immigration policies (for example 270–73).

[12] In section 7, however, I will discuss the most plausible general rationale, based on collective autonomy, for thinking that states might have the right to do wrong.

[13] Here I am referring to Miller's description of the right (2016, p. 163).

[14] Walzer, *Spheres of Justice*, 61–62; Wellman, "Freedom of Association," e.g., 137. (For Wellman's allusion to this as a claim-right against interference, see, for example, 111–12, and for his suggestion of the unilateral understanding, see the top of 114.) Blake, "Immigration, Jurisdiction, and Exclusion," 120–21; Miller, *Strangers in Our Midst*, 33, 57, 62–63, chap. 6. As we will see, sometimes these authors refer to the idea of the right to exclude as a liberty-right and at other times as a claim-right against interference, and it will be important to distinguish these different senses.

antidiscrimination duties and thus can be morally wrong, haven't I *already* argued that states lack the right to exclude as defined above? In fact, I have not; nor have most authors arguing either that certain immigration criteria are wrong or that states' borders must be open. Moreover, arguments that appear explicitly to criticize the idea of a right to exclude have also not necessarily argued against the right to exclude *as defined above*.[15] The idea of a *claim*-right is critical for seeing why. A claim-right to do X (a right that correlates with a duty of others not to interfere with one's doing of X) is distinct from a liberty-right (or permission-right) to do X, which means there is no duty not to do X.[16] If a state has the claim-right to exclude, others have a duty not to interfere in the state's immigration policies and decisions. But the idea of states' choice examined in previous chapters refers to broad *liberty*-rights to choose immigration criteria, under which excluding people (on most or all grounds) is not morally wrong (that is, there is no moral duty not to exclude in most cases). Most arguments against a state's right to decide its membership as it chooses (including mine up to now) attempt to demonstrate why many bases for immigration restrictions, or almost all bases in the case of open-borders views, are morally wrong and thus that states lack the liberty-right to exclude on many, or almost all, bases.

But these arguments have not shown that states lack the *claim*-right to exclude people—the sense in which "right to exclude" is used in this book.[17] And perhaps the most significant implication of this right, thus far unchallenged, is, as we will see, that states would have the right against interference to make and implement *morally wrong* immigration decisions.[18]

3. States' Right to Do Wrong

As we will explore in depth in this section and the next, the right to exclude implies that states have a right against interference to make morally wrong immigration decisions. Indeed, this is the conventional position regarding both (1) excluding people on the basis of identity criteria and, relatedly, (2) excluding refugees and others with urgent admission needs.

---

[15] For instance, Sarah Fine's paper that challenges the self-determination rationales for a "right to exclude" nicely argues that such rationales fail to establish the *moral permissibility* of states excluding people. As I discuss in the next paragraph, the latter is distinct from "right to exclude" as defined above. Fine, "Ethics of Immigration." Also see Carens, "Migration and Morality"; Huemer, "Right to Immigrate?"; Oberman, "Immigration as Human Right."

[16] Waldron, "Right to Do Wrong," 29.

[17] A notable exception is Abizadeh, "Democratic Theory"; however, Abizadeh doesn't examine the claim-right's implications for *wrongful* exclusions (discussed next).

[18] Thus, states could lack a liberty-right to exclude in some cases (that is, exclusion may be morally wrong in those cases) and yet have a claim-right to exclude in those same cases.

I describe this as the conventional position for two reasons. First, by most accounts this is the way the right to exclude is interpreted in international law, which grants states a robust claim-right to exclude while also insisting that states have obligations to admit refugees and asylum seekers.[19] As two international law experts have recently noted, even the core principle of non-refoulement—the duty not to expel refugees and asylees to territories where they face serious risk of harm or persecution[20]—can give way to the state's right to exclude.[21]

Second, many of the notable immigration scholars we have surveyed in this book maintain that the two categories of exclusions above are almost always morally wrong while also suggesting that *legitimate* states—more on this below—nonetheless have the right against interference to construct their immigration policies as they choose, including in these two categories.[22] The view seems to comes down to the idea that, when it comes to their admission decisions, states have the right against interference to do wrong, or the right to wrongfully exclude.

Before going further, it is important to clarify what proponents of the right to exclude mean by "legitimate" states. Recently, there have been numerous compelling accounts of what makes an individual state legitimate which depend on the global system of states being legitimate. These accounts argue that a legitimate state system must include a global, cooperative migration scheme, which might specifically refer to refugee protection,[23] decisions concerning irregular migrants and identity-based immigration selection,[24] or even immigration selection more generally.[25] Such accounts argue that whether some state's immigration decision or set of decisions is right or wrong cannot be determined from the perspective of that individual state alone but must be considered from the collective perspective of the state system. The end result of this sort of approach is that states' admission decisions must be subject to international regulatory and enforcement mechanisms and institutions, and thus that states lack the right to exclude.[26]

Another way to demonstrate that states lack the right to exclude would be to argue that legitimate states must protect the basic human rights not only of their own members but that of nonmembers as well.[27] For, if, in order to be legitimate,

---

[19] Song, "Why Does the State Have the Right to Control Immigration"; Wyman, "Limiting the National Right to Exclude"; and Criddle and Fox-Decent, "The Authority of International Refugee Law".

[20] Convention Relating to the Status of Refugees Article 33(1), July 28, 1951, 19 U.S.T. 6259, 189 U.N.T.S. 150

[21] Criddle and Fox-Decent, "The Authority of International Refugee Law", 1096–97.

[22] Concerning stances on identity criteria, see, for example, Carens, *Ethics of Immigration*, 179, 174–75; Blake, "Discretionary Immigration"; Wellman, "Freedom of Association"; Miller, *Strangers in Our Midst*, 104–6. Shortly, I will discuss stances on refugees and others with urgent needs.

[23] See Owen, *What Do We Owe to Refugees*.   [24] See Brock, *Justice for People on the Move*.

[25] See Bertram, *Do States Have the Right to Exclude Immigrants*.

[26] See a recent paper ("Immigration and State System Legitimacy") by Daniel Sharp for helpful discussion and critical analyses of these positions.

[27] For a prominent description of state legitimacy along these lines, see the work of Allen Buchanan, 193, 266, chaps 4 and 6.

states must protect the basic human rights of nonmembers, then excluding people with urgent needs, such as refugees, might typically violate a state's legitimacy and hence not be something that a state would have a right against interference to do.[28]

I will take a different approach to arguing against the right to exclude that accepts the minimal conception of state legitimacy represented in international norms—one that depends neither on the state-system being legitimate nor on states protecting nonmembers' basic human rights. As reflected in international human rights norms, legitimate states are those which protect the basic human rights of all their members and merely do not violate the basic human rights of nonmembers.[29] As we saw in Chapter 1, states'-choice theorists construe state legitimacy in these terms. And this is also how proponents of the right to exclude construe legitimate states,[30] with the result being that a state that wrongfully excludes does not forfeit its right against interference to exclude.[31]

This is most obvious for authors who agree with this book's claim that certain criteria, such as race, can (also) wrong the excluded nonmembers. For these authors, the appeal to the right to wrongfully exclude is fairly explicit and their understandings of legitimacy do not rule it out. For instance, even though, as we saw in Chapter 1, Miller claims that racial criteria are wrong primarily because they wrong nonmembers,[32] he suggests that states have the moral right to decide their criteria on their own, even when wrong.[33] He discusses state legitimacy in terms of protecting the basic human rights of those within the state's territory, but when it comes to people outside the territory, legitimate states are those which merely do not violate basic human rights.[34] And he suggests that, under this idea of legitimacy, a state's legitimacy is not forfeited when it wrongfully excludes. For example, although he argues that racial and ethnic criteria are wrong,[35] he suggests that states have the moral right to choose any admission criteria against even "in principle" interference by "third parties."[36] Similarly, he writes that "a self-determining political community ... must have the *right* to control its borders."[37]

---

[28] Additionally, if there were a human right against discrimination, and excluding people on the basis of racial, ethnic, or other identity criteria would amount to the relevant discrimination, this would also violate a state's legitimacy and thus not be something that it has a right against interference to do. However, see (e.g.) Miller's discussion of this idea, which he rejects (*Strangers in Our Midst*, 103–4).

[29] Blake, Justice, *Migration and Mercy*, 68–71.

[30] This is also how Criddle and Fox-Decent ("The Authority of International Refugee Law", 1093–96) read these authors.

[31] As I discuss below in note 54, it seems for these authors that only disastrous consequences forfeit a state's right against interference, such as if excluding migrants triggers a war.

[32] Altman and Wellman, *Liberal Theory*, 104.

[33] Miller, *Strangers in Our Midst*, 33. Similarly, he writes, as long as it is not violating basic human rights, "a self-determining political community ... must have the *right* to control its borders" (62, emphasis in original).

[34] Miller, 59–62.   [35] Miller, 104–6.   [36] Miller, 33.

[37] Miller, 62, original emphasis. He writes, "my intention is not to lay down any particular immigration policy ... These are matters to be decided by democratic means within each state" (57). Also see 163.

Moreover, Miller seems to extend this position to people with urgent needs, concluding (reluctantly[38]) that a state that fails in its responsibility to admit refugees "could not be forced to comply, either by the refugees themselves, or by third parties."[39] More generally, in describing his aims concerning immigration selection, he writes, "my intention is not to lay down any particular immigration policy... These are matters to be decided by democratic means within each state. Instead my aim here is to show that policies that involve selecting some migrants and excluding others are [il]legitimate."[40] Importantly, "[il]legitimate" here does not refer to his view of the conditions which make a *state* legitimate or not; rather he is referring to his view about which immigration policies are morally wrong or not. Thus, Miller is suggesting that even when, according to his arguments, certain immigration policies are wrong, they are nonetheless "matters to be decided... within each state."

Carens appears to adopt a similarly minimal notion of legitimacy,[41] and is even more explicit in discussing the right to wrongfully exclude.[42] For instance, when considering whether moral questions about immigration conflict with the notion that "states must be free to construct their own immigration and citizenship policies, free from external interference," Carens writes that such a concern "confuses the question of who ought to have authority to determine a policy with the question of whether a given policy is morally acceptable."[43] He proceeds to say that, in general, "one can think that someone has the moral right to make a decision and still think that the decision itself is morally wrong,"[44] and he says that when it comes to states, "the decisions of a sovereign state may be morally wrong even if the state is morally entitled to make those decisions."[45] As we will see, it seems that Carens ultimately endorses this position, and moreover, like Miller, extends this position even to decisions to admit refugees and others with urgent needs.[46]

---

[38] Miller, 162–63. Miller expresses great moral concern with this position but seems to regard it as unavoidable.

[39] Miller, 163. More generally, here and elsewhere (e.g., 92) he suggests it's up to a state to decide how many refugees it admits.

[40] Miller, 57. In this next sentence, he proceeds to say, "instead my aim here is to show that policies that involve selecting some migrants and excluding others are [il]legitimate." But here, he is not referring to his view of the conditions which make a *state* legitimate or not; rather he is referring to his view about which immigration policies are morally *wrong* or not.

[41] See Carens, *Ethics of Immigration*, 7–8 where he describes the idea of sovereign democratic states in the context of human-rights obligations (also see 90–93).

[42] Carens, 174–75 and 179.   [43] Carens, 6.   [44] Carens, 6.

[45] Carens, 7. Also see 270–73. Chandran Kukathas, another open-borders proponent, appears to accept the realist perspective adopted by both Carens and Miller, though it is not entirely clear whether he construes the right to exclude only in legal terms or whether he also thinks it is a moral right. For instance, he claims that Miller's defense of a right to exclude is not necessary, given that "we live in a world of states and states have the authority and usually also the capacity to control their borders. Better from this starting point to turn to the question of whether they should exercise this power to open or close their borders, and how open those borders should be." Kukathas, "On David Miller," 714.

[46] Carens, *Ethics of Immigration*, 218–20.

Finally, though less explicit, Altman and Wellman also seem to endorse the right to wrongfully exclude. They argue that wealthy states have moral duties to rescue refugees, which can often only be satisfied by admitting them.[47] Moreover—as discussed (in the case of Wellman) in Chapters 1 and 4—they argue that certain identity criteria, especially race and ethnicity, are almost always wrong because they wrong the state's own members with the disfavored criteria.[48] But they also claim that legitimate states—which they define as those which "protect [their] own members against 'substantial and recurrent threats' to a decent human life...and refrain from imposing such threats on outsiders"[49]— have the right against interference in their decisions as part of their right of self-determination.[50] Importantly, wrongfully excluding people would not seem to constitute the sorts of things that violate this understanding of state legitimacy, such as "the arbitrary deprivation of life or liberty, and the infliction of torture."[51] Thus, it would seem for these authors that states enjoy the right against interference to exclude people even when excluding someone is morally wrong.

It might seem that the position described above is merely that outsiders may not interfere with a state's wrongful exclusions because doing so would either have worse consequences or entail more wrongs. However, this does not seem to be the position. In fact, citing John Stuart Mill, Carens even suggests that *criticism* (not just coercion) might be an impermissible form of interference. He writes that "there is something to the claim that freedom from external criticism is an important component of state autonomy and democratic self-determination."[52] More generally, as indicated in the quoted passages, these authors stress the *right* against interference, not only the moral impermissibility of interference. And, while the fact that interference in a state's wrongdoing may entail greater moral wrongs might well be a reason against interference and thus may provide states a measure of de facto freedom to wrongfully exclude people, that is not equivalent to saying, nor does it establish, that states possess the *right* against interference. In the case of the right against interference, there is a duty (seemingly an all-things-considered duty, as discussed shortly) owed to the right-holder not to interfere.[53] In general, questions about the feasibility or permissibility of interference can arise in any kind of wrongdoing, and not just those purportedly protected by a right. As Galston argues, "Even if an outbreak of looting can only be quelled through a draconian shoot-to-kill policy, it is by no means clear that it is proper to employ such a policy. But our qualms about its permissibility obviously do not stem from

---

[47] Altman and Wellman, *Liberal Theory*, 182–82.   [48] Altman and Wellman, 186–87.
[49] Altman and Wellman, 4. See the earlier discussion of legitimacy in this book's Chapter 1, section 2.
[50] Altman and Wellman, 7.   [51] Altman and Wellman, 4.
[52] Carens, *Ethics of Immigration*, 8.
[53] This is true of the right to do wrong generally. As Herstein writes, "The cutting edge of the right to do wrong is that it gives the right-holder a *moral claim to enforce the duty of non-interference* on others." Herstein, "Right to Do Wrong," 18. See also Galston, "Alleged Right to Do Wrong"; Enoch, Right to Violate One's Duty."

any suspicion that the looters had a right to do what they did."[54] It is one thing to say that (some form of) interference is morally wrong, but quite another to say that one has the right against (that form of) interference. In the next section, I discuss why this distinction is important.

4. What Is at Stake?

At this point, one might have a number of questions. Is the difference between having the right against interference even in wrongdoing, on the one hand, and interference being morally wrong, on the other, merely a conceptual distinction? Is it at most a trivial substantive distinction? Moreover, notice that under the idea of a right to do wrong, acting within one's right does not make a wrong action any *less* wrong. As Enoch writes, "It is important to note that it does not follow from the thesis [of a right to do wrong] that a right to violate one's duty gets one off the (moral) hook."[55] Thus, one might ask, if, independently of states having the right against interference to wrongfully exclude, we can discuss whether interference in a state's wrongful exclusions is morally wrong, and if we can speak intelligently in the first place about states committing moral wrongs when they make certain immigration decisions, why the fuss in this chapter about demonstrating that states lack the *right* against interference to wrongfully exclude? More generally, one might wonder what exactly the bite is of arguing that states lack the right to exclude.

To highlight the significance of this issue, the first thing to note is that the idea that states have the right to exclude does not seem to be that states have only the right against interference to make morally *permissible* decisions or even decisions that are only *pro tanto wrong* (or violate a prima facie duty).[56] Second, the idea does not seem to be that states have merely a *prima facie right* to exclude. Let's take each part in turn.

First, it is not plausible to interpret proponents of the right to exclude as maintaining merely that states have the right against interference to do something either that is morally permissible or that is only pro tanto wrong. If that were the position, it would be hard to see how the question of outside interference might even arise. This is obvious in the case of doing something that is morally permissible: why would we need to defend states having the moral right against interference when they do nothing wrong? But the point also holds for exclusions that are only pro tanto wrong. For X's being only pro tanto wrong is compatible

---

[54] Galston, "Alleged Right to Do Wrong," 321.   [55] Enoch, "Right to Violate One's Duty," 363.
[56] Generally speaking, if the thesis of a right to do wrong were that there is a prima facie right to commit a pro tanto wrong or violate a prima facie duty, it would be trivial. As Enoch notes, "Thus understood even the thesis that one can have a moral duty to do something and a moral duty not to do it is right" (360–61).

with X's being all-things-considered *not wrong*. So, if states merely had the right against interference to commit only pro tanto-wrong exclusions, states would have the right against interference to exclude in cases that are, when everything is morally tallied, not wrong. But, again, why would the idea that others have a duty not to interfere even arise if we are considering exclusions that are, at the end of the day, not wrong? For even those who deny the right to exclude, or state sovereignty entirely, would likely readily agree that committing a pro tanto-wrong exclusion that is overall *not wrong* would not warrant any even in-principle interference by outsiders. Thus, the idea of the right to exclude really seems to be that, when making decisions about immigration, a state has the right against interference to commit even an all-things-considered-wrong exclusion.

For similar reasons, the idea does not seem to be that states have merely a prima facie right against interference to wrongfully exclude that can be overridden or outweighed by other considerations, for this too would seem rather uncontentious.[57] Sometimes authors do seem to be suggesting that the right to exclude can be overridden in some circumstances, especially urgent circumstances. For instance, Miller suggests that there are cases in which people's urgent claims for admission "may override the state's right to exclude them."[58] But at such times, immigration theorists seem to be implicitly referring to the idea of a *liberty*-rights to exclude—basically suggesting that, sometimes, a state's excluding of others is, all things considered, morally wrong. For instance, we have seen that it may, according to these authors, often be wrong to exclude someone with urgent needs. If so, a liberty-right to exclude would be overridden in those cases. But this does *not* mean that they think that outsiders (whether those with urgent needs themselves or third parties) may interfere.[59] In fact, even when Carens eventually goes on to challenge the conventional position in the second half of his book, he is only challenging the view of *states' choice*—again, the view that states have broad liberty-rights to decide their immigration policies how they choose[60]—not the position that they have the right against interference to exclude even when making wrong immigration policies.[61] For instance, in referring to his view that there is a moral right to international freedom of movement, he claims that it does not conflict with the idea of state sovereignty. He writes, "As a concept, sovereignty

[57] Enoch (360–61) suggests that such a right would be uncontroversial. And Herstein ("Right to Do Wrong," 18) writes, "The cutting edge of the right to do wrong is that it gives the right-holder a moral claim to enforce the duty of non-interference on others."

[58] Miller, *Strangers in Our Midst*, 58.

[59] Indeed, Miller (*Strangers in Our Midst*, 163) suggests that if a state were to fail in its obligations to admit refugees ("under a fair distribution"), it "could not be forced to comply, either by the refugees themselves, or by third parties."

[60] For instance, see Carens, *Ethics of Immigration*, 226.

[61] Carens, 270–71. For another example, Carens says states' "discretionary authority" is limited by duties not to use (e.g.) racial criteria (see, e.g., p.174). But, again, he's suggesting that states lack not the claim-right but the liberty-right to use certain criteria (i.e., he is stating that such criteria are morally wrong).

only requires that states themselves be the ones to decide what their immigration policies will be. It does not entail the idea that their immigration policies must be morally unconstrained."[62] The suggestion is that the moral rationales for freedom of movement provide the relevant moral constraints but do not imply that outsiders may enforce a state's compliance with those moral constraints.[63]

When discussing the *claim*-right to exclude, such theorists seem to be carving out a special realm of decision-making—regarding the state's admission decisions—as something that is to be (virtually) entirely insulated from the interference of outsiders. That is, perhaps barring disastrous circumstances such as if excluding migrants were to trigger a war,[64] such authors seem to maintain that states have the all-things-considered right to exclude; if so, it would seem that interference in a state's wrongful exclusion *cannot* be justified.[65]

Now, to fully understand what is at stake in arguing against this position, it will be helpful to examine how the project undertaken in this chapter is different from some other recent work. Some authors have recently argued that individuals' noncompliance with immigration restrictions,[66] even if it involves the use of force,[67] *can* sometimes be justified. My analysis is different for several reasons, beginning with some relatively minor issues.

First, I am concerned with *collective* interference in a state's immigration decisions, not individual acts. Second, and more relevantly, interference is distinct from resistance or noncompliance—the topic of these authors' recent work. Interference seems to have the goal of altering the agent's conduct, whether by trying to prevent the agent from choosing an option they might otherwise choose or forcing them to choose an option they might otherwise not choose. Resistance or noncompliance, in contrast, doesn't necessarily aim to coercively alter agents' behavior so much as it evades that behavior. Indeed, aside from using force against (especially) border guards, states would arguably not even be aware of the kinds of resistance or noncompliance highlighted by recent authors as potentially permissible, such as evading and deceiving immigration officials.[68]

---

[62] Carens, 273.

[63] Carens, 270. Similarly, Carens says states' "discretionary authority" is limited by duties not to use (for example) racial criteria (see, for example, 174). But he's suggesting that states lack not the claim-right but the liberty-right to use certain criteria (that is, such criteria are morally wrong).

[64] Altman and Wellman (*Liberal Theory*, 6–7) say the right to exclude is not absolute, but it seems defeated only if a state's exclusion decision causes disastrous consequences (the example they give of an individual's right being defeated is when their decision would cause a world war) (165). Since standard exclusion decisions aren't likely to provoke such consequences, we can leave this qualification aside.

[65] Clear expressions of this are found in Altman and Wellman (6–7), who describe deontic reasons not to interfere with the state's decisions as "exclusionary reasons." See my previous note for a possible exception. Also see Carens, *Ethics of Immigration*, 6; Miller, *Strangers in Our Midst*, 163.

[66] In particular, see Hidalgo, "Unjust Immigration Restrictions."

[67] Hidalgo, "Unjust Immigration Restrictions."

[68] A related point is worth stressing. One key theme in these recent arguments is that immigrants lack content-independent duties to obey the admitting state's immigration laws. But the question

The third and most important difference between my project and recent work, especially a valuable paper by Hidalgo,[69] remains even if we ignore the distinction between individual and collective action and we assume that resistance or non-compliance amounts to (external) interference. Namely, Hidalgo's project, which is concerned with demonstrating that interference can be justified, simply seems to reject the possibility of the right to exclude. After noting that border guards and other state agents "can cause [migrants] harm or risks of harm,"[70] he claims that when threats of harm are undertaken to enforce wrongful immigration restrictions, they are "unjustified threats."[71] He then maintains that agents (or states) that pose unjustified threats of harm forfeit any right against interference, including against physical interference;[72] thus, in such cases, if certain conditions are satisfied (proportionality and necessity), physical interference is permissible.[73] Hidalgo provides compelling arguments for the latter, but, on his understanding, it seems that whenever an immigration restriction is morally wrong, the state's enforcing it is unjustified, and it thus forfeits the right against interference.[74] However, if states have the right to exclude, wrongfully excluding would not itself forfeit the right against interference.[75] I am not asserting that states have the right to exclude nor, if they do, that there are not conditions under which they forfeit this right. But maintaining that wrongfully excluding *itself* forfeits that right simply denies the possibility of the right since, as we have seen, the right to exclude seems to entail (whether explicitly or implicitly) the all-things-considered right against interference to have all-things-considered-wrongful policies.

To examine whether interference in wrongful exclusions is permissible in certain cases, then, the prior issue that must be addressed, and, moreover, the one that constitutes the first line of defense against interference in a state's immigration decisions, is whether states have the right to exclude. For no matter how compelling arguments in favor of interference in a particular kind of wrongful immigration decision are, if states have the all-things-considered right against interference, then others' interference is morally prohibited at the outset since others are seemingly under an *all-things-considered duty* (owed to the state) not to interfere. So, before we can arrive at the question whether particular forms of interference may be permissible in particular cases, we must first demonstrate that

---

whether a state has political authority over its laws is largely distinct from whether it has the right to exclude. The purported grounds for a duty to obey the law (that is, the state's authority) include notions such as fair play, reciprocity, and democratic respect. (See Hidalgo's ("Unjust Immigration Restrictions") clear discussion of these issues.) But these grounds are strongest or most apt with respect to a state's members (see Huemer, *Problem of Political Authority*). The right to exclude, however, pertains only to interference by outsiders.

[69] Hidalgo, "Unjust Immigration Restrictions."   [70] Hidalgo, 5, 1.

[71] Hidalgo, 6. He focuses on one type of wrongful exclusion—roughly, not admitting people with urgent needs (4)—but says his analysis applies to any kind of wrong exclusion (see 4, 5n16).

[72] Hidalgo, 6, 9, 20.   [73] Hidalgo, 8–9.   [74] Hidalgo, 18.

[75] To preempt a possible objection: the right to have wrongful policies is not simply the right to design and implement them but also to enforce them.

states lack the all-things-considered right against interference to commit an all-things-considered wrong—that is, that they lack the right to exclude.

5. The Autonomy to Wrong the State's Members?

Focusing first only on cases of identity criteria, in this section and the next we will begin to see what a successful defense of the right to wrongfully exclude requires and, eventually, why that defense is concerning. The focus in this section is exploring the idea of the right within the framework of the Wrong to Members view (WM).

Recall that Blake, Wellman, and Altman claim that racial criteria are wrong when and because they express a demeaning message about or treat as second-class citizens the states' members of the disfavored race.[76] And importantly, as we saw in section 3, (at least) Altman and Wellman maintain that states enjoy the right against interference to wrongfully exclude. Putting the two positions together, states would have the right against interference to make immigration decisions that wrong their own members.

One might think that it is easy to justify states having the right to wrongfully exclude when such decisions only wrong the state's own members. Perhaps defenders would say that since the relevant wrong would be committed against the state's own collective self, this insulates it from *external* interference. However, from the mere fact that the wrong is an internal one—that the aggrieved party is the self—it does not follow that outsiders are barred from interfering. This can be seen by examining the individual case: let's presume that if, out of curiosity, I were to ingest several gallons of gasoline, I would, all things considered, wrong myself. Even though the action would wrong myself (and thus represent an internal moral wrong), it does not seem that others would have an all-things-considered duty to me not to interfere with my action. The opposite seems true: they would have a duty to try to prevent me from drinking the gasoline. To clarify, there may be a variety of all-things-considered wrongs to the self that outsiders are barred from interfering with; examples might include consuming a lot of unhealthy food or never exercising. But to claim that others have an all-things-considered duty not to interfere with one's wrongdoing, it is not enough to point out that the wrong is committed against *oneself*. Substantive argument is needed.

---

[76] Wellman, "Freedom of Association," 139; Blake, "Discretionary Immigration," 284–85. It looks like Carens (*Ethics of Immigration*) accepts a similar sort of view when it comes to states' membership decisions regarding family admission criteria. For instance, he writes that "the right of human beings to live with their immediate family members imposes a moral limit on the state's right simply to set its admissions policy as it chooses" (188). For Carens, the moral limits in this case come from within—from the claims of people already in the society.

Returning to states, it is implausible to think that just because the wronged in a given case are the state's own members, other states are under a duty to that state not to interfere. If the majority in some state were to begin systematically killing the minority, not only would other states not have a duty to refrain from intervening, but they would have a *positive* duty to intervene. To clarify, I am not stating that in the case of, say, racial immigration criteria, the wrong done to members who share the disfavored race is of equal moral significance with killing members; demeaning members or undermining the social bases of their self-respect, while important, are certainly not as serious as killing members. This might often mean that the potential harm or wrong done by outsiders attempting to intervene—such as by attempting to coerce the state not to use racial criteria—would clearly outweigh the harm or wrong that occurs when immigration decisions disfavor some members' race.

However, it is first worth remembering that external interference need not come in the form of the use of force but could consist in trade sanctions or other economic, political, or diplomatic measures to attempt to alter the state's immigration policies. And because of the availability of these other methods, it might not always even be true that interference with a state's wrongful immigration decisions would result in more harm or wrongs. More importantly, as we have seen in the previous two sections, just because interfering with a state's wrongful immigration decisions might generate greater harm or wrongs does not imply that states have the right to make wrongful immigration decisions that wrong their members.

The upshot is that a defense of the right to wrongfully exclude that appeals to the idea that only the state's members are wronged when it uses certain immigration criteria must do more than show that interference is either infeasible or impermissible. It must provide substantive reasons in favor of the view that states have the right against interference to wrong their members when making immigration decisions. In section 7, we will survey the primary rationale for maintaining that individuals are thought to have a right to do certain wrongs and assess whether it is plausible that this rationale applies to states and, if so, what this means.

6. A Right to Exclude and Wronging Nonmembers?

Before proceeding to discuss the primary rationale for the right to do wrong, the issue I want to explore now concerns why, or in what way, states that have the right to exclude, and hence the right to wrongfully exclude, would, by employing wrongful identity criteria, be doing something morally wrong. In short, despite it being intuitive that such criteria would often wrong nonmembers, it's difficult to see why that is the case if states in fact have the right to exclude. As mentioned, both Carens and Miller believe that certain identity criteria primarily wrong nonmembers. Since something close to Miller's argument may be the intuitive view, let's focus on it.

It will be helpful to recall Miller's explanation, briefly explored in Chapter 1. Miller believes that since people have strong interests at stake when it comes to immigration, states must show people equal consideration absent relevant differences between them, implying that a state must give someone relevant reasons if they are excluded while others are admitted.[77] He suggests that racial or ethnic preferences are not tied to morally permissible goals for democratic states, and so they can never be relevant reasons for exclusion; thus, such exclusions wrong the excluded nonmembers.[78] In Chapter 1, I discussed problems facing Miller's view, such as determining what counts as a relevant reason, and throughout this book I have argued that it sometimes is morally permissible to use racial or ethnic criteria. But here, let's assume that we are only considering cases in which such criteria are indeed wrong and, to sidestep concerns about how to understand "relevant reason," assume it refers to a morally good reason. Nonetheless—setting aside nonmembers with either urgent or special claims for admission[79]—it is unclear why states owe nonmembers morally good reasons, or even owe it to them to have such reasons, if states actually have the right to exclude.

Consider the position that it is at the sole moral discretion of property owners to deny others access to their property, and imagine the following scenario:

> Prisha, who is a Sinhalese (Sri Lankan), would like to start a business harvesting rare herbs, which requires a particular combination of soil, rain, and sun exposure. The only nearby suitable land belongs to a local homeowner, Adnan, who is Punjabi (Pakistani). Adnan owns several acres, so Prisha requests permission to use a small part of his land. Adnan harbors racist beliefs and, based on those beliefs, denies her request without explaining his reasons.

Supposing there is a unilateral right to exclude others from one's personal property, what exactly does Adnan owe to Prisha? Specifically, does he owe it to her to have a morally good reason for excluding her? If so, and since he fails to have one, does he wrong her (and perhaps all Sinhalese people) by excluding her?

---

[77] Miller, *Stranger in Our Midst*, 105.

[78] Miller, 104–6. Miller says that racial criteria cannot be tied to "goals that a democratic state might legitimately wish to pursue" (106), and he says he's relying on an intuitive understanding of which goals are legitimate (197n35). While I agree it's intuitive that racial selection isn't legitimate, appealing to democratic considerations doesn't obviously explain how racial criteria wrong *nonmembers* (though they might explain how they wrong members). And insofar as democratic obligations are thought to extend outside the state, different arguments from those here place pressure on the right to exclude (for instance, see Abizadeh, "Democratic Theory and Border Coercion").

[79] Again, the category of urgent needs includes people like refugees. By "special claims" I mean people with whom the admitting state has special relationships or has made promises or commitments.

Certainly, Adnan's beliefs are deplorable and reveal something very objectionable about his character. But, if Adnan has the right to exclude, then (aside from urgent or special claims for access[80]), it is not obvious that he has a duty to Prisha or any other person to have a morally good reason, or any reason at all, for refusing people access. Adnan does not seem to wrong Prisha by excluding her from his property for the same reason that he would not wrong *anyone* by excluding them, whether for racial reasons or otherwise: it is simply his right to control his property.

To clarify, the idea is not that having the right to exclude others from one's property serves as a reason *in favor* of excluding on wrongful (or any particular) grounds.[81] It is rather that, apart from urgent cases and special cases (more on this below), the idea of the right to exclude is so intricately bound with the idea of freedom from interference that it seems one does not *owe* any sort of explanation—morally good or otherwise—for excluding anyone. It could be that the right generates a noninterference claim of an especially robust sort: a right not only against coercive interference but against even having to have (and, so provide) a reason for excluding someone. This might set the right apart from a variety of other claim-rights, such as a right to choose how to discharge one's charitable obligations, a right to expression, or a right to decide one's employment. Take a right to expression. It often seems one owes it to others to have a morally good reason for making certain statements, even if others must not coercively interfere with their expression. But thinking that people must have a good reason for excluding others from their property seems to commit a category mistake about what the idea of the right to exclude entitles one to do: namely, (aside from urgent and special cases) exclude for *any* or *no* reason at all.

Suppose another stranger, Farah (who, like Adnan, is Punjabi), also asks to use a portion of Adnan's land and that based on his racist preferences, he grants Farah access but not Prisha. Does he now wrong Prisha by failing to treat her equally with Farah? Once again, his actions reveal something quite objectionable about his character, and perhaps by failing to live up to certain standards for a virtuous person, he commits a wrong. But that is very different from saying that he has *wronged* someone.[82] Again, there is a directionality to wronging someone, whereby the wrongdoer violates a duty *to* the wronged person, giving the wronged person a certain moral standing in relation to the wrongdoer—to complain, seek redress, or demand accountability or apology. It could be that Adnan has done *something* that fails to treat Prisha equally with others and that thereby wrongs her

---

[80] We can imagine analogs to state admissions. See my previous note.

[81] This is important, as having a right against interference in one's wrongdoing does not provide a reason in favor of doing wrong. The issue is further discussed in section 8.

[82] Owens. *Shaping the Normative Landscape.* Also see Cornell's discussion ("Wrongs, Rights, and Third Parties").

(and other Sinhalese people): having racist beliefs about them.[83] And for this, Prisha may have standing to demand of Adnan accountability and that he work to change his beliefs. But if Adnan has the right to exclude, it is far from obvious Prisha has any moral standing with respect to Adnan's act of *excluding* her from his land, even while admitting someone else—no matter whether she is excluded because of his racist beliefs.

Finally, we could imagine that multiple people own the land along with Adnan, and it would not seem to alter anything: if, collectively, they have the right to exclude others from their property, excluding Prisha on the basis of her race would still not seem to wrong her. Thus, the implication seems to be that if a state's members have the collective right to exclude, it would be difficult to explain why identity criteria would ever wrong the excluded nonmembers—presenting a problem for authors, such as Miller and Carens, maintaining both that states have such a right and that the primary wrong of certain identity criteria is against excluded nonmembers.

Now there could certainly be special circumstances in which we can make sense of how Adnan wrongs Prisha by excluding her from his property—if he had, say, previously committed to allowing her onto his land, or if he owes her access as repayment for some favor. The same is true of states. For instance, imagine that state A has entered into a particular agreement or relationship with another state, B, or has made a promise to admit any of B's members. But then A implements racial criteria with the effect that some of B's members—those falling into the disfavored racial category—will not be admitted. In that case, we can make sense of how state A wrongs certain nonmembers even if it has the right to exclude: it has violated a special commitment to those nonmembers. The concern, however, is how we can make sense of any moral grievance against nonmembers absent either special or urgent circumstances.

To clarify, just as with our property example, and as suggested in both Chapters 4 and 5, it may often be the case that a state's act of wrongfully excluding people on racial grounds would express that it has flawed values or poor moral character. And by failing to have the character of a virtuous state or live up to certain standards for a just state, the state has done something morally wrong. But that is very different from saying that the state wrongs the excluded nonmembers or that it violates a relevant duty to nonmembers.[84]

---

[83] I'm uncertain which, if any, beliefs are inherently morally wrong to *have/token* (i.e., apart from acting on them), but granting that the present belief is inherently wrong doesn't damage my argument.

[84] The difficulty here might be at least partly explained by the common understanding of what *sorts* of wrongs one might have a right to commit. The canonical examples are things like the right not to give any lottery winnings to charity, the right not to help people requesting directions, and the right to vote for a racist political party. (For such examples, see Waldron, "Right to Do Wrong," 21; Enoch, "Right to Violate One's Duty"; Quong, "Rights of Unreasonable Citizens," 332; Herstein, "Right to Do Wrong," 2.) What these examples may have in common is that they all seem to involve the violation of nondirectional duties—that is, duties not owed *to* anyone in particular. Without wading into the debate

7. The Right to Wrongfully Exclude, and State Autonomy

I have not conclusively shown that the right to exclude does not permit saying that states can wrong nonmembers when using wrongful criteria, but I hope to have provided reason to doubt that possibility. However, perhaps many defenders of the right to exclude would happily accept a character-based explanation for how some wrongful exclusion is wrong. They might think that, as in the landowner example, when a state excludes on racial or ethnic grounds, it often expresses that it (or its members) has morally reprehensible values or poor moral character. And it is by failing to have the character of a virtuous state or live up to standards for a just state that the state commits a wrong.

The previous section demonstrated that this sort of character-based explanation of some exclusion's wrong does seem coherent with thinking that an agent has a right to undertake that exclusion. But we must still explore whether there are plausible grounds for states' having the right. We will see that not only can the wrong of wrongful identity criteria, and, more importantly, wrongfully excluding people with urgent needs, be explained in terms of morally objectionable character, but objectionable character ends up providing the moral *defense* for having the right to undertake these wrong exclusions in the first place. For this reason, I will conclude, we should reject that states have such a right.

---

about the best understanding of rights—specifically, whether it is possible for a right to consist only of a claim or whether it must also involve a privilege—some authors note that it may be conceptually difficult to reconcile having a right to violate one's duty if the duty is owed to the same person or people the right is against, since that may amount to saying that one has a right against person X in one's ø-ing to violate a duty to X *not* to ø. Depending on one's view of rights, it may be conceptually implausible to say that one has a moral right (against another) to violate one's duty to someone. For instance, see Enoch's ("Right to Violate One's Duty," 370–72) discussion of the Hart-Hohfeldian understanding of a right to ø. Hart argues that the proper understanding of a right to ø implies a privilege (or liberty) to ø in conjunction with a claim against interference in one's ø-ing. But a privilege to ø means that one has no duty not to ø. Thus, under the Hart-Hohfeldian understanding of a right to ø, to reconcile the conceptual possibility of having a right to ø, where ø-ing involves violating one's duty, it must be that the duty is not owed to the same person or people the right is against. For otherwise, we would be saying that one has a privilege *against* X to ø and a duty *to* X *not* to ø. For instance, Enoch writes, "According to Hohfeld, privileges, much like claims, are directional. A privilege *against* X to ø is indeed incompatible with a duty *to* X not to ø. But a privilege *against* X to ø is perfectly compatible with a duty *to* Y (where Y is not X) not to ø, or with a non-directional duty not to ø It follows, then, that even if the best understanding of a right to ø is as involving a privilege to ø, it is still possible to have a right to violate one's duty, so long as the duty is not owed to the same person the right (and so also the privilege) is against" (370). Such concerns seem to have motivated the most prominent defender of a right to do wrong, Waldron, to suggest that the strongest candidates for wrong acts that we might have a right to commit are not wrongs that violate duties to others, but rather wrongs that are "subject to moral criticism for other and more subtle reasons" such as wrongs that "may be seen as wrong because they are vicious, or because they fall short of the standard required by some ideal or principle" (Waldron, "Right to Do Wrong," 24–25). Waldron equates violating a duty to another with the idea that the other person has a right, but this is because he is (here) discussing the idea of violating duties owed to others in terms of Mackie's understanding of Hohfeld's rights analysis, under which a duty to someone corresponds to a right of theirs.

We can start by considering the primary reason that individuals are thought to have certain rights to do wrong. The main rationale is related to the idea of individual autonomy, or self-governance and self-determination over one's own life. Jeremy Waldron, perhaps the most prominent figure in the right-to-do-wrong discussion, argues that in order to be autonomous, one must have a protected range of choices in domains of decision-making that are especially important to self-determination, and that, given few to no morally permissible options in those important domains, genuine choice must also include the choice to do certain wrongs.[85] And, as we saw, although others' interference in a decision may be wrong for any number of reasons, Waldron argues that having the right against such interference provides a special (and all-things-considered) reason for others' noninterference—one that originates in the right-holders' claims. Thus, the idea is that if one has few to no morally permissible options in central matters of decision-making, then, to be autonomous, one must have the special protection afforded by the right to do wrong.

We can invoke a similar understanding of autonomy for states, appealing to the idea of a collective right (discussed in Chapter 1) of a group of people to define for themselves the terms of their political association or community. Moreover, we can grant that immigration decisions are especially significant to a state's collective autonomy since authors seem to regard them as such; indeed, it seems few other decisions are considered as relevant for a state's self-constitution. For instance, Altman and Wellman write that "because the members of a group can change, an important part of group self-determination is having control over what the 'self' is. In other words, unlike individual self-determination, a significant component of group self-determination is having control over the group which in turn gets to be self-determining."[86] In a similar vein, Walzer has written that "admission and exclusion are at the core of communal independence. They suggest the deepest meaning of self-determination."[87] As suggested throughout this book, I more or less accept the importance of membership decisions for collective autonomy, including, under certain conditions, for states' autonomy. But does this imply that there is an autonomy-based rationale for states having the right to wrongfully exclude?

---

[85] Waldron's ("Right to Do Wrong," 34–37) view is that since everything is either morally required, morally indifferent, or morally prohibited, without the right to do wrong, one ultimately only has the right to choose the required option (because the prohibited one is ruled out and the required one dominates the indifferent one). This view has been contested by others, who (I believe, rightly) argue that it fails to capture the full space of moral life. In particular, it fails to properly distinguish morally permissible from morally indifferent. As Enoch ("Right to Violate One's Duty," 365–66) notes, "From the fact that an action is morally permissible but not required it does *not* follow that it is morally indifferent. There are many things we have moral reasons to do (and not to do) that are neither morally impermissible nor morally required."

[86] Altman and Wellman, *Liberal Theory*, 163.   [87] Walzer, *Spheres of Justice*, 62.

Recall that under the view defended in this book, states may often be permitted to use not only security, safety, and resource considerations in their immigration decisions, but also a variety of professional, skills, and language considerations and accessible test requirements for the public political culture (as long as none of the above are used as proxies for wrongful identity-based decisions); even identity criteria, including racial and ethnic criteria, might not always be wrong. Moreover, although (as we have seen) prominent immigration theorists suggest that states have the right to wrongfully exclude in cases of identity criteria and people with urgent needs, many of the same theorists maintain that states also have a range of morally permissible options for exclusion. Indeed, as we saw in previous chapters, under a wide variety of views—even Carens's understanding of open borders— states may be morally permitted to exclude on the basis of security, safety, capacity, resource, and way-of-life considerations and also often based on professional, skills, and language considerations (as long as none of these serve as proxies for wrongful identity criteria or wrongfully excluding urgent cases).[88] Moreover, when some of these issues are present, including way-of-life concerns, identity criteria might not be all-things-considered wrong,[89] and excluding people with urgent needs might not be all-things-considered wrong when other issues are present, such as significant safety, capacity, and resource concerns.[90] Though such immigration decisions might be considered *pro tanto* wrong under the views surveyed in this book, recall that the right to do wrong concerns all-things-considered wrongs: if it is not all-things-considered wrong to (say) use resource or capacity considerations to exclude urgent cases, such decisions do not concern the right to wrongfully exclude.

Based, then, not only on the antidiscrimination view I have defended but also a wide range of other views on the ethics of immigration, states are morally permitted to make the immigration decisions just described; at most, such decisions are pro tanto wrong. Do states also have the right to do wrong when excluding?

A preliminary point is that even for individuals, there is not the right to commit *any* wrong: no one thinks there is a right against interference to murder. For defenders of individuals' right to do wrong, their interest is in arguing only that one might have the right to commit certain wrongs. Which wrongs? Canonical examples include the right not to give any lottery winnings to charity or the right to vote for racist parties.[91] To account for why individuals might have the right to do these sorts of wrongs but not a right to murder, proponents seem to implicitly rely on a balance-of-reasons approach—weighing (a) the autonomy reasons in favor of the right to choose wrongful options against (b) the reasons those options are wrong.

---

[88] Carens suggests that these options, though often pro tanto wrong, might not be all-things-considered wrong in our actual world. "Migration and Morality," 40; *Ethics of Immigration*, 276–87.

[89] Carens, "Migration and Morality," 37–39; Blake, "Distributive Justice," 286; Miller, "Immigration," 204; Wellman, "Freedom of Association," 140–41.

[90] See (for example) Miller, *Strangers in Our Midst*, chap. 5; Carens, *Ethics of Immigration*, 220.

[91] See my note 85 for discussion.

Now, to argue that states lack the right to wrongfully exclude in cases involving identity criteria and urgent needs, I could focus only on (b). I might attempt demonstrating that the wrongful options violate moral rights or are on a moral par with acts like murder, thereby ruling out the possibility that states have the right to choose those options even without assessing (a). For instance, some understandings of rights might rule out having claim-rights to violate other moral rights, and perhaps excluding people with urgent needs violates their basic human rights (at least their remedial rights, as explained in Chapter 6); if so, states might not have a claim-right to deny them. Or I might argue that when a state fails to admit people with urgent needs, it is responsible for their dire needs' going unmet, thereby *causing* them substantial harm[92]—something so egregious that it is obvious states do not have the right to do so. However, there are problems with such strategies. Under some rights conceptions, it seems there can be claim-rights to violate other moral rights,[93] and I wish to remain neutral on the best understanding of rights. Likewise, determining whether not admitting migrants with urgent needs causes harm or instead fails to prevent harm depends on many of the prior (unresolved) debates on immigration that we have examined throughout this book and on potential moral distinctions between doing and allowing.[94] Moreover, it doesn't seem that all of the relevant wrongful options are so obviously horrendous that there cannot possibly be a right to choose them;[95] racial or ethnic criteria may express a demeaning message about people or perpetuate their subordination, but seem much less morally weighty than, say, acts like murder. To clarify, I believe the relevant immigration wrongs are *capable* of outweighing the autonomy reasons in favor of states' having the right to commit those wrongs, but we must first examine what those reasons are; that is, we must examine (a).

8. The Right to Wrongfully Exclude, and Objectionable State Character

In considering (a), we must not start by exploring whether there is something morally in favor of any particular (kinds of) wrongful immigration decisions or

---

[92] This is distinct from Hidalgo's focus discussed above—namely, border agents causing migrants (threats of) physical harm.

[93] Enoch, "Right to Violate One's Duty."

[94] If a state's members have morally legitimate ownership rights over the relevant territory or public goods and resources (as discussed in Chapters 4 and 6), it seems more accurate to say excluding urgent cases *fails to prevent* substantial harm. And though the latter can be wrong, it might not be as egregious as causing people substantial harm, and so it's not obvious that the wrong manifestly outweighs the reasons for a right to make wrongful decisions. Consider that it's commonly thought there is a claim-right not to donate one's property to charity (even when the stakes of not donating are high), presumably because the wrong is not conceived of in terms of *causing* harm.

[95] The right's defenders likely also conceive of these wrongs this way (since we can assume they wouldn't think there's a right to commit them otherwise).

even of having the choice to make those particular decisions. The autonomy defense for the right to do wrong consists not in defending the significance of having some specific choice but in defending the importance of having choices in an area of decision-making especially important to autonomy.[96] So the claim that states have the right to wrongfully exclude would need to be defended not on the merits of any particular acts of exclusion or policies but on the basis of their connection to the wider freedom to have a range of choices in membership decisions.

However, since states have a range of morally permissible options to exclude people, states already have a range of choices for making membership decisions, and so, in *general* terms, their autonomy is secured. This means that, although we do not start with the question whether the choice to make particular wrongful decisions is important to state autonomy, we will nonetheless end up at that question—providing the basis of my argument against the right to exclude.

Before demonstrating my argument, let me explain the basic idea: if states had very few to no morally permissible options for excluding people, then any potential wrongful option's significance for state autonomy would arguably be sizable. In that case, especially if there's little variation among the few morally permissible options, the autonomy rationale for having some wrongful option may be fairly weighty.[97] The reason would not be that some particular choice is distinctively important for autonomy; rather, the reason would be that the choice simply adds to the number and variety of options, helping to secure state autonomy in general terms. But when the range of morally permissible options for excluding people includes more than just a few similar options, and so when state autonomy is protected in general terms, the distinctive significance of any one wrongful option whose absence is under consideration becomes important. In that case, what is required to defend a state's having the wrongful option is an important reason for protecting its autonomy in the *specific* way(s) entailed by having the choice to make particular (kinds of) wrongful decisions. Thus, we end up asking whether it would undermine a state's autonomy in any special, important sense if it was to lack the right to make those particular (kinds of) wrongful decisions.[98] And the answer, it turns out, depends on what a state's moral character *already* is.

---

[96] Waldron, "Right to Do Wrong," 32, 35.

[97] In Akhtar "The Claim-Right to Exclude", I examine the implications for the right to exclude if states do not have a range of permissible exclusion options (as some open-border views maintain). And I argue that even this would not suggest that states have the right to exclude in cases involving identity criteria and refusing people with urgent needs.

[98] Bolinger makes a different (very effective) point when considering whether for "an agent to freely choose to be virtuous" ("Revisiting the Right to Do Wrong," 51), they must have the right to do wrong. She shows that if moral valence differs among the morally permissible choices, one *is* free to choose to be virtuous; thus, justifying the right to do wrong requires demonstrating why freely choosing to be virtuous also requires at least one wrong (not inferior) option (esp. 51–52). My argument

To see this, let's start with wrongful identity criteria and consider three variations of the following case:

> State S is predominantly composed of a racial group that enjoys a significantly powerful global status ("Powerful Race"). Powerful Race's population continues to grow, and its way of life flourishes in numerous states. Moreover, its members have almost never been subject to exploitation or oppression on the basis of race, and their racial identity has almost never been the object of prejudice or contempt; thus, the social bases of the group's self-respect remain strong. Finally, Powerful Race enjoys significant comparative advantages in material terms and exercises substantial power over global military, political, and economic institutions (such as the United Nations Security Council and the World Bank), especially in issues concerning armed conflict, treaty negotiations, climate agreements, and trade. S is considering having an immigration policy favoring the admission of others belonging to Powerful Race (on the basis of race), which, we will presume for now, would be wrong.

In variation (1) assume S does *not* define itself centrally by its racial identity. Would the state's autonomy be more than trivially threatened—that is, beyond the loss of *an* option for immigration decisions—by denying that it has the right to choose this sort of immigration policy? Put differently, what would be gained for S's autonomy by protecting its choice to have this type of policy? Since we have granted it has a range of permissible options and since its identity is *not* defined in racial or ethnic terms, it is difficult to see why the choice to have such a policy is important enough to its ability to define its collective self that it warrants protection by a right. Thus, there doesn't seem to be a plausible autonomy defense for the state having the right to choose the sort of wrongful policy in question.

But this reply raises the possibility that if S *did* define itself in racial or ethnic terms, the choice to have such a policy would be distinctively important to its autonomy. And that is precisely what is troubling. In variation (2), imagine that S centrally conceives of its collective identity in terms of Powerful Race. At stake now in denying a right to choose the wrongful policy (again, favoring the admission of others in Powerful Race) is the state's autonomy to choose a policy that reflects the *central* way it defines itself. But S's defining itself racially is surely objectionable: because of Powerful Race's secure global status, this racial self-definition would seem to reflect some sort of vainglory or belief in the superiority of Powerful Race over other races, perhaps misconstrued or masquerading as pride or, more directly, a kind of hostility or animus toward (at least certain) other

---

(demonstrated next) is that if there's a range of morally permissible options, justifying the right to do wrong requires that some *particular* wrong option be morally significant to autonomy, which, I argue, is only true of states (or, by extension, individuals) with very bad character.

groups.[99] In any case, it would be difficult to come up with an *un*objectionable interpretation and thus easy to demonstrate that the state's collective character is reprehensible. But this means that S has an autonomy-based rationale for having the right to choose this sort of wrongful racial policy if it (quite objectionably) defines itself by its racial identity but not if it does not define itself so.

Thus, a state's morally objectionable character ends up being centrally implicated in the *defense* of the state's right to choose wrongful identity criteria in the first place. This is troubling. If we are attempting to diagnose the moral concern of wrongfully excluding in terms of states' having bad character, presumably it is because we care that states *not* have such character. But if states with very objectionable character have plausible moral claims to a right to wrongfully exclude, while more decent states—states that do not objectionably define themselves in racial or ethnic terms—do not, the former are rewarded, practically speaking (more on this in the next section).

To clarify, the point I have tried to illustrate is *not* that a state with objectionable character would have a stronger right to wrongfully exclude than a state with unobjectionable character; the point is rather that it seems a plausible *defense* for the right to wrongfully exclude in the relevant scenario can only be made when the state in question, S, has objectionable character—something that is morally perverse.

Moreover, this concern is independent of character-based explanations of the wrong of wrongful criteria. Consider again WM, under which, say, racial criteria are wrong only when and because they wrong a state's disfavored members. Imagine now variation (3): S is predominantly composed of Powerful Race and, as under (2), conceives of its identity centrally in these terms but now has a minority Uyghur population. Since, as we have seen, Uyghurs have a significantly vulnerable global status,[100] S's favoring the admission of others in Powerful Race would wrong its minority Uyghur members (and proponents of WM would likely easily agree). But since the choice to have this sort of racial policy seems distinctively important to S's autonomy, there nonetheless remains a strong autonomy-based rationale for its right to have it. However, this seems like an especially morally troubling instance in which a state's criteria wrong its members: not only does the state's policy disfavor members belonging to a significantly vulnerable group, but they are disfavored because the state defines itself in terms of the identity of a powerful racial group to which they do not belong. The policy would seem to deeply demean S's Uyghur members. All of this is because of how S objectionably views racial or ethnic identity as central to its self-understanding.

---

[99] Chapters 3 and 5 provide more discussion on these points.
[100] For recent discussion, see Chan, "I Never Thought China"; Wong and Buckley, "U.S. Says China's Repression"; *Economist*, "Persecution of Uyghurs"; Serhan, "Saving Uighur Culture."

Thus, the very thing that makes the policy especially morally troublesome appears to morally *support* the state's right to choose this sort of policy.

I believe that my normative interpretation of both the immigration policy and the state's character in the different variations is correct. But one might disagree and think either that the immigration policy is not wrong or that conditions exist under which its being wrong would not impugn the state's character. In the next section, I will explain why even if these stances are correct, they do not pose a problem for my central argument.

Here, let me clarify that none of what I have said means that any state that centrally defines itself in racial or ethnic terms has, for that reason, morally objectionable character. Recall our Navajo state discussed in several previous chapters: a hypothetical state in which the majority of members are Navajo and the minority white. Race or ethnicity is arguably important to the collective identity of the state, but we saw that this is not necessarily objectionable, nor is the state's hypothetical immigration policy favoring the admission of other Navajo. Given the Navajo's own history of significant mistreatment, there is an antidiscrimination rationale both for defining themselves centrally in terms of a racial or ethnic identity and for an immigration policy designed around those characteristics—based on their own global disadvantages. Moreover, the Navajo lack the powerful global status needed for putting others down, subordinating them, or compromising the social bases of their self-respect. Thus, although racial or ethnic belonging is arguably central to the collective identity of the Navajo state, this does not suggest the state has poor character and its immigration policy does not seem wrong.[101]

For another case, consider again Kiribati—the state, made up of three small Pacific Island groups, expected to be the first to lose its territory because of changing climate patterns. As we saw in the book's introduction, since gaining independence in 1979, it has favored the admission of anyone whose ancestry is linked to the I-Kiribati people, automatically conferring them citizenship.[102] Although racial or ethnic belonging seems central to the Kiribati state's collective identity, given the significant climate-related threat to its dominant way of life coupled with the fact that the i-Kiribati are globally vulnerable in economic and political terms,[103] the state defining itself in such terms does not suggest the state

---

[101] This doesn't mean that *no* use of racial/ethnic criteria by the Navajo would suggest poor character. Consider the hypothetical from Chapter 5 whereby they explicitly exclude Muslims. It was difficult to find a rationale for such a policy based on the Navajo's global vulnerability. That fact, combined with Muslims' disadvantages in self-respect, meant the policy was wrong. Given the range of permissible immigration options, to argue that they have the right to make wrongful decisions, including to wrongfully exclude Muslims, it seems we would again need to demonstrate this particular policy's importance to the state's collective autonomy. But it is easy to see how such a policy's distinctive importance *would* reflect poorly on the Navajo's character.

[102] Constitution of Kiribati, Articles 19 and 23.

[103] https://www.countryreports.org/country/Kiribati/economy.htm; https://data.worldbank.org/country/KI.

has objectionable character. But, because of its threatened way of life, it also seems its immigration policy is *not* all-things-considered wrong.[104] And if it is not wrong, the state's character does not support its right to do *wrong*. It merely supports its right against interference to do things that are morally permissible; but that was never in doubt.

Importantly, we can now see how the analysis generalizes to the wrongful exclusion of refugees and others with urgent admission needs. There may be a variety of morally permissible reasons to exclude urgent cases, especially in large numbers. Imagine a state such as Pakistan, which is at (or past) the limits of its infrastructure for handling the population's basic needs, has weak economic, political, and legal institutions, and already hosts a vast refugee population; excluding refugees and others with urgent needs may not be even pro tanto wrong. For more complicated examples, consider again Kiribati, where admitting many people with urgent needs who do not share the central identity might significantly threaten its already-compromised way of life, or imagine a wealthy state that would experience significant domestic unrest if it accepted many people with urgent needs: even if exclusion wrongs the denied people in such cases and is therefore pro tanto wrong, it may not be all-things-considered wrong.[105] And once again, there is no problem accepting that states have the right against interference to exclude when excluding is not all-things-considered wrong.

But now consider instances in which it seems obvious that excluding urgent cases is all-things-considered wrong. Suppose there are no legitimate resource, capacity, way-of-life, or related concerns, and suppose both the risk and consequences of domestic backlash are low. Why might states have the right to wrongfully exclude in such instances? In answering this, recall that we must weigh (a) the autonomy reasons in favor of the right to choose wrongful options against (b) the reasons those options are wrong.

Since, as we have seen, states already have a range of permissible options, this again means that, for (a), we must examine whether having the choice to make particular (kinds of) wrongful decisions is distinctively important to state autonomy. Moreover, turning to (b), the wrong of this option is substantial: we are no longer talking about denying nonurgent admissions based on wrongful identity criteria but wrongfully excluding refugees, forcibly displaced persons, and others whose basic human rights are significantly and urgently threatened—people with *urgent* needs for admission. This raises the bar for what sorts of reasons under (a) could potentially outweigh (b). And it is difficult to imagine reasons significant enough that do not come down to how the state, or its dominant population, centrally defines itself, whether racially, ethnically, nationally, religiously, or some

---

[104] Even under Carens's open-borders view, it seems at most pro tanto wrong (see, for example, "Migration and Morality," 40).
[105] See discussion in section 7.

combination. Moreover, if the state's excluding people with urgent needs is in fact all-things-considered *wrong*, then the state's defining itself centrally in identity terms would seem quite objectionable: perhaps it is a state whose dominant identity is like that of Powerful Race, or perhaps the relevant state's manner of conceiving of its identity engenders hostility or unwarranted fear toward the race or ethnicity of those with urgent needs. But however this explanation goes, it is unlikely to be a state (perhaps like Kiribati) that *un*objectionably defines itself in identity terms, and so it is plausible to assume the state has reprehensible character. Once again, then, the defense for the right to wrongfully exclude turns on objectional state character.

9. The Right to Exclude Revisited

As mentioned earlier, one might think that the examples I provided illustrating wrongful exclusions are not actually all-things-considered wrong. I disagree,[106] but the analysis does not depend on those examples. Anyone wanting to defend the right to wrongfully exclude in cases involving identity criteria and urgent needs must grant that there are some such all-things-considered wrongful decisions. And the analysis suggests, first, that the wrongful exclusions will most plausibly express that the state has objectionable character; but this is not terribly surprising, since doing wrong often, though not necessarily always (more on this soon), exhibits or expresses bad character.[107] Thus, the more central point is that the *defense* for the state's right to wrongfully exclude turns on the state's objectionable character. So, even if one disagrees with my examples and provides different examples of wrongful exclusion decisions in cases involving identity criteria and urgent needs, the analysis suggests that justifying the right to make those wrongful decisions rests on objectionable state character.

One might wonder whether there are some conditions under which a state's excluding someone via identity criteria or with urgent needs is wrong yet does not require a defense appealing to the state's having objectionable character. In particular, they might think there are certain conditions which would morally excuse a state's wrongfully excluding someone in those cases and thus not impugn the state's character in any way.

---

[106] Moreover, the views surveyed thus far would likely interpret the examples as I have. See: Carens, "Migration and Morality," 37–39; Blake, "Distributive Justice," 286; Blake, "Immigration," 232–33; Wellman, "Freedom of Association," 139–40.

[107] The state's vicious character may even partly explain the exclusion's being wrong. On several accounts, an action is right iff it is what a virtuous agent would (characteristically) do in those circumstances. See, for example, Oakley, "Varieties of Virtue Ethics"; Hursthouse, *On Virtue Ethics*, 28. For an alternative view that retains the tight connection between wrong action and vicious character, see Kawall, "Virtue Theory and Ideal Observers."

To reply to this concern, we must again first distinguish exclusions that are all-things-considered wrong from those that are pro tanto wrong. As we have seen, there might be certain issues, especially way-of-life concerns, that morally excuse a state's wrongfully using identity criteria, and there might be a variety of other issues, including safety, infrastructure, or resource concerns, that excuse a state's wrongfully excluding urgent cases; when such issues arise, the state's character might not be impugned. But, again, when states have many permissible exclusion options, as they do not only under the antidiscrimination view but also under a wide variety of other views on the ethics of immigration,[108] such issues at most make excluding someone via identity criteria or with urgent needs only pro tanto wrong.

Thus, we must ask under what sorts of conditions a state might be morally excused for an *all-things-considered*-wrong exclusion in either category. And, as when an individual commits all-things-considered wrongs but is morally excused, most plausibly such conditions include things such as unfortunate or unforeseen circumstances, nonculpable ignorance, inability to predict the relevant consequences, coercion, and manipulation.[109] The presence of any such issues, however, would suggest that a state accidentally, mistakenly, or involuntarily wrongfully excluded. But a justification for unintentionally doing wrong, even a justification against interference for doing so, doesn't require the right to do wrong. The right to do wrong entails one's having the right to *choose* to do wrong, so it presumes that the agent knows a given act is wrong and can autonomously choose to do it or not.[110] So while there could be circumstances in which an all-things-considered-wrongful

---

[108] One might wonder about the implications for my analysis if states do not have such options. For instance, under a strong version of open borders, perhaps the only permissible reasons for exclusion are substantial safety and security concerns. Excluding people because they lack certain qualifications or because of resource, capacity, or way-of-life concerns might be all-things-considered wrong, not just pro tanto wrong. If a strong version is correct, then states have few to no permissible exclusion options and little to no variation between them; if so, the autonomy-based rationale for a right to make wrongful decisions might indeed be more straightforward. However, even under such a view of open borders, this does not mean there is an autonomy-based rationale specifically for a right to make wrongful decisions in cases concerning identity criteria or urgent needs. Instead, there might be a defense for states' having a right to choose from a greater number and variety of options *in general*; and given the greater moral concerns associated with identity criteria and excluding people with urgent needs, it is hard to see why these options would be on the table rather than other sorts of options considered wrong. That is, if a strong version of open borders is correct, there might be a good argument for states' having a right to make wrongful decisions (in the absence of urgent needs and when not using proxies to exclude based on identity) regarding people who, say, lack certain professional, educational, or language qualifications—more generally, for having a right to choose any non-identity or non-urgent exclusions considered wrong under a strong version. However, the autonomy rationale for states' having a right to choose such wrongful options would simply be that those options add to the *number* and *variety* of choices for a state's membership decisions; the defense would not depend on their being distinctively important to any state's autonomy. So, despite such options' being *wrong* (under a strong view), defending states' right to choose such options would not turn on objectionable state character. I explore these issues further in Akhtar "The Claim-Right to Exclude".

[109] See especially Kawall, "Virtue Theory and Ideal Observers."

[110] Herstein, "Right to Do Wrong," 12, 20. Also, note common right-to-do-wrong examples (for example, Waldron, "Right to Do Wrong," 21).

instance of excluding someone in cases involving identity criteria or urgent needs would not express or exhibit objectionable state character at all, these would seem to be circumstances in which the state does not actually *choose* to do wrong; if so, these circumstances are not the sort at stake in the examination of whether states have a right against interference to exclude. For, as with morally permissible immigration decisions or decisions that are only pro tanto wrong, critics of the right to exclude would not likely suggest that states' immigration policies may be coercively interfered with when those policies are *genuinely* mistaken or involuntary.

I have demonstrated that, given a range of permissible immigration policies, a state with objectionable character has a stronger autonomy-based rationale for the right against interference to wrongfully exclude in cases of identity and urgent needs than do states that do not have objectionable character. I believe this morally perverse implication is sufficient reason to reject the idea that states have the right to exclude, where, again, this means the unilateral right against interference to exclude—even wrongfully. But there are also two more practical reasons to reject the right that I want to briefly touch on.

The first reason is more tentative than the second but still worth mentioning. Namely, it could be that having the right to exclude influences how a state constructs its immigration policies. As Herstein notes, "As is demonstrated in the numerous instances of people invoking their rights to ϕ against allegations of their wrongdoing through ϕ-ing, rights often have a strong liberating and insulating (even if not justifying) effect," giving one "some measure of empowerment to ignore the judgment of others."[111] Second, and more importantly, if states have the right to exclude, there is at the very least an additional justificatory burden associated with interfering with a state's wrongful exclusions. As we have seen, even if a state's excluding certain people is morally wrong and there are strong arguments for interfering in those instances, if states have the right to exclude, then outsiders have a duty—and seemingly an all-things-considered duty—to the state not to interfere. But if, as I have argued, a plausible autonomy defense for the right to wrongfully exclude in cases of identity and urgent needs can only be made for states with objectionable character, the right to exclude would insulate the very states we should be most concerned about. Without the right in those cases, a major moral hurdle for demonstrating the permissibility of interference is cleared.

So where does this leave us regarding the idea that states have the right to exclude more generally? After all, I have focused my analysis in this chapter on arguing that states lack the right to exclude in cases of identity, and relatedly, urgent needs, but not in all cases.[112] However, as we saw in the introductory chapter, since cases involving identity are often at the *heart* of immigration

---

[111] Herstein, "Right to Do Wrong," 18.   [112] See my note 98.

concerns, even if states only lack the right to exclude in those cases, that is a significant result. Moreover, an implication of this result is that states are *not* unilaterally entitled to make their membership decisions. In other words, external interference in states' membership decisions (at least in the relevant cases) is permissible.

Though the goal of this chapter was not to provide an account of when or under what conditions interference is permissible, I do wish to reemphasize that external interference need not come in the form of physical force, especially by a single international authority.[113] It might come in many forms, including direct sanctions, trade policy, tariffs, or, perhaps most plausibly, outsiders' collective input in states' immigration decisions (perhaps through international associations).[114] This would not necessarily mean outsiders have a direct say in any state's particular decisions, but rather it could involve outsiders' indirect consultation, such as by all states collectively establishing international norms or guidelines governing admission decisions. This would be similar to the domestic context, where although forcefully interfering with an association's membership decisions might not be permissible—because of the greater harms generated by doing so— for a variety of associations, such as large businesses, we nonetheless do *not* think that they have the moral right to create whatever membership criteria they choose free from deliberative or regulative input from outsiders. Likewise, the morally appropriate way for states' membership decisions to be made might most plausibly involve the collective establishment of international rules governing states' admission decisions in the relevant cases, with violation triggering economic or political penalties and sanctions. And, importantly, it seems it is mainly through such collective coordination and enforcement that addressing the pressing concern of helping people with urgent admission needs becomes a meaningful aim.[115]

---

[113] Carens (*Ethics of Immigration*) seems to interpret the issue of interference along these sort of lines.

[114] Phillip Cole (*Philosophies of Exclusion*) observes that the international nature of the problem of immigration suggests a non-unilateral approach to solving it.

[115] See (for example) Cole, *Philosophies of Exclusion*; Gibney, "Refugees and Justice"; Owen, "Refugees, Fairness"; Song, *Immigration and Democracy*. Also see: Bertram, *Do States Have the Right to Exclude Immigrants*; Brock, *Justice for People on the Move*; Owen, *What Do We Owe to Refugees*.

References

ABC News. "New Zealand Citizens Face 'Endemic' Discrimination in Australia, Activist David Faulkner Says." *ABC News*, February 10, 2015. https://www.abc.net.au/news/2015-02-11/new-zealanders-face-endemic-discrimination-in-australia-activist/6085162.

Abizadeh, Arash. "Cooperation, Pervasive Impact, and Coercion: On the Scope (Not Site) of Distributive Justice." *Philosophy & Public Affairs* 35, no. 4 (2007): 318–58. doi:10.1111/j.1088-4963.2007.00116.x.

Abizadeh, Arash. "Democratic Theory and Border Coercion: No Right to Unilaterally Control Your Own Borders." *Political Theory* 36, no. 1 (2008): 37–65. doi:10.1177/0090591707310090.

Acemoglu, Daron, Simon Johnson, and James A. Robinson. "The Colonial Origins of Comparative Development: An Empirical Investigation." *American Economic Review* 91, no. 5 (2001): 1369–401. doi:10.1257/aer.91.5.1369.

Acemoglu, Daron, and James A. Robinson. "Unbundling Institutions." *Journal of Political Economy* 113, no. 5 (2005): 949–95. doi:10.1086/432166.

Acemoglu, Daron, and James A. Robinson. *Why Nations Fail*. New York: Crown Business, 2013.

Aid to the Church in Need. *Religious Freedom in the World 2018*. Aid to the Church in Need, 2018. https://www.churchinneed.org/wp-content/uploads/2018/11/RFR-2018-Exec-Summary-Web-version.pdf.

Akhtar, Sahar. "Being at Home in the World: International Relocation (Not Open Borders)." *Public Affairs Quarterly* 30, no. 2 (2016): 103–28.

Akhtar, Sahar. "Stripping Citizenship: Does Membership Have Its (Moral) Privileges?" *Australasian Journal of Philosophy* 95, no. 3 (2017): 419–34. doi:10.1080/00048402.2016.1238496.

Akhtar, Sahar. "Race Beyond our Borders: Is Racial and Ethnic Immigration Selection Always Morally Wrong?" *Ethics* 132, no. 2 (2022): 322–51.

Akhtar, Sahar. "The Claim-Right to Exclude and the Right to Do Wrong." *Critical Review of International Social and Political Philosophy* (2023). doi:10.1080/13698230.2023.2265288.

Albahari, Maurizio. *Crimes of Peace: Mediterranean Migrations at the World's Deadliest Border*. Philadelphia, PA: University of Pennsylvania Press, 2015.

Aleem, Zeeshan. "These Statistics Show Why Silicon Valley Is Terrified of Trump's Next Immigration Crackdown." *Vox*, February 8, 2017. https://www.vox.com/world/2017/2/8/14547212/trump-executive-order-h1b-silicon-valley.

Alesina, Alberto, and Marco Tabellini. "The Political Effects of Immigration: Culture or Economics?" Harvard Business School Working Paper 21–069, 2020.

Alexander, Larry. "What Makes Wrongful Discrimination Wrong? Biases, Preferences, Stereotypes, and Proxies." *University of Pennsylvania Law Review* 141, no. 1 (1992): 149–219. doi:10.2307/3312397.

Alexander, Laura, Jane Hong, Karen Hooge Michalka, and Luis A. Romero. "How Race and Religion Have Always Played a Role in Who Gets Refuge in the US." *Conversation*, April 28, 2022. https://theconversation.com/how-race-and-religion-have-always-played-a-role-in-who-gets-refuge-in-the-us-181700.

Altman, Andrew. "Discrimination." In *The Stanford Encyclopedia of Philosophy*, (Winter 2020 Edition) edited by E. N. Zalta. Stanford, CA: The Metaphysics Research Lab. https://plato.stanford.edu/archives/win2020/entries/discrimination.

Altman, Andrew, and Christopher Wellman. *A Liberal Theory of International Justice.* Oxford: Oxford University Press, 2009. doi:10.1093/acprof:oso/9780199564415.001.0001.

American Civil Liberties Union. "Caged in Solitary Confinement's Devastating Harm on Prisoners with Physical Disabilities." American Civil Liberties Union. https://www.aclu.org/sites/default/files/field_document/010916-aclu-solitarydisabilityreport-single.pdf.

American Psychiatric Association. "Lesbian, Gay, Bisexual, Transgender and Queer/Questioning." American Psychiatric Association, 2017. https://www.psychiatry.org/psychiatrists/cultural-competency/education/lgbtq-patients.

American Psychiatric Association. *Mental Health Disparities: LGBTQ.* American Psychiatric Association, 2017. https://www.psychiatry.org/File%20Library/Psychiatrists/Cultural-Competency/Mental-Health-Disparities/Mental-Health-Facts-for-LGBTQ.pdf.

Amundson, R. "Disability, Handicap, and the Environment." *Journal of Social Philosophy* 23, no. 1 (1992): 105–19.

Anderson, Carol. *White Rage.* New York: Bloomsbury, 2016.

Anderson, Elizabeth. "What Is the Point of Equality?" *Ethics* 109, no. 2 (1999): 287–337. doi:10.1086/233897.

Anderson, Elizabeth, and Richard Pildes. "Expressive Theories of Law: A General Restatement." *University of Pennsylvania Law Review* 148, no. 5 (2000): 1503–76. doi:10.2307/3312748.

Anderson, Elizabeth. *The Imperative of Integration.* Princeton, NJ: Princeton University Press, 2010. doi:10.1515/9781400836826.

Appiah, Anthony. *The Ethics of Identity.* Princeton, NJ: Princeton University Press, 2005. doi:10.1515/9781400826193.

Arneson, Richard. "What Is Wrongful Discrimination?" *San Diego Law Review* 43, no. 4 (2006): 775–807.

Baker, John. "Conceptions and Dimensions of Social Equality." In *Social Equality: What It Means to Be Equals*, edited by C. Fourie, F. Schuppert, and I. Wallimann-Helmer, pp. 65–86. Oxford: Oxford University Press, 2015. doi:10.1093/acprof:oso/9780199331109.003.0004.

Bard, Mitchell. "Arab Funding of American Universities: Donors, Recipients and Impact." Jewish Virtual Library, November 2021. https://www.jewishvirtuallibrary.org/arab-funding-of-american-universities-donors-recipients-and-impact#_Toc57043867.

Baskin, Gershon. "Israel Should Give East Jerusalem Palestinians Israeli Passports." *Jerusalem Post*, March 17, 2021. https://www.jpost.com/opinion/israel-should-give-east-jerusalem-palestinians-israeli-passports-opinion-662341.

Batalova, Jeanne, Mary Hanna, and Christopher Levesque. "Frequently Requested Statistics on Immigrants and Immigration in the United States." Migration Policy Institute, February 11, 2021. https://www.migrationpolicy.org/article/frequently-requested-statistics-immigrants-and-immigration-united-states-2020#immig-now-historical.

BBC News. "Trump Travel Ban: What Does This Ruling Mean?" BBC News, June 26, 2018. https://www.bbc.com/news/world-us-canada-39044403.

BBC News. "What's Happening in Assam in India?" BBC News, July 31, 2018. https://www.bbc.co.uk/newsround/45007750.

BBC News. "Who Are the Kurds?" BBC News, October 15, 2019. https://www.bbc.com/news/world-middle-east-29702440.

BBC News. "Europe and Right-Wing Nationalism: A Country-by-Country Guide." BBC News, November 13, 2019. https://www.bbc.com/news/world-europe-36130006.

Beauvais, F. "Trends in Drug Use among American Indian Students and Dropouts." *American Journal of Public Health* 86, no. 11 (1996): 1594–9. doi:10.2105/AJPH.86.11.1594.

Becker, Jo. "The Global Machine behind the Rise of Far-Right Nationalism." *New York Times*, August 10, 2019. https://www.nytimes.com/2019/08/10/world/europe/sweden-immigration-nationalism.html.

Becker, L. *Habilitation, Health, and Agency: A Framework for Basic Justice*. New York: Oxford University Press, 2012.

Behrendt, Sven. "When Money Talks Arab Sovereign Wealth Funds in the Global Public Policy Discourse." Carnegie Papers, Carnegie Middle East Center, Carnegie Endowment for International Peace, October 2008. https://carnegieendowment.org/files/arab_sovereign_wealth_funds.pdf.

Beitz, Charles R. *Political Theory and International Relations*. Princeton, NJ: Princeton University Press, 1979.

Bertram, Christopher. *Do States Have the Right to Exclude Immigrants?* Cambridge: Polity Press, 2018.

Bickel, Alexander. *The Morality of Consent*. New Haven, CT: Yale University Press, 1974.

Bier, David. "U.S. Citizens Targeted by ICE: U.S. Citizens Targeted by Immigration and Customs Enforcement in Texas." Policy Brief 8. Cato Institute, 2018. https://www.cato.org/publications/immigration-research-policy-brief/us-citizens-targeted-ice-us-citizens-targeted.

Blake, Michael. "Discretionary Immigration." *Philosophical Topics* 30, no. 2 (2002): 273–89. doi:10.5840/philtopics200230219.

Blake, Michael. "Distributive Justice, State Coercion, and Autonomy." *Philosophy & Public Affairs* 30, no. 2 (2002): 257–96.

Blake, Michael. "Immigration." In *A Companion to Applied Ethics*, edited by R.G. Frey and Christopher Heath Wellman, pp. 224–37. Malden, MA: Blackwell, 2005. doi:10.1002/9780470996621.ch17.

Blake, Michael. "Immigration and Political Equality." *San Diego Law Review* 45, no. 4 (2008): 963–80.

Blake, Michael. "Immigration, Association, and Antidiscrimination." *Ethics* 122, no. 4 (2012): 748–62. doi:10.1086/666327.

Blake, Michael. "Immigration, Jurisdiction, and Exclusion." *Philosophy and Public Affairs* 41, no. 2 (2013): 103–30. doi:10.1111/papa.12012.

Blake, Michael. *Justice, Migration, and Mercy*. New York: Oxford University Press, 2020. doi:10.1093/oso/9780190879556.001.0001.

Blinder, S., and W. Allen. *UK Public Opinion toward Immigration: Overall Attitudes and Level of Concern*. Oxford: Migration Observatory, 2020.

Bolinger, Renee. "Revisiting the Right to Do Wrong." *Australasian Journal of Philosophy*, 95(1): 43–57, 2017.

Boorse, C. "Concepts of Health." In *Health Care Ethics: An Introduction*, edited by D. VanDeveer and T. Regan, pp. 359–93. Philadelphia, PA: Temple University Press, 1987.

Borodak, Daniela, and Matloob Piracha. "Who Moves and For How Long: Determinants of Different Forms of Migration." IZA Discussion Paper No. 7388, Institute of Labor Economics, May 2013.

Bowles, Samuel, and Herbert Gintis. "Reciprocity, Self-Interest and the Welfare State." *Nordic Journal of Political Economy* 26 (2000): 33–53.

Boxill, Bernard. *Blacks and Social Justice*. Revised Edition. Lanham, MD: Rowman and Littlefield, 1992.

Brave Heart, M.Y.H. "Oyate Ptayela: Rebuilding the Lakota Nation through Addressing Historical Trauma among Lakota Parents." *Journal of Human Behavior in the Social Environment* 2, no. 1 (1999): 109–26. doi:10.1300/J137v02n01_08.

Brave Heart, M.Y.H., and M. Lemyra. "DeBruyn, 'The American Indian Holocaust: Healing Historical Unresolved Grief.'" *American Indian and Alaska Native Mental Health Research* 8, no. 2 (1998): 56–78.

Brennan, Jason, and Bas van der Vossen. *In Defense of Openness: Why Global Freedom Is the Humane Solution to Global Poverty*. New York: Oxford University Press, 2018.

Bretton Woods Project. *IMF and World Bank Decision-Making and Governance*: Bretton Woods Project, 2020, https://www.brettonwoodsproject.org/2020/04/imf-and-world-bank-decision-making-and-governance-2/.

Brock, Gillian. *Justice for People on the Move: Migration in Challenging Times*. Cambridge: Cambridge University Press, 2020.

Buchanan, Allen. "Theories of Secession." *Philosophy & Public Affairs* 26, no. 1 (1997): 31–61. doi:10.1111/j.1088-4963.1997.tb00049.x.

Buchanan, Allen. "Rawls' Law of Peoples: Rules for a Vanished Westphalian World." *Ethics* 110, no. 4 (2000): 697–721. doi:10.1086/233370.

Buchanan, Allen. *Justice, Legitimacy, and Self-Determination: Moral Foundations for International Law*. Oxford: Oxford University Press, 2004.

Buchanan, Allen. *Justice, Legitimacy, and Self-Determination: Moral Foundations for International Law*. Oxford: Oxford University Press, 2007.

Buckinx, Barbara, Jonathan Trejo-Mathys, and Timothy Waligore (Eds). *Domination and Global Political Justice: Conceptual, Historical and Institutional Perspectives*. New York: Routledge, 2015. doi:10.4324/9781315757506.

Budiman, Abby. "Key Findings about US Immigrants." Pew Research Center, August 20, 2020. https://www.pewresearch.org/fact-tank/2020/08/20/key-findings-about-u-s-immigrants/.

Budnik, Katarzyna Barbara. "Temporary Migration in Theories of International Mobility of Labour." National Bank of Poland Working Paper 89, 2011.

Bündnis Entwicklung Hilft. *WorldRiskReport 2019*. Bündnis Entwicklung Hilft. https://reliefweb.int/sites/reliefweb.int/files/resources/WorldRiskReport-2019_Online_english.pdf.

Bush, S. "Varieties of International Influence and the Middle East." *PS: Political Science & Politics* 50, no. 3 (2017): 668–71. doi:10.1017/S1049096517000361.

Butt, Daniel. *Rectifying International Injustice: Principles of Compensation and Restitution between Nations*. Oxford: Oxford University Press, 2009.

Caplan, Bryan (author) and Zach Weinersmith (illustrator). *Open Borders: The Science and Ethics of Immigration*. New York: First Second, 2019.

Carens, Joseph. "Aliens and Citizens: The Case for Open Borders." *Review of Politics* 49, no. 2 (1987): 251–73. doi:10.1017/S0034670500033817.

Carens, Joseph. "Migration and Morality: A Liberal Egalitarian Perspective." In *Free Movement: Ethical Issues in the Transnational Migration of People and of Money*, edited by Brian Barry and Robert Goodin, pp. 23–48. University Park, PA: Pennsylvania State University Press, 1992.

Carens, Joseph. "Who Should Get In? The Ethics of Immigration Admissions." *Ethics & International Affairs* 17, no. 1 (2003): 95–110. doi:10.1111/j.1747-7093.2003.tb00421.x.

Carens, Joseph. "A Contextual Approach to Political Theory." *Ethical Theory and Moral Practice* 7, no. 2 (2004): 117–32. http://www.jstor.org/stable/27504304.

Carens, Joseph. *The Ethics of Immigration*. New York: Oxford University Press, 2013.

Carr, James. *Experiences of Islamophobia: Living with Racism in the Neoliberal Era*. New York: Routledge, 2015. doi:10.4324/9781315723921.

Cavallero, Eric. "Coercion, Inequality and the International Property Regime." *Journal of Political Philosophy* 18, no. 1 (2010): 16–31. doi:10.1111/j.1467-9760.2009.00343.x.

Cavanagh, Matt. *Against Equality of Opportunity*. Oxford: Oxford University Press, 2002.

Center for Human Rights in Iran. "Christian Property in Iran to Be Taken Over by Supreme Leader's Organization." Center for Human Rights in Iran, March 29, 2018. https://www.iranhumanrights.org/2018/03/christian-property-in-iran-to-be-taken-over-by-supreme-leaders-organization/.

Chan, Melissa. "'I Never Thought China Could Ever Be This Dark.'" *Atlantic*, April 8, 2021. https://www.theatlantic.com/international/archive/2021/04/uyghur-women-china-xinjiang/618531/.

Cherem, Max, "Refugee Rights: Against Expanding the Definition of a 'Refugee' and Unilateral Protection Elsewhere." *Journal of Political Philosophy* 24, no. 2 (2016): 183–205.

Christiano, Thomas. "Immigration, Political Community, and Cosmopolitanism." *San Diego Law Review* 45 (2008): 933–62.

Chung, Erin Aeran. *Immigration and Citizenship in Japan*. Cambridge: Cambridge University Press, 2010. doi:10.1017/CBO9780511711855.

Clark, Ximena, Timothy J. Hatton, and Jeffrey G. Williamson. "Where Do US Immigrants Come From, and Why?" NBER Working Paper Series no. 8998, 2002. http://www.nber.org/papers/w8998.

Clemens, Michael. "Economics and Emigration: Trillion-Dollar Bills on the Sidewalk?" *Journal of Economic Perspectives* 25, no. 3 (2011): 83–106. doi:10.1257/jep.25.3.83.

Clemens, Michael. "The Emigration Life Cycle: How Development Shapes Emigration from Poor Countries." IZA Discussion Paper No. 13614, August 24, 2020. doi: http://dx.doi.org/10.2139/ssrn.3679020. Available at SSRN: https://ssrn.com/abstract=3679020.

Clemens, Michael, and Sami Bazzi. "Don't Close the Golden Door: Making Immigration Policy Work for Development." In *The White House and the World: A Global Development Agenda for the Next US President*, edited by N. Birdsall, pp. 241–72. Washington, DC: Center for Global Development, 2008.

Clodfelter, M. *Warfare and Armed Conflicts: A Statistical Reference to Casualty and Other Figures, 1494–2007*. 3rd ed. Jefferson, NC: McFarland, 2008.

Cohen, Joshua, and Charles Sabel. "Extram Republicam Nulla Justitia?" *Philosophy & Public Affairs* 34, no. 2 (2006): 147–75. doi:10.1111/j.1088-4963.2006.00060.x.

Cole, Phillip. *Philosophies of Exclusion: Liberal Political Theory and Immigration*. Edinburgh: Edinburgh University Press, 2000.

Cole, Phillip. "Open Borders: An Ethical Defense." In *Debating the Ethics of Immigration: Is There a Right to Exclude?*, edited by Christopher Heath Wellman and Phillip Cole, pp. 159–313. Oxford: Oxford University Press, 2011.

Coleman, Jule, and Sarah Harding. "Citizenship, the Demands of Justice, and the Moral Relevance of Political Borders." In *Justice in Immigration*, edited by Warren F. Schwartz, pp. 18–62. Cambridge: Cambridge University Press, 1995. doi:10.1017/CBO9780511663789.002.

Colker, Ruth. "Anti-subordination above All: Sex, Race, and Equal Protection." *New York University Law Review* 61 (1986): 1003.

Collier, Paul. *Exodus: How Migration Is Changing Our World.* Oxford University Press, 2013.

Cornell, Nicholas. "Wrongs, Rights, and Third Parties." *Philosophy & Public Affairs* 43, no. 2 (2015): 109–43. doi:10.1111/papa.12054.

Credit Suisse Group. *Global Wealth Report 2020.* October 2020. https://www.credit-suisse.com/media/assets/corporate/docs/about-us/research/publications/global-wealth-report-2020-en.pdf.

Crenshaw, Kimberle. "Demarginalizing the Intersection of Race and Sex: A Black Feminist Critique of Antidiscrimination Doctrine, Feminist Theory and Antiracist Politics." *University of Chicago Legal Forum* 1989, no. 1 (1989): 139.

Criddle, Evan J. and Evan Fox-Decent. "The Authority of International Refugee Law." *William and Mary Law Review*, 62 (2021): 1067–1136.

Crush, J., and W. Pendleton. "Regionalizing Xenophobia? Citizen Attitudes to Immigration and Refugee Policy in Southern Africa." SAMP Migration Policy Series no. 30, Southern African Migration Programme, Waterloo, ON, 2004.

Convention Relating to the Status of Refugees Article 33(1), July 28, 1951, 19 U.S.T. 6259, 189 U.N.T.S. 150.

d'Appollonia, Ariane Chebel, and Simon Reich. *Immigration, Integration and Security: America and Europe in Comparative Perspective.* Pittsburgh, PA: University of Pittsburgh Press, 2008.

Dash, Sanchita. "Meet this successful bunch of Indian-Americans behind some of the most popular startups and technology firms in the US." *Business Insider India*, April 3, 2021. https://www.businessinsider.in/business/startups/news/indian-americans-behind-some-of-the-most-popular-startups-and-technology-firms-in-the-us/slidelist/81884255.cms.

De Haas, H. "The Internal Dynamics of Migration Processes: A Theoretical Inquiry." *Journal of Ethnic and Migration Studies* 36, no. 19 (2010): 1587–1617.

De Haas, H. "The Determinants of International Migration." ORA Working Paper, University of Oxford, 2011.

de Oliveira, Cleuci. "Is Neymar Black? Brazil and the Painful Relativity of Race." *New York Times*, June 30, 2018. https://www.nytimes.com/2018/06/30/opinion/is-neymar-black-brazil-and-the-painful-relativity-of-race.html.

de Soto, Hernando. *The Mystery of Capital.* New York: Basic Books, 2000.

Dempster, Helen, Amy Leach, and Karen Hargrave. "Public Attitudes towards Immigration and Immigrants." ODI Working Paper 588, ODI, September 2020. https://cdn.odi.org/media/documents/Public_attitudes_towards_immigration_and_immigrants_what_people_think_why_and_how.pdf.

Desai, S. and V. Kulkarni. "Changing Educational Inequalities in India in the Context of Affirmative Action." *Demography* 45, no. 2 (2008): 245–70. doi: 10.1353/dem.0.0001.

Dickerson, Caitlin. "The Secret History of Family Separation." *Atlantic*, August 7, 2022. https://www.theatlantic.com/magazine/archive/2022/09/trump-administrationfamily-separation-policy-immigration/670604/.

Disabled World. "Disability Statistics: Information, Charts, Graphs and Tables." Disabled World, February 9, 2021. https://www.disabled-world.com/disability/statistics/.

Dogauchi, Masoto. "Private International Law on Intellectual Property: A Civil Law Overview." WIPO Forum on Private International Law and Intellectual Property, 2001.

Doña-Reveco, Cristián. "Amid Record Numbers of Arrivals, Chile Turns Rightward on Immigration." Migration Policy Institute, January 17, 2018. https://www.migrationpolicy.org/article/amid-record-numbers-arrivals-chile-turns-rightward-immigration.

Dorf, Michael C. "A Partial Defense of an Anti-discrimination Principle". *Cornell Law Faculty Publications* 2, no. 1 (2002): 116. doi:10.2202/1539-8323.1006.

Dorf, Michael C. "Equal Protection Incorporation." *Virginia Law Review* 88, no. 5 (September 2002): 1014–15.

Dubois, W.E.B. *Black Reconstruction in America*. New York: Free Press, 1962.

Economist. "From Pearls to Black Gold: How Oil Transformed the Gulf." *Economist*, June 23, 2018.

Economist. "Right-Wing Anti-immigrant Parties Continue to Receive Support in Europe." *Economist*. September 10, 2018. https://www.economist.com/graphic-detail/2018/09/10/right-wing-anti-immigrant-parties-continue-to-receive-support-in-europe.

Economist. "Millions of Millionaires." *Economist*, October 22, 2019. https://www.economist.com/graphic-detail/2019/10/22/millions-of-millionaires.

Economist. "The Persecution of the Uyghurs Is a Crime against Humanity." *Economist*, October 17, 2020. https://www.economist.com/leaders/2020/10/17/the-persecution-of-the-uyghurs-is-a-crime-against-humanity.

Edmond, Charlotte, "Global Migration, by the Numbers: Who Migrates, Where They Go and Why." World Economic Forum, January 10, 2020.

Eidelson, Benjamin. *Discrimination and Disrespect*. Oxford: Oxford University Press, 2015. doi:10.1093/acprof:oso/9780198732877.001.0001.

Ely, John Hart. *Democracy and Distrust*. Cambridge, MA: Harvard University Press, 1980.

Enoch, David. "A Right to Violate One's Duty." *Law and Philosophy* 21, no. 4/5 (2002): 355–84.

Epstein, Daniel C. "Black and White and Gray All Over: How Anticlassification Theory Can Endorse Race-Based Affirmative Action Policies." *University of Pennsylvania Journal of Constitutional Law* 20 (2017): 433.

Esipova, Neli, Julie Ray, and Anita Pugliese. "Syrian Refugees Not Welcome in Eastern Europe." Gallup, May 5, 2017. https://news.gallup.com/poll/209828/syrian-refugees-not-welcome-eastern-europe.aspx.

Esipova, Neli, Julie Ray, and Anita Pugliese. "World Grows Less Accepting of Migrants." Gallup, September 23, 2020. https://news.gallup.com/poll/320678/world-grows-less-accepting-migrants.aspx.

European Parliament. "Assistive Technologies for People with Disabilities." European Parliament, January 2018. https://www.europarl.europa.eu/RegData/etudes/IDAN/2018/603218/EPRS_IDA(2018)603218(ANN2)_EN.pdf.

Eyal, N. "'Perhaps the Most Important Primary Good': Self-Respect and Rawls's Principles of Justice." *Politics, Philosophy & Economics* 4, no. 2 (2005): 195–219. doi:10.1177/1470594X05052538.

Fasulo, Linda. *An Insider's Guide to the UN*. New Haven, CT: Yale University Press, 2004.

Fehr, Ernst, Urs Fischbacher, and Simon Gächter. "Strong Reciprocity, Human Cooperation, and the Enforcement of Social Norms." *Human Nature (Hawthorne, N.Y.)* 13, no. 1 (2002): 1–25. doi:10.1007/s12110-002-1012-7.

Fine, Sarah. "Freedom of Association Is Not the Answer." *Ethics* 120, no. 2 (2010): 338–56. doi:10.1086/649626.

Fine, Sarah. "The Ethics of Immigration: Self-Determination and the Right to Exclude." *Philosophy Compass* 8, no. 3 (2013): 254–68. doi:10.1111/phc3.12019.

Fine, Sarah. "Immigration and Discrimination." In *Migration in Political Theory: The Ethics of Movement and Membership*, edited by Sarah Fine and Lea Ypi, pp. 125–50. Oxford: Oxford University Press, 2016.

Fiss, Owen. "Groups and the Equal Protection Clause." *Philosophy and Public Affairs* 5, no. 2 (1976): 107–77.

FocusEconomics. "The World's Top 5 Largest Economies in 2024." FocusEconomics. https://www.focus-economics.com/blog/the-largest-economies-in-the-world.

Follesdal, Andreas. "The Distributive Justice of a Global Basic Structure: A Category Mistake?" *Politics, Philosophy & Economics* 10, no. 1 (2011): 46–65. doi:10.1177/1470594X10396302.

Fourie, C., F. Schuppert, and I. Wallimann-Helmer. "The Nature and Distinctiveness of Social Equality: An Introduction." In *Social Equality: On What It Means to Be Equals*, edited by C. Fourie, F. Schuppert, and I. Wallimann-Helmer, pp. 1–18. Oxford: Oxford University Press, 2015.

Fourie, C., F. Schuppert, and I. Wallimann-Helmer. *Social Equality: On What It Means to Be Equals*. Oxford: Oxford University Press, 2015.

Fourie, Carina "What Is Social Equality? An Analysis of Status Equality as a Strongly Egalitarian Ideal." *Res Publica* 18, no. 2 (2012): 107–26. doi:10.1007/s11158-011-9162-2.

Fox, Caroline. "Jeff Bezos Created Amazon from his Garage—Here Are 14 of the Most Successful Companies That Started in Basements, Sheds, and Bedrooms." *Business Insider*, February 4, 2021. https://www.businessinsider.com/successful-companies-started-in-basements-garages-bedrooms-2020-4.

Friedberg, Rachel, and Jennifer Hunt. "The Impact of Immigrants on Host Country Wages, Employment and Growth." *Journal of Economic Perspectives* 9 (1995): 23–44. doi:10.1257/jep.9.2.23.

Gaikwad, Nikhar, and Gareth Nellis. "The Majority-Minority Divide in Attitudes toward Internal Migration: Evidence from Mumbai." *American Journal of Political Science* 61, no. 2 (2017): 456–72. doi:10.1111/ajps.12276.

Galston, William A. "On the Alleged Right to Do Wrong: A Response to Waldron." *Ethics* 93, no. 2 (1983): 320–4. doi:10.1086/292437.

Gardner, Frank. "Iraq's Christians 'Close to Extinction.'" BBC News, May 23, 2019. https://www.bbc.com/news/world-middle-east-48333923.

Gardner, John. "On the Ground of Her Sex(uality)." *Oxford Journal of Legal Studies* 18, no. 1 (1998): 167–87. doi:10.1093/ojls/18.1.167.

Gibney, Matthew. *The Ethics and Politics of Asylum: Liberal Democracy and the Response to Refugees*. Cambridge: Cambridge University Press, 2004. doi:10.1017/CBO9780511490248.

Gibney, Matthew. "Refugees and Justice between States." *European Journal of Philosophy* 14, no. 4 (2015): 448–63.

Givens, Terri E. "Immigrant Integration in Europe: Empirical Research." *Annual Review of Political Science* 10, no. 1 (June 2007): 67–83. doi:10.1146/annurev.polisci.9.062404.162347.

Givens, Terri E., and Rhonda Evans Case. *Legislating Equality: The Politics of Antidiscrimination Policy in Europe*. Oxford: Oxford University Press, 2014. doi:10.1093/acprof:oso/9780198709015.001.0001.

Givens, Terri E., Gary P. Freeman, and David L. Leal. *Immigration Policy and Security: U.S., European and Commonwealth Perspectives*. New York: Routledge, 2009.

Goldman, Alan. *Justice and Reverse Discrimination*. Princeton, NJ: Princeton University Press, 1979.

Gone, J. P. "'We Never Was Happy Living Like a Whiteman': Mental Health Disparities and the Postcolonial Predicament in American Indian Communities." *American Journal of Community Psychology* 40, no. 3–4 (2007): 290–300. doi:10.1007/s10464-007-9136-x.

Gonzalez-Barrera, Ana, and Phillip Connor. "Around the World, More Say Immigrants Are a Strength than a Burden." Pew Research Center, March 14, 2019. https://www.pewresearch.org/global/2019/03/14/around-the-world-more-say-immigrants-are-a-strength-than-a-burden/.

Goodwin, Matthew, and Thomas Raines. "What Do Europeans Think about Muslim Immigration?" Chatham House, February 7, 2017.

Gosepath, Steven. "The Principles and Presumption of Equality." In *Social Equality: On What It Means to Be Equals*, edited by C. Fourie, F. Schuppert, and I. Wallimann-Helmer, pp. 167–85. Oxford: Oxford University Press, 2015. doi:10.1093/acprof:oso/9780199331109.003.0009.

Götz, Norbert. "Western Europeans and Others: The Making of Europe at the United Nations." *Alternatives* 33, no. 3 (2008): 359–81. doi:10.1177/030437540803300305.

Government of Canada. *Excessive Demand: Calculation of the Cost Threshold, 2018*. Government of Canada, 2018. https://www.canada.ca/en/immigration-refugees-citizenship/corporate/publications-manuals/excessive-demand.html.

Government of Canada. "Program Delivery Update: Update to the Cost Threshold for Excessive Demand on Health and Social Services." Government of Canada, 2022. https://www.canada.ca/en/immigration-refugees-citizenship/corporate/publications-manuals/operational-bulletins-manuals/updates/2022-cost-threshold.html.

Government of India. Ministry of Home Affairs. Office of the Registrar General and Census Commissioner. *Census of India 2001*. https://www.censusindia.gov.in/Data_Products/Data_Highlights/Data_Highlights_link/data_highlights_D1D2D3.pdf.

Guardian. "Brazil Census Shows African-Brazilians in the Majority for the First Time." *Guardian*, November 17, 2011. https://www.theguardian.com/world/2011/nov/17/brazil-census-african-brazilians-majority.

Guerreiro, Joao, Sergio Rebelo, and Pedro Teles. "What Is the Optimal Immigration Policy? Migration, Jobs and Welfare." Carnegie-Rochester-NYU Conference Series 113, 2020.

Guglielmo, Thomas. *White on Arrival: Italians, Race, Color, and Power in Chicago, 1890–1945*. New York: Oxford University Press, 2003.

Hainmueller, Jens, and Daniel J. Hopkins. "Public Attitudes toward Immigration." *Annual Review of Political Science* 17, no. 1 (2014): 225–49. doi:10.1146/annurev-polisci-102512-194818.

Hammond, Robin. "To Fight Poverty, We Need to Fight Homophobia and Transphobia." World Bank, May 17, 2016. https://www.worldbank.org/en/news/feature/2016/05/17/to-fight-poverty-we-need-to-fight-homophobia-and-transphobia

Harper, Jennifer. "Gallup Research Estimate: 42 Million Latin Americans 'Want to Come to the U.S.'" Associated Press, February 11, 2019. https://apnews.com/article/845433de9afd2a78b3435a2806da14fb

Harvard Medical School. Harvard Health Publishing. "Urinary Tract Infection in Women." Harvard Health Publishing, February 25, 2020. https://www.health.harvard.edu/womens-health/urinary-tract-infection-in-women-a-to-z.

Haslanger, Sally. "Gender and Race: (What) Are They? (What) Do We Want Them to Be?" *Noûs* 34, no. 1 (2000): 31–55. doi:10.1111/0029-4624.00201.

Haslanger, Sally. "Future Genders? Future Races?" *Philosophic Exchange* 34, no. 1 (2004): 1–24.

Healthcare Global Magazine. "Why the Pacific Islands Are the Most Obese Nations in the World." *Healthcare Global Magazine*, May 17, 2020. https://www.healthcareglobal.com/hospitals/why-pacific-islands-are-most-obese-nations-world.

Hellman, Deborah. *When Is Discrimination Wrong?* Cambridge, MA: Harvard University Press, 2008.

Hellman, Deborah. "Two Concepts of Discrimination." *Virginia Law Review* 102, no. 47 (2016): 895–952.

Heritage Foundation. "Japan." Heritage Foundation, 2021. https://www.heritage.org/index/country/japan.

Herstein, Ori. "Defending the Right to Do Wrong." *Cornell Law Faculty Publications* 339. 2012. http://scholarship.law.cornell.edu/facpub/339.

Hidalgo, Javier. "Resistance to Unjust Immigration Restrictions." *Journal of Political Philosophy* 23, no. 4 (2015): 450–70. doi:10.1111/jopp.12051.

Hidalgo, Javier. "The Ethics of People Smuggling." *Journal of Global Ethics* 12, no. 3 (2016): 311–26.

Higgins, Peter W. *Immigration Justice*. Edinburgh: Edinburgh University Press, 2013. doi:10.3366/edinburgh/9780748670260.001.0001.

Hing, Bill Ong. "Institutional Racism, ICE Raids, and Immigration Reform." *University of San Francisco Law Review* 44, no. 1 (2009): 1–49.

Hosein, Adam. "'Where Are You Really From?' Ethnic and Linguistic Immigrant Selection Policies in Liberal States." In *Citizenship and Immigration—Borders, Migration and Political Membership in a Global Age*, edited by Ann Cudd and Win-Chiat Lee, pp. 191–202. New York: Springer, 2016.

Hosein, Adam. "Do Outsiders Have Legal Rights?" *Boston Review*, March 15, 2017.

Hosein, Adam. "Racial Profiling and a Reasonable Sense of Inferior Political Status." *Journal of Political Philosophy* 26, no. 3 (2018): 1–20.

Hosein, Adam. *The Ethics of Migration: An Introduction*. New York: Routledge Press, 2019.

Martin, Matthew, and Nicolas Parasie. "Gulf Sovereign Funds Seen Shedding $300 Billion in Market Mayhem." *Bloomberg*, March 26, 2020. https://www.bloomberg.com/news/articles/2020-03-26/gulf-sovereign-funds-seen-shedding-300-billion-in-market-mayhem

Howard, Dana, and Sean Aas. "On Valuing Impairment." *Philosophical Studies* 175, no. 5 (2018): 1113. doi:10.1007/s11098-018-1074-y.

Huemer, Michael. "Is There a Right to Immigrate?" *Social Theory and Practice* 36, no. 3 (2010): 429–61. doi:10.5840/soctheorpract201036323.

Huemer, Michael. *The Problem of Political Authority: An Examination of the Right to Coerce and the Duty to Obey*. London: Palgrave Macmillan, 2013. doi:10.1057/9781137281661.

Human Rights Watch. *Group Denial: Repression of Kurdish Political and Cultural Rights in Syria*. Human Rights Watch, November 26, 2009. https://www.hrw.org/report/2009/11/26/group-denial/repression-kurdish-political-and-cultural-rights-syria.

Human Rights Watch. "Saudi Arabia: Christians Arrested at Private Prayer." Human Rights Watch, January 30, 2012. https://www.hrw.org/news/2012/01/30/saudi-arabia-christians-arrested-private-prayer.

Human Rights Watch. "'Shoot the Traitors': Discrimination against Muslims under India's New Citizenship Policy." Human Rights Watch, April 9, 2020. https://www.hrw.org/report/2020/04/09/shoot-traitors/discrimination-against-muslims-under-indias-new-citizenship-policy.

Hursthouse, Rosalind. *On Virtue Ethics*. New York: Oxford University Press, 1999.

Hutt, Rosamond. "A Woman Would Have to Be Born in the Year 2255 to Get Equal Pay at Work." World Economic Forum, December 17, 2019. https://www.weforum.org/agenda/2019/12/global-economic-gender-gap-equality-women-parity-pay/.

Institute for Middle East Understanding. "Palestinian Christians in the Holy Land." Institute for Middle East Understanding, December 17, 2012. https://imeu.org/article/palestinian-christians-in-the-holy-land.

Institute on Disability. "The Power of Statistics." Institute on Disability, March 3, 2020. https://iod.unh.edu/vision-voice/article/2020/03/power-statistics.

International Diabetes Federation. *IDF Diabetes Atlas*. International Diabetes Federation. 2019. https://www.diabetesatlas.org/data/en/region/8/wp.html.

International Labour Organization. "Agricultural Wage Workers: The Poorest of the Rural Poor." International Labour Organization, September 23, 1996. https://www.ilo.org/global/about-the-ilo/newsroom/news/WCMS_008067/lang–en/index.htm.

International Labour Office, International Organization for Migration, and Office of the United Nations High Commissioner for Human Rights. *International Migration, Racism, Discrimination and Xenophobia*. Geneva, Switzerland: UNHCR, 2001.

International Monetary Fund. *World Economic Outlook Database*. https://www.imf.org/en/Publications/WEO/weo-database/2019/October/weo-report?c=218,223,233,248,336,288, 293,366,299,&s=PPPSH,&sy=2017&ey=2024&ssm=0&scsm=1&scc=0&ssd=1&ssc= 0&sic=0&sort=country&ds=.&br=1.

Ip, Kevin K. W. *Egalitarianism and Global Justice: From a Relational Perspective*. London: Palgrave Macmillan, 2016.

Janus, A. L. "The Influence of Social Desirability Pressures on Expressed Immigration Attitudes." *Social Science Quarterly* 91, no. 4 (2010): 928–46. doi:10.1111/j.1540-6237.2010.00742.x.

Jodhka, Surinder S., and Ghanshyam Shah. "Comparative Contexts of Discrimination: Caste and Untouchability in South Asia." *Economic and Political Weekly* 45, no. 48 (2010): 99–106.

Johnson-Ahorlu, Robin Nicole. "The Academic Opportunity Gap: How Racism and Stereotypes Disrupt the Education of African American Undergraduates." *Race Ethnicity and Education* 15, no. 5 (2012): 633–52. doi: 10.1080/13613324.2011.645566.

Johnston, Eric. "Is Japan Becoming Extinct?," *Japan Times*, May 16, 2015. https://www.japantimes.co.jp/news/2015/05/16/national/social-issues/japan-becoming-extinct/#.XTD5cy2ZPOQ.

Jones, Garett. *Culture Transplant: How Migrants Make the Economies They Move To a Lot Like the Ones They Left*. Stanford, CA: Stanford University Press, 2023.

Julius, A. J. "Nagel's Atlas." *Philosophy & Public Affairs* 34, no. 2 (2006): 176–92. doi:10.1111/j.1088-4963.2006.00061.x.

Kahlenberg, Richard. *The Remedy*. New York: Basic Books, 1996.

Kates, Michael, and Ryan Pevnick. "Immigration, Jurisdiction, and History." *Philosophy & Public Affairs* 42, no. 2 (Spring 2014): 179–94. doi:10.1111/papa.12030.

Kaufmann, Eric. *Whiteshift: Populism, Immigration, and the Future of White Majorities*. New York: Abrams Press, 2019.

Kawall, Jason. "Virtue Theory and Ideal Observers." *Philosophical Studies* 109, no. 3 (2002): 197–222.

Keirans, Denis. *Who Migrates to the UK and Why?* Oxford: Migration Observatory at University of Oxford, 2020. https://migrationobservatory.ox.ac.uk/resources/briefings/who-migrates-to-the-uk-and-why/.

Khaitan, Tarunabh. *A Theory of Discrimination Law*. Oxford: Oxford University Press, 2015. doi:10.1093/acprof:oso/9780199656967.001.0001.

Khoo, Siew-Ean, Graeme Hugo, and Peter McDonald. "Which Skilled Temporary Migrants Become Permanent Residents and Why?" *International Migration Review* 42, no. 1 (2008): 193–226. doi:10.1111/j.1747-7379.2007.00118.x.

Kim, Anna. "The New Nationalism in Modi's India." *Diplomat*, December 11, 2019. https://thediplomat.com/2019/12/the-new-nationalism-in-modis-india/.

Kim, In Song, and Helen V. Milner. "Multinational Corporations and Their Influence through Lobbying on Foreign Policy." In *Global Goliaths: Multinational Corporations in a Changing Global Economy*, edited by C. Fritz Foley, James Hines, and David Wessel, pp. 497–536. Washington, DC: Brookings Institution, 2021.

Kimalainen, Sieni. "15 Countries with the Largest White Population outside of Europe." *Yahoo! Finance*, September 13, 2020. https://finance.yahoo.com/news/15-countries-largest-white-population-195712421.html.

Kolodny, Niko. "Rule over None II: Social Equality and the Justification of Democracy." *Philosophy & Public Affairs* 42, no. 4 (2014): 287–336. doi:10.1111/papa.12037.

Kordos, Marcel, and Sergej Vojtovic. "Transnational Corporations in the Global World Economic Environment." *Procedia: Social and Behavioral Sciences* 230 (2016): 150–8. doi:10.1016/j.sbspro.2016.09.019.

Korte, Gregory, and Alan Gomez. "Trump Ramps Up Rhetoric on Undocumented Immigrants: 'These Aren't People. These Are Animals.'" *USA Today*, May 16, 2018. https://www.usatoday.com/story/news/politics/2018/05/16/trump-immigrants-animals-mexico-democrats-sanctuary-cities/617252002/.

Kotkin, Joel. *Tribes: How Race, Religion and Identity Determine Success in the New Global Economy*. New York: Random House, 1992.

Kotkin, Joel. "Rise of the Hans." *Foreign Policy*, January 17, 2011.

Kukathas, Chandran. "The Case for Open Immigration." In *Contemporary Debates in Applied Ethics*, edited by Andrew I. Cohen and Christopher Heath Wellman, pp. 207–20. Oxford: Blackwell Publishing, 2005.

Kukathas, Chandran. "On David Miller on Immigration Control." *Critical Review of International Social and Political Philosophy* 20, no. 6 (2017): 712–8. doi:10.1080/13698230.2016.1231833.

Kuttab, Daoud. "Israel Urged to Reverse Confiscation of Church Land." *Arab News*, November 28, 2018. https://www.arabnews.com/node/1412211/middle-east.

Kymlicka, Will. *Liberalism, Community, and Culture*. Oxford: Clarendon Press, 1989.

Kymlicka, Will. *Multicultural Citizenship: A Liberal Theory of Minority Rights*. Oxford: Clarendon Press, 1995.

Laine, J. "Ambiguous Bordering Practices at the EU's Edges." In *Borders and Border Walls: In-Security, Symbolism, Vulnerabilities*, edited by A. Bissonnette and É. Vallet, pp. 69–87. London: Routledge, 2020.

Lake, Marilyn, and Henry Reynolds. *Drawing the Global Colour Line: White Men's Countries and the Question of Racial Equality*. New York: Cambridge University Press, 2008. doi:10.1017/CBO9780511805363.

Lallemant-Moe, R. H. "The Polynesian Political Awakening in Response to Climate Change." *Interdisciplinary Perspectives on Equality and Diversity* 4, no. 1 (2018).

Lauter, David. "How Do Americans View Poverty?" *Los Angeles Times*, August 14, 2016. https://www.latimes.com/projects/la-na-pol-poverty-poll/.

Lichter, Daniel T., and Martha L. Crowley. *Poverty in America: Beyond Welfare Reform*. Vol. 57, no. 2. Washington, DC: Population Reference Bureau, 2002.

Lim, Desiree. "Selecting Immigrants by Skill: A Case of Wrongful Discrimination?" *Social Theory and Practice* 43, no. 2 (2017): 369–96. doi:10.5840/soctheorpract20172157.

Lindbeck, Assar, S. Nyberg, and J. W. Weibull. "Social Norms and Economic Incentives in the Welfare State." *Quarterly Journal of Economics* 114, no. 1 (1999): 1–35. doi:10.1162/003355399555936.

Lipka, Michael. "Most Americans Express Support for Taking in Refugees, but Opinions Vary by Party and Other Factors." Pew Research Center, September 19, 2022. https://www.pewresearch.org/fact-tank/2022/09/19/most-americans-express-support-for-taking-in-refugees-but-opinions-vary-by-party-and-other-factors/.

Lippert-Rasmussen, Kasper. "The Badness of Discrimination." *Ethical Theory and Moral Practice* 9, no. 2 (2006): 167–85. doi:10.1007/s10677-006-9014-x.

Lippert-Rasmussen, Kasper. *Born Free and Equal: A Philosophical Inquiry into the Nature of Discrimination*. New York: Oxford University Press, 2014.

Lippert-Rasmussen, Kasper. "Affirmative Action, Historical Injustice, and the Concept of Beneficiaries." *Journal of Political Philosophy* 25, no. 1 (2017): 72–90. doi:10.1111/jopp.12092.

Lister, Matthew. "Who Are Refugees?" *Law and Philosophy* 32, no. 5 (2013): 645–71. doi:10.1007/s10982-012-9169-7.

Lomasky, Loren, and Fernando Tesón. *Justice at a Distance*. Cambridge: Cambridge University Press, 2015. doi:10.1017/CBO9781316336267.

Loury, Glenn. *The Anatomy of Racial Inequality*. Cambridge, MA: Harvard University Press, 2002.

Lynch, A., H. Bond, and J. Sachs. *In the Red: The US Failure to Deliver on a Promise of Racial Inequality*. New York: SDSN, 2021.

Ma, Haiyun. *The Anti-Islamic Movement in China*. Washington, DC: Hudson Institute, 2019.

Maaka, Roger, and Augie Fleras. "Engaging with Indigeneity: Tino Rangatiratanga in Aotearoa." In *Political Theory and the Rights of Indigenous Peoples*, edited by Duncan Ivison, Paul Patton, and Will Sanders, pp. 89–112. New York: Cambridge University Press, 2000.

MacKay, Doug. "Immigration Selection, Health Requirements, and Disability Discrimination." *Journal of Ethics and Social Philosophy* 14, no. 1 (2018): 66–7. doi:10.26556/jesp.v14i1.370.

Maqbool, Aleem. "Don't Shoot, I'm Disabled." BBC News, October 4, 2018. https://www.bbc.com/news/stories-45739335.

Massey, D., A. Arango, G. Hugo, A. Kouaouci, A. Pellegrino, and J.E. Taylor. *Worlds in Motion: Understanding International Migration at the End of the Millennium*. Oxford: Clarendon Press, 2005.

McAuliffe, Marie, and Anna Triandafyllidou (Eds). *The World Migration Report 2022*. Geneva: International Organization for Migration, 2022.

McCarthy, Julie. "Why These World War II Sex Slaves Are Still Demanding Justice." NPR, December 20, 2020. https://www.npr.org/sections/goatsandsoda/2020/12/04/940819094/photos-there-still-is-no-comfort-for-the-comfort-women-of-the-philippines.

Mendoza, José Jorge. "Discrimination and the Presumptive Rights of Immigrants." *Critical Philosophy of Race* 2, no. 1 (2014): 68–83. doi:10.5325/critphilrace.2.1.0068.

Mendoza, José Jorge. *The Moral and Political Philosophy of Immigration: Liberty, Security, and Equality*. Lanham, MD: Lexington Books, 2016.

Meredith, Martin. *The Fate of Africa: A History of the Continent Since Independence*. London: Simon & Schuster, 2011.

Miller, David. "Equality and Justice." *Ratio* 10, no. 3 (1997): 222–37. doi:10.1111/1467-9329.00042.

Miller, David. *Principles of Social Justice*. Cambridge, MA: Harvard University Press, 2001. doi:10.2307/j.ctv1pdrq04.

Miller, David. "Immigration: The Case for Limits." In *Contemporary Debates in Applied Ethics*, edited by Andrew I. Cohen and Christopher Heath Wellman, pp. 193–207. Oxford: Blackwell Publishing, 2005.

Miller, David. "Immigrants, Nations, and Citizenship." *Journal of Political Philosophy* 16, no. 4 (2008): 371–390. doi:10.1111/j.1467-9760.2007.00295.x.

Miller, David. *National Responsibility and Global Justice*. Oxford: Oxford University Press, 2008.

Miller, David. *Strangers in Our Midst: The Political Philosophy of Immigration*. Cambridge, MA: Harvard University Press, 2016. doi:10.4159/9780674969827.

Mills, Charles W. "Race and Global Justice." In *Domination and Global Political Justice: Conceptual, Historical, and Institutional Perspectives*, edited by Barbara Buckinx, Jonathan Trejo-Mathys, and Timothy Waligore, pp. 172–92. New York: Routledge, 2015.

Mills, Charles. *The Racial Contract*. Ithaca, NY: Cornell University Press, 1990.

Moagi, Miriam M., Anna E. van Der Wath, Priscilla M. Jiyane, and Richard S. Rikhotso. "Mental Health Challenges of Lesbian, Gay, Bisexual and Transgender People: An Integrated Literature Review." *Healh SA* 26 (January 2021): 1487. https://www.ncbi. nlm.nih.gov/pmc/articles/PMC7876969.

Moreau, Sophia. "What Is Discrimination?" *Philosophy and Public Affairs* 38 (2010): 143–79. doi:10.1111/j.1088-4963.2010.01181.x.

Moreau, Sophia. "Discrimination and Subordination." In *Oxford Studies in Political Philosophy*, vol. 5, edited by David Sobel, Peter Vallentyne, and Steven Wall, pp. 117–46. New York: Oxford University Press, 2019.

Moreau, Sophia. "Equality and Discrimination." In *Cambridge Companion to the Law*, edited by John Tasioulas, pp. 171–90. Cambridge: Cambridge University Press, 2020. doi:10.1017/9781316104439.010.

Mukeredzi, Tonderayi. "Zimbabwe's New Land Reforms Don't Go Far Enough." *Foreign Policy*, July 31, 2019. https://foreignpolicy.com/2019/07/31/zimbabwes-new-land-reforms-dont-go-far-enough-mugabe-mnangagwa-white-farmers/.

Müller, J. F. "The Ethics of Commercial Human Smuggling." *European Journal of Political Theory* 20 (2021): 138–56. https://doi.org/10.1177/1474885118754468.

Murphy, Dominic. "Concepts of Disease and Health." In *Stanford Encyclopedia of Philosophy*. Last updated March 18, 2020. edited by E. N. Zalta and Uri Nodelman, Stanford, CA: The Metaphysics Research Lab. https://plato.stanford.edu/entries/health-disease/.

Mydans, Seth. "Japanese Veteran Writes of Brutal Philippine War." *New York Times*, September 2, 2001. https://www.nytimes.com/2001/09/02/world/japanese-veteran-writes-of-brutal-philippine-war.html.

Nagel, Thomas. "The Problem of Global Justice." *Philosophy & Public Affairs* 33, no. 2 (2005): 113–47. doi:10.1111/j.1088-4963.2005.00027.x.

Nath, Rekha. "Equal Standing in the Global Community." *Monist* 94, no. 4 (2011): 593–614. doi:10.5840/monist201194431.

Nath, Rekha. "On the Scope and Grounds of Social Equality." In *Social Equality: On What It Means to Be Equals*, edited by C. Fourie, F. Schuppert, and I. Wallimann-Helmerm, pp. 186–208. Oxford: Oxford University Press, 2015. doi:10.1093/acprof:oso/9780199331109.003.0010.

National Community Reinvestment Coalition. *Racial Wealth Snapshot: Asian Americans and the Racial Wealth Divide*. National Community Reinvestment Coalition, May 2020. https://ncrc.org/wp-content/uploads/2020/05/Racial-Wealth-Snapshot_Asian-American.pdf.

Nickel, James W. *Making Sense of Human Rights*. 2nd ed. Oxford: Blackwell, 2007.

Nine, Cara. "Do Territorial Rights Include the Right to Exclude?" *Politics, Philosophy & Economics* 18, no. 4 (2019): 307–22. doi:10.1177/1470594X18788345.

Norman, Richard. "The Social Basis of Equality." *Ratio* 10, no. 3 (1997): 238–52.

North, Douglass. *Institutions, Institutional Change, and Economic Performance*. Cambridge: Cambridge University Press, 1990. doi:10.1017/CBO9780511808678.

Novosad, P., and E. Werker, "Who Runs the International System? Nationality and Leadership in the United Nations Secretariat." *Review of International Organizations* 14 (2019): 1–33 doi:10.1007/s11558-017-9294-z.

Nowrasteh, Alex. "Terrorism and Immigration: A Risk Analysis." Policy Analysis no. 798, Cato Institute, September 13, 2016.

Nowrasteh, Alex, and Andrew Forrester. "Trust Doesn't Explain Regional U.S. Economic Development and Five Other Theoretical and Empirical Problems with the Trust Literature." Cato Working Paper No. 57, Cato Institute, January 6, 2020.

Nowrasteh, Alex, and Benjamin Powell. *Wretched Refuse; The Political Economy of Immigration and Institutions.* New York: Cambridge University Press, 2021.

Oakley, Justin. "Varieties of Virtue Ethics." *Ratio* 9 (1996): 128–52.

Obasanjo, Olusegun. "Xenophobic Attacks: Equivocation by South Africa Is a Silent Nod of Approval." *Daily Maverick*, October 2, 2019.

OECD. *International Migration Outlook 2010.* Paris: OECD Publishing, 2010. https://doi.org/10.1787/migr_outlook-2010-en.

OECD. *International Migration Outlook 2018.* Paris: OECD Publishing, 2018. https://doi.org/10.1787/migr_outlook-2018-en.

O'Neill, Martin. "What Should Egalitarians Believe?" *Philosophy & Public Affairs* 36, no. 2 (2008): 119–56. doi:10.1111/j.1088-4963.2008.00130.x.

O'Neill, Onora. 1992. "Commentary: Magic Associations and Imperfect People." In *Free Movement: Ethical Issues in the Transnational Migration of People and of Money*, edited by Brian Barry and Robert Goodin, pp. 115–23. University Park, PA: Pennsylvania State University Press, 1992.

Oberman, Kieran. "Immigration as a Human Right." In *Migration in Political Theory: The Ethics of Movement and Membership*, edited by Sarah Fine and Lea Ypi, pp. 32–56. Oxford University Press, 2016. doi:10.1093/acprof:oso/9780199676606.003.0003.

Organisation of Islamic Cooperation. *OIC Health Report 2019.* Ankara, Turkey: Organisation of Islamic Cooperation, 2019. https://www.sesric.org/files/article/699.pdf.

Organisation of Islamic Cooperation. *OIC Economic Outlook 2020.* Ankara, Turkey: Organisation of Islamic Cooperation, 2020. https://www.sesric.org/files/article/735.pdf.

Organization of American States. Inter-American Commission on Human Rights. "IACHR Expresses Concern over Pervasiveness of Violence against LGBTI Persons and Lack of Data Collection by OAS Member States." Organization of American States, December 17, 2014. https://www.oas.org/en/iachr/media_center/PReleases/2014/153.asp.

Øverland, Gerhard and Christian Barry. "Do Democratic Societies Have a Right to Do Wrong?" *Journal of Social Philosophy* 42, no. 2 (2011): 111–31.

Owens, David. *Shaping the Normative Landscape.* Oxford: Oxford University Press, 2012. doi:10.1093/acprof:oso/9780199691500.001.0001.

Owen, David. "Refugees, Fairness and Taking Up the Slack: On Justice and the International Refugee Regime." *Moral Philosophy and Politics* 3, no. 2 (2016): 141–64.

Owen, David. *What Do We Owe to Refugees?* Cambridge: Polity Press, 2020.

Parekh, Bhikhu. *Rethinking Multiculturalism: Cultural Diversity and Political Theory.* Basingstoke: Macmillan, 2000.

Pasternak, Judy. "Bias Blights Life outside Appalachia." *Los Angeles Times*, March 29, 1994. https://www.latimes.com/archives/la-xpm-1994-03-29-mn-39810-story.html.

Paxson, Monia Rix. "How Healthcare in Mexico Ranks in the World." Expats in Mexico, August 13, 2020. https://www.expatsinmexico.com/how-healthcare-in-mexico-ranks-in-the-world.

Pevnick, Ryan. *Immigration and the Constraints of Justice.* Cambridge: Cambridge University Press, 2011. doi:10.1017/CBO9780511975134.

Pew Research Center. "The 10 Largest Hispanic Origin Groups: Characteristics, Rankings, Top Counties." Washington, DC: Pew Research Center, 2012.

Pew Research Center. "Modern Immigration Wave Brings 59 Million to U.S., Driving Population Growth and Change through 2065." Pew Research Center, September 28, 2015. https://www.pewresearch.org/hispanic/2015/09/28/modern-immigration-wave-brings-59-million-to-u-s-driving-population-growth-and-change-through-2065/.

Plan International. "LGBTIQ+ Inclusion." https://plan-international.org/sexual-health/lgbtiq-inclusion.

Pogge, Thomas W. *Realizing Rawls*. Ithaca, NY: Cornell University Press, 1989.

Pogge, Thomas W. *World Poverty and Human Rights: Cosmopolitan Responsibilities and Reforms*. Cambridge: Polity Press, 2002.

Pogge, Thomas W. *World Poverty and Human Rights*. 2nd ed. Oxford: Polity Press, 2008.

Poitras, Colin. "The 'Global Closet' Is Huge—Vast Majority of World's Lesbian, Gay, Bisexual Population Hide Orientation, YSPH Study Finds." Yale School of Medicine, June 13, 2019. https://medicine.yale.edu/news-article/20510/.

Quong, Jonathan. "The Rights of Unreasonable Citizens." *Journal of Political Philosophy* 12, no. 3 (2004): 314–35. doi:10.1111/j.1467-9760.2004.00202.x.

Raj, Suhasini, and Jeffrey Gettleman. "A Mass Citizenship Check in India Leaves 2 Million People in Limbo." *New York Times*, August 31, 2019. https://www.nytimes.com/2019/08/31/world/asia/india-muslim-citizen-list.html.

Rawls, John. *A Theory of Justice*. Revised Edition. Cambridge, MA: Harvard University Press, 1999. First published 1971.

Rawls, John. *The Law of Peoples*. Cambridge, MA: Harvard University Press, 1999.

Rawls, John. *Justice as Fairness: A Restatement*. Cambridge, MA: Harvard University Press, 2001.

Reed-Sandoval, Amy. "The New Open Borders Debate." In *The Ethics and Politics of Immigration: Core Issues and Emerging Trends*, edited by Alex Sager, pp. 13–28. New York: Rowman and Littlefield, 2016.

Reuters. "Factbox: The Kurdish Struggle for Rights and Land." Reuters, October 9, 2019. https://www.reuters.com/article/us-syria-security-kurds-factbox/factbox-the-kurdish-struggle-for-rights-and-land-idUSKBN1WO19X.

Rhee, William, and Stephen C. Scott. "Geographic Discrimination: Of Place, Space, Hillbillies, and Home." *West Virginia Law Review* 121 (2018): 121.

Rich, Timothy S., Kaitlyn Bison, and Aleksandra Kozovic. "Survey: South Koreans Oppose a More Open Refugee Policy." *News Lens*, June 8, 2020. https://international.thenewslens.com/article/136149.

Rudolph, Christopher. *National Security and Immigration: The United States and Western Europe since 1945*. Stanford, CA: Stanford University Press, 2006.

Sager, Alex. "Private Contractors, Foreign Troops, and Offshore Detention Centers: The Ethics of Externalizing Immigration Controls." *APA Newsletter on Hispanic/Latino Issues in Philosophy* 17, no. 2 (2018): 12–15.

Sandel, Michael J. *Liberalism and the Limits of Justice*. 2nd ed. Cambridge: Cambridge University Press, 1999.

Sangiovanni, Andrea. "Global Justice, Reciprocity, and the State." *Philosophy & Public Affairs* 35, no. 1 (2007): 3–39. doi:10.1111/j.1088-4963.2007.00097.x.

Scanlon, T. M. "The Diversity of Objections to Inequality." In *The Ideal of Equality*, edited by Matthew Clayton and Andrew Williams, pp. 41–59. Basingstoke: Palgrave Macmillan, 2002.

Scanlon, T. M. *Moral Dimensions: Permissibility, Meaning, Blame*. Cambridge, MA: Harvard University Press, 2008. doi:10.4159/9780674043145.

Scheffler, Samuel. "What Is Egalitarianism?" *Philosophy & Public Affairs* 31, no. 1 (2003): 5–39. doi:10.1111/j.1088-4963.2003.00005.x.

Scheffler, Samuel. "Immigration and the Significance of Culture." *Philosophy & Public Affairs* 35, no. 2 (2007): 93–125. doi:10.1111/j.1088-4963.2007.00101.x.

Scheffler, Samuel. *Equality and Tradition: Questions of Value in Moral and Political Theory.* Oxford: Oxford University Press, 2010.

Scheffler, Samuel. "The Practice of Equality." In *Social Equality: On What It Means to Be Equal,* edited by C. Fourie, F. Schuppert, and I. Wallimann-Helmer. Oxford: Oxford University Press, 2015, 21–45.

Schemmel, Christian. "Distributive and Relational Equality." *Politics, Philosophy & Economics* 11, no. 2 (September 2012): 123–48. doi:10.1177/1470594X11416774.

Segawa, Nakisanze. "Tension between Indians, Blacks in Uganda Continues, Sometimes Leading to Violence." *Global Press Journal,* October 16, 2016. https://globalpressjournal.com/africa/uganda/tension-indians-blacks-uganda-continues-sometimes-leading-violence/

Sellers-Diamond, Alfreda A. "Serving the Educational Interests of African-American Students at *Brown* Plus Fifty: The Historically Black College or University and Affirmative Action Programs." *Tulane Law Review* 78 (2004): 1877.

Sen, Amartya. *Inequality Reexamined.* Cambridge, MA: Harvard University Press, 1995.

Sen, Amartya. *The Idea of Justice.* Cambridge, MA: Harvard University Press, 2009. doi:10.2307/j.ctvjnrv7n.

Serhan, Yasmeen. "Saving Uighur Culture from Genocide." *Atlantic,* October 4, 2020. https://www.theatlantic.com/international/archive/2020/10/chinas-war-on-uighur-culture/616513/.

Shachar, Ayelet. "Shifting Borders: Invisible, but Very Real." *UNESCO Courier,* July-September 2020. https://www.law.utoronto.ca/sites/default/files/users/ashachar/2020-08_unescocourier_shachar.pdf.

Shacknove, A. E. "Who Is a Refugee?" *Ethics* 95, no. 2 (1985): 274–84. doi:10.1086/292626.

Shakespeare, T. *Disability Rights and Wrongs.* Abingdon: Routledge, 2006.

Shane, Scott. "Immigration Ban Is Unlikely to Reduce Terrorist Threat, Experts Say." *New York Times,* January 28, 2017.

Sharp, Daniel. "Immigration and State System Legitimacy," *Critical Review of International Social and Political Philosophy* 23, no.1 (2020): 1–11.

Shear, Michael D., and Helen Cooper. "Trump Bars Refugees and Citizens of 7 Muslim Countries," *New York Times,* January 27, 2017. https://www.nytimes.com/2017/01/27/us/politics/trump-syrian-refugees.html.

Shin, Patrick. "The Substantive Principle of Equal Treatment." *Legal Theory* 15, no. 2 (2009): 149–72. doi:10.1017/S1352325209090090.

Siegel, Reva B. "Equality Talk: Anti-subordination and Anti-classification Values in Constitutional Struggles over Brown." *Harvard Law Review* 117, no. 5 (2004): 1470–547. doi:10.2307/4093259.

Siegel, Reva B. "From Colorblindness to Antibalkanization: An Emerging Ground of Decision in Race Equality Cases." *Yale Law Journal* 120 (2011): 1288–89.

Singh, Priyansha, and Rohini Mitra. "Millions of Indians Seek Better Lives Abroad, but India Treats Immigrants Poorly, New Study Shows." *IndiaSpend,* January 7, 2021. https://www.indiaspend.com/governance/millions-of-indians-seek-better-lives-abroad-but-india-treats-immigrants-poorly-study-711347.

Smith, Nathanael. "Open Borders with Migration Taxes Are the Optimal Policy." Unpublished manuscript, last modified March 15, 2012. Available at SSRN: https://ssrn.com/abstract=2035616.

Song, Sarah. "Why Does the State Have the Right to Control Immigration", in NOMOS LVII: Immigration, Emigration and Migration, edited by Jack Knight. New York: New York University Press, 2017, pp. 3–50, 7, 11–13.

Song, Sarah. *Immigration and Democracy*. New York: Oxford University Press, 2018. doi:10.1093/oso/9780190909222.001.0001.

Sönmez, Sevil, Yorghos Apostopoulos, Diane Tran, and Shantyana Rentrope. "Human Rights and Health Disparities for Migrant Workers in the UAE." *Health and Human Rights Journal* 13, no. 2 (August 2013). https://www.hhrjournal.org/2013/08/human-rights-and-health-disparities-for-migrant-workers-in-the-uae/.

Soufan Center. *White Supremacy Extremism: The Transnational Rise of the Violent White Supremacist Movement*. Soufan Center, September 2019. https://thesoufancenter. org/wp-content/uploads/2019/09/Report-by-The-Soufan-Center-White-Supremacy-Extremism-The-Transnational-Rise-of-The-Violent-White-Supremacist-Movement.pdf.

Stahnke, Tad, Paul LeGendre, Innokenty Grekov, Michael McClintock, Alexis Aronowitz, and Vanessa Petti. *Violence against Muslims: 2008 Hate Crime Survey*. New York: Human Rights First, 2008. https://www.humanrightsfirst.org/sites/default/files/FD-081103-hate-crime-survey-2008.pdf.

Stilz, Anna. "Occupancy Rights and the Wrong of Removal." *Philosophy & Public Affairs* 41, no. 4 (2013): 324–56. doi:10.1111/papa.12018.

Stokes, Bruce. "How Indians See Their Place in the World." Pew Research Center, September 19, 2016. https://www.pewresearch.org/global/2016/09/19/3-how-indians-see-their-place-in-the-world/.

Suk, Julie C. "Quotas and Consequences: A Transnational Re-evaluation." In *Philosophical Foundations of Discrimination Law*, edited by Deborah Hellman and Sophia Moreau, pp. 228–49. New York: Oxford University Press, 2018.

Somerville, K. "Strategic Migrant Network Building and Information Sharing: Understanding 'Migrant Pioneers' in Canada." *International Migration* 53, no. 4 (2011): 135–54.

Sunstein, Cass. "The Anticaste Principle." *Michigan Law Review* 92, no. 8 (1994): 2410–55. doi:10.2307/1289999.

Tannenbaum, Jessie, Anthony Valcke, Andrew McPherson, Leah Mueller, and Simon Conté. "Analysis of the Aliens and Nationality Law of the Republic of Liberia." Unpublished manuscript, last modified May 1, 2009. Available at SSRN: https://ssrn. com/abstract=1795122.

Taylor, Charles. *Sources of the Self: The Making of the Modern Identity*. Cambridge, MA: Harvard University Press, 1989.

Tebbe, Nelson. *Religious Freedom in an Egalitarian Age*. Cambridge, MA: Harvard University Press, 2017. doi:10.2307/j.ctvc2rms2.

Telles, E. "Demography of Race in Brazil." In *The International Handbook of the Demography of Race and Ethnicity*, edited by R. Sáenz, D. Embrick, and N. Rodríguez, pp. 151–67. Vol. 4 of *International Handbooks of Population*. Dordrecht: Springer, 2015.

Tienda, Marta, and Faith Mitchell (Eds). *Hispanics and the Future of America*. Washington, DC: National Academies Press, 2006.

US Bureau of Economic Analysis. "Direct Investment by Country and Industry, 2019." US Bureau of Economic Analysis, July 23, 2020. https://www.bea.gov/news/2020/direct-investment-country-and-industry-2019.

US Congress. House. *Expressing the Sense of the House of Representatives in Support of Full Membership of Israel in the Western European and Others Group at the United Nations."* HR 615. Introduced in House April 30, 2004.

US Department of Education. Federal Student Aid. *Foreign Gift and Contract Report*. https://studentaid.gov/data-center/school/foreign-gifts.

US Department of Education. *Status and Trends in the Education of Racial and Ethnic Groups 2018*. February 2019. https://nces.ed.gov/pubs2019/2019038.pdf.

US Department of Labor. Bureau of Labor Statistics. "Four States and D.C. Had Labor Force That Was More than 30 Percent African American in 2020." *Economics Daily*, February 19, 2021. https://www.bls.gov/opub/ted/2021/four-states-and-dc-had-labor-force-that-was-more-than-30-percent-african-american-in-2020.htm.

US News & World Report. "Mexico." https://www.usnews.com/news/best-countries/mexico#country-ranking-details.

Ubertazzi, Benedetta. *Exclusive Jurisdiction in Intellectual Property*. Max Planck Institute, 2012. doi:10.1628/978-3-16-152087-7.

UNCTAD. "80% of Trade Takes Place in 'Value Chains' Linked to Transnational Corporations, UNCTAD Report Says." UNCTAD, February 27, 2013. https://unctad.org/press-material/80-trade-takes-place-value-chains-linked-transnational-corporations-unctad-report.

UNICEF. "Girls' Education." https://www.unicef.org/education/girls-education.

United Nations. Department of Economic and Social Affairs. Division for Inclusive Social Development. *Toolkit on Disability in Africa: Culture, Beliefs, and Disability*. https://www.un.org/esa/socdev/documents/disability/Toolkit/Cultures-Beliefs-Disability.pdf.

United Nations. Department for General Assembly and Conference Management. "United Nations Regional Groups of Member States."

US Council of Economic Advisers. *Changing America: Indicators of Social and Economic Well-Being by Race and Hispanic Origin*. Minneapolis, MN: University of Minnesota, 1998.

US Department of State. *Saudi Arabia 2018 Human Rights Report*. Washington, DC: US Department of State. https://www.state.gov/wp-content/uploads/2019/03/SAUDI-ARABIA-2018.pdf.

Valente, Marcela. "Argentina: Deep-Rooted Prejudice against Immigrants." Inter Press Service, June 24, 2011. http://www.ipsnews.net/2011/06/argentina-deep-rooted-prejudice-against-immigrants/.

Ventura, Luca. "Richest Countries in the World 2021." *Global Finance*, May 13, 2021. https://www.gfmag.com/global-data/economic-data/richest-countries-in-the-world.

Ventura, Luca. "The World's Richest and Poorest Countries 2021." *Global Finance*, May 12, 2021. https://www.gfmag.com/global-data/economic-data/worlds-richest-and-poorest-countries

Viehoff, Daniel. "Democratic Equality and Political Authority." *Philosophy & Public Affairs* 42, no. 4 (2014): 337–64. doi:10.1111/papa.12036.

Viehoff, Daniel. "Power and Equality." In *Oxford Studies in Political Philosophy*, vol. 5, edited by David Sobel, Peter Vallentyne, and Steven Wall, pp. 3–38. New York: Oxford University Press, 2019.

Vucetic, Srdjan. *The Anglosphere: A Genealogy of a Racialized Identity in International Relations*. Stanford, CA: Stanford University Press, 2011. doi:10.1515/9780804777698.

Waldron, Jeremy. "A Right to Do Wrong." *Ethics* 92, no. 1 (1981): 21–39. doi:10.1086/292295.

Waldron, Jeremy. "Superseding Historic Injustice." *Ethics* 103, no. 1 (1992): 4–28. doi:10.1086/293468.

Waligore, Thomas. "Rawls, Self-Respect and Assurance: How Past Injustice Changes What Publicly Counts as Justice." *Politics, Philosophy & Economics* 15, no. 1 (2016): 42–66. doi:10.1177/1470594X15599100.

Walzer, Michael. *Spheres of Justice: A Defense of Pluralism and Equality*. New York: Basic Books, 1983.

Warner, Gregory. "As New Zealand Police Pledge to Stay Unarmed, Maori Activists Credit U.S. Protests." NPR, June 11, 2020. https://www.npr.org/sections/live-updates-protests-for-racial-justice/2020/06/11/874851593/as-new-zealand-police-pledge-to-stay-unarmed-maori-activists-credit-u-s-protests.

Wasserman, D. "Discrimination, Concept of." In *Encyclopedia of Applied Ethics*, edited by Ruth Chadwick, pp. 805–14. San Diego, CA: Academic Press, 1998.

Wasserman, D., A. Asch, J. Blustein, and D. Putnam. "Disability: Definitions, Models, Experience." In *The Stanford Encyclopedia of Philosophy*, edited by E.N. Zalta. 2013. Stanford, CA: The Metaphysics Research Lab.

Watson, Maya K. "The United States' Hollow Commitment to Eradicating Global Racial Discrimination." *Human Rights* 44, no. 4 (2020). https://www.americanbar.org/groups/crsj/publications/human_rights_magazine_home/black-to-the-future-part-ii/the-united-states-hollow-commitment-to-eradicating-global-racia/.

Weeden, L. D. "Historically Black Colleges Advance Reverse Academic Diversity." *CUNY Law Review* 13, no. 1 (2009): 1. doi:10.31641/clr130101.

Wellman, Christopher Heath. "Immigration and Freedom of Association." *Ethics* 119, no. 1 (2008): 109–41. doi:10.1086/592311.

Wellman, Christopher Heath. "Freedom of Association and the Right to Exclude." In *Debating the Ethics of Immigration: Is There a Right to Exclude?*, edited by Christopher Heath Wellman and Phillip Cole, part I, 13–158. Oxford: Oxford University Press, 2011.

Wendell, S. "Unhealthy Disabled: Treating Chronic Illnesses as Disabilities." *Hypatia* 16 (2001): 17–33.

Wertheimer, Alan. "Jobs, Qualifications, and Preferences." *Ethics* 94, no. 1 (1983): 99–112. doi:10.1086/292512.

White, Stuart. "Freedom of Association and the Right to Exclude." *Journal of Political Philosophy* 5, no. 4 (1997): 373–91. doi:10.1111/1467-9760.00039.

Wilkinson, Richard, and Kate Pickett. *The Spirit Level: Why Greater Equality Makes Societies Stronger*. London: Allen Lane, 2009.

Wintour, Patrick. "Persecution of Christians 'Coming Close to Genocide' in Middle East—Report." *Guardian*, May 2, 2019. https://www.theguardian.com/world/2019/may/02/persecution-driving-christians-out-of-middle-east-report

Wolff, Jonathan. "Social Equality and Social Inequality." In *Social Equality: On What It Means to Be Equals*, edited by C. Fourie, F. Schuppert, and I. Wallimann-Helmer, 209–25. Oxford: Oxford University Press, 2015. doi:10.1093/acprof:oso/9780199331109.003.0011.

Wong, Edward, and Chris Buckley. "U.S. Says China's Repression of Uighurs Is 'Genocide.'" *New York Times*, January 19, 2021. https://www.nytimes.com/2021/01/19/us/politics/trump-china-xinjiang.html.

Wong (Omowale), Dwayne. *The Devastation and Economics of the African Holocaust*. Self-published, CreateSpace, 2016.

World Health Organization. *State of the Art on the Initiatives and Activities Relevant to Risk Assessment and Risk Management of Nanotechnologies in the Food and Agriculture Sectors*. World Health Organization, September 9, 2013. https://www.who.int/publications/i/item/9789241564649.

World Health Organization. *Human Health and Climate Change in Pacific Island Countries*. Manilla: World Health Organization, 2015.

World Health Organization. "Maternal Mortality." World Health Organization, September 19, 2019. https://www.who.int/en/news-room/fact-sheets/detail/maternal-mortality.

World Watch Monitor. "Turkey Seizes Six Churches as State Property in Volatile Southeast." World Watch Monitor, April 6, 2016. https://www.worldwatchmonitor.org/2016/04/turkey-seizes-six-churches-as-state-property-in-volatile-southeast/.

Wyman, Katrina M. "Limiting the National Right to Exclude." *University of Miami Law Review* 72 (2018): 425–75.

Yeginsu, Ceylan. "Turkey's Seizure of Churches and Land Alarms Armenians." *New York Times*, April 23, 2016. https://www.nytimes.com/2016/04/24/world/europe/turkeys-seizure-of-churches-and-land-alarms-armenians.html.

Young, Iris Marion. *Justice and the Politics of Difference.* Princeton, NJ: Princeton University Press, 1990.

Young, Iris Marion. *The Imperative of Integration.* Princeton, NJ: Princeton University Press, 2010.

Index